SUNSHINE AND LAUGHTER

LOUIS BARFE is an expert on all aspects of the entertainment industry. He is the author of *Where Have All the Good Times Gone? The Rise and Fall of the Record Industry* (2004), *Turned Out Nice Again: The Story of British Light Entertainment* (2008), *The Trials and Triumphs of Les Dawson* (2012), and *Happiness and Tears: The Ken Dodd Story* (2019).

SUNSHINE AND LAUGHTER

THE STORY OF MORECAMBE AND WISE

Louis Barfe

HEAD
ZEUS

An Apollo Book

First published in the UK in 2021 by Head of Zeus Ltd
This paperback edition first published in 2022 by Head of Zeus Ltd,
part of Bloomsbury Publishing Plc

9 7 5 3 1 2 4 6 8

A catalogue record for this book is available from
the British Library.

Plate section credits:
6. Popperfoto via Getty Images; 7. George Stroud/Daily Express/Getty Images;
8. Don Smith/Radio Times via Getty Images; 9. Don Smith/Radio Times via Getty
Images; 11. Dick Barnatt/Getty Images; 13. United News/Popperfoto via
Getty Images; 14. Mike Moore/Evening Standard/Hulton Archive/Getty
Images; 15. Landmark Media/Alamy; 16. Dave Hogan/Getty Images;
all other materials from the author's collection.

ISBN (PB): 9781838933388
ISBN (E): 9781838933395

Typeset by Ben Cracknell Studios

Printed and bound in Great Britain by
CPI Group (UK) Ltd, Croydon CR0 4YY

Head of Zeus Ltd
5–8 Hardwick Street
London EC1R 4RG
WWW.HEADOFZEUS.COM

Contents

Introduction

The peak of British television light entertainment began at 8.55 p.m. on Sunday 25 December 1977, and lasted for sixty-five minutes, sandwiched between Mike Yarwood's Christmas show and Angela Rippon reading the news.

Ratings measurement being even more of an inexact science then than now, viewer figures vary. The BBC's own figures place the audience at 28 million, whereas the JICTAR* figures commissioned by ITV say 21.3 million people were viewing, 100,000 fewer than watched Yarwood. However, even if Yarwood won the day, who can remember a single sketch from that top-rating show? This is no reflection on Yarwood's considerable talent, it's just that impressions of Jim Callaghan have not tended to have a long shelf life.

However, the show that came after is packed with moments that still provoke laughter and fond memories. The main event was the *Morecambe and Wise Christmas Show*, an annual occurrence on BBC1 since 1969, and, from 1971 onwards,

* Joint Industry Committee for Television Audience Research.

the jewel of the festive schedules. That was the year when Shirley Bassey donned a pair of brown boots and Andrew Preview failed to conduct Grieg's Piano Concerto, turning the show from an extended edition of a big hit into the one that everybody wanted to be on.

As it transpired, this was the last show Eric and Ernie were to make for the BBC, but they left on a high. Although both men were only just in their fifties, this show was the culmination of forty years in the business. During those four decades, they had amassed a lot of experience, some of it in the hardest possible way. Most importantly, though, those years had made them indivisible. Their brains were in perfect synchronisation. They loved each other like brothers, and the audience repaid that love.

However, their career wasn't a straightforward, linear, rags-to-riches story. Both became famous at an early age, as protégés of the bandleader Jack Hylton, before fading into obscurity. That could have been the highest their star ever ascended, but they emerged again, bigger, better, brighter, reaching a level unlikely ever to be equalled, and which, thirty-eight years after their last television show, displays no sign of abating.

Being a child star is almost always the recipe for a disastrous and sometimes tragic adulthood. Those who shine brightest earliest find it hard to keep the flame from guttering. Often the public is unwilling to accept the adult version, leading to bitterness and rancour. Sometimes the experience of childhood stardom was so abusive and damaging that adult life becomes impossible. Lena Zavaroni and Judy Garland are the obvious extreme examples of this.

Eric Morecambe and Ernie Wise were two of the greatest exceptions. Young Ernest Wiseman's London stage debut at the age of thirteen was front-page news. He was billed as the next Jack Buchanan.* When another talented young lad joined Jack Hylton's company, he too made news, with his outsize lollipop and his Lancashire 'gowk' act. It would have been very easy for both boys to get too big for their boots, but Eric's mother, Sadie, was on hand to make sure that neither did. The long years of struggle to make their names as adults sealed the matter. However, even when they made it, arriving at rehearsals in their Rolls-Royces, they remained working-class entertainers. They might have had luxury houses in well-heeled areas, but they were of the people. They were two of us.

Eric Morecambe died in 1984, and Ernie Wise rejoined his partner in 1999. Just what is it that makes Eric and Ernie endure all these years later? Between 1979 and 1988, Thomas Derbyshire and Robert Harper, better known as Tommy Cannon and Bobby Ball, were London Weekend Television's big double act. Their catchphrases – not least 'Rock on, Tommy' – became currency in playgrounds and workplaces the nation over. They remained active as a partnership until Ball's untimely death in 2020 during the Covid-19 pandemic, Ball having also carved out a niche as a comic actor in shows like *Not Going Out*. However, their shows languish unrepeated.

Other double acts have been and gone. Mike Hope and Albie Keen, Lennie Bennett and Jerry Stevens, Gareth Hale and Norman Pace, Mike and Bernie Winters, Bernie Winters and Schnorbitz†. All were good turns, yet none come close to the affection in which Morecambe and Wise were, and are, held.

For whatever reason, the tall handsome one with glasses

* (1891–1957) – a celebrated song and dance man who owned theatres.
† Schnorbitz was the St Bernard dog, or rather, fleet of St Bernard dogs, who became Bernie Winters' comedy partner, replacing his brother Mike when the act split acrimoniously.

and the one with the short fat hairy legs continue to work their charm on audiences. Maybe it's their authenticity? Once refined to its essence in its later years, theirs was no longer really an act. They were playing themselves. They were two very old, close friends having fun and inviting millions to join in with them. Eric and Ernie were inclusive. They were the nation's best friends.

If Eric Morecambe's first heart attack, in 1968, had been fatal, it's unlikely that Morecambe and Wise would be remembered so fondly or intensely. The best of the work they did at ATV,* with writers Dick Hills and Sid Green, was ratings-topping comedy in its day, but it lacks the depth and warmth of their work with Eddie Braben. The Liverpudlian fruiterer-turned-writer expanded the double act into a triumvirate with a non-performing partner to create the Eric and Ernie we continue to love and celebrate. Braben wrote surrealism with a basis of essential truth and integrity. When they met in Bill Cotton Jr's office at Television Centre, something happened, something magical.

Hills and Green had mined for comic purposes the contrast between Lancastrian warmth and Yorkshire sharpness. Braben mixed up both with his own Liverpool wit, and made the boys non-specifically Northern. He created a mythical world where Eric and Ernie had grown up together, as indeed they almost had. He called it Tarryasson Street. He made Wise much

---

* Associated Television (ATV) was the ITV programme contractor for weekends in London from 1955 to 1968 and weekdays in the Midlands from 1956 to 1968. Then from 1968 to 1981, it provided programmes to the Midlands all week. Throughout, it was an extension of the personality of its chairman, former Charleston dancer Lew (later Lord) Grade. On 1 January 1982, it was restructured and renamed to become Central Independent Television, now ITV Central.

gentler and warmer, closer to the man he actually was, but with the genius addition of comic meanness, when he wasn't mean at all. He made Morecambe much stronger and sharper, not always the fall guy. He saw the warmth that existed between these two men, a love closer than many brothers, and made it into comic gold.

That magic, that chemical reaction, created a phenomenon that transcended and continues to transcend conventional popularity. The Beatles had, and have, it. Eric and Ernie had, and have it. Their work can be repeated endlessly because so little of it is even slightly problematic. There is something comforting and safe about Morecambe and Wise, but this isn't cosy nostalgia. They always were comforting and safe. They were and are a constant in an increasingly uncertain world. This is their story.

1

Parallel lives

Calling them Wise and Morecambe or Ernie and Eric sounds wrong, but it was Ernie that came first. Born on 27 November 1925 in Bramley on the outskirts of Leeds, Ernest was the first child of Harry and Connie Wiseman. Harry worked for the London and North Eastern Railway as a porter and signal lampman, while Connie had worked in the local mills before her marriage.

Wiseman had come from a poor family. His father died when he was fourteen, and his mother was blind. Harry lied about his age to join the Army in the First World War. He met the relatively well-to-do Constance Wright on a tram when he tripped over her umbrella. Connie's father – in Ernie's words, 'a dour man... of the sort that only Yorkshire breeds'[1] – took an instant dislike to the young man, and when it became clear that his daughter was falling for Harry, he issued her with an ultimatum. Drop Wiseman or be abandoned by her family. Connie chose Harry, and her father cut her out of his will. They married on 25 June 1924, and moved into a single room with only her piano joining them from her former family life.

Ernest was followed by brother Gordon, sisters Ann and Constance, and another brother, Arthur, who died aged only two. By the time Ernie was five, the family was installed in a railway cottage at 12 Station Terrace, East Ardsley, hard by Ardsley station where Harry worked. 'Whenever a train went past, the place shook,' Ernie recalled. Life was hard on £2 a week, and made harder by Harry's inability to manage his finances. 'He was a wonderful personality,' his devoted son said, 'a big bone of contention with my mother who was always a very thrifty person.' Indeed, Connie had saved for her precious piano from the five shillings a week that her father allowed her from her £3 a week wages at the mill.

'We were a railway family,' Ernie said proudly, many years later, but to Harry, the railways were just a job. His real passion was for entertainment, and he supplemented his railway wages by performing in local pubs and clubs as a singer. The young Ernie idolised his father and, after seeing Harry perform at a working men's club, asked his mother to teach him a song. Connie went to her piano and they worked on 'The Sheik of Araby'.* When Harry got home, his boy showed him what he had learned. He glowed with pride. He also immediately realised the potential of building an act with his son. In Hollywood, this was the age of Shirley Temple and Mickey Rooney. Talented children were gold dust. Soon Wiseman and son began working on a turn for the local clubs, billing themselves as Carson and Kid, or Bert Carson and his Little Wonder. Ernie was the comic, his father was the straight man.

The sort of comedy material the Wisemans were using was fairly basic. One gag had Ernest talking about a pair of miners (or whatever was the main employment of the area they were

* Later to become Tommy Cooper's theme music.

performing in) tossing a coin to decide what to do with their day. 'If it comes down heads, we'll go to the football match. If it comes down tails, we'll go dog racing. And if it stands on edge, we'll go to work.'[2] It might seem risky trading on the work-shy angle just a few years after the General Strike, but the jokes seemed to get a laugh of recognition wherever the pair went.

However, it wasn't the gags that went down best. 'We used to sing the songs and do the dancing, and I also had the sentimental bit as well. I used to come on and sing "It's my mother's birthday today", and I had them all crying in their beer.'

Harry needed the money to supplement his railway wages, but very soon Ernie was feeling aggrieved that he wasn't getting a share of the proceeds. He hit upon the idea of giving his friends a few coppers to chuck on stage when he was doing his solo section of the act. This was a sprat to catch a mackerel and it usually resulted in other members of the audience joining in, with Ernie gathering up the donations gratefully.

There was only one thing getting in the way of Ernie and Harry's progress. Ernie's school work suffered and the local education authority soon found out he was spending evenings out performing in clubs with his father. Harry was ordered to stop. He took the stricture very seriously indeed. He and young Ernest stopped working the clubs of Leeds. Instead they concentrated on Bradford, just out of reach of the local education authority's inspectors. Then, when the inspectors realised they were working the Bradford circuit, they returned to the Leeds clubs, managing to stay one step ahead.

Another outlet for Ernie's burgeoning talents came through one of the local newspapers, the *Bradford Telegraph and Argus*, which printed a regular syndicated column by Derek

McCulloch, 'Uncle Mac' of the BBC's Children's Hour. McCulloch included stories about a pair of imps called Nig and Nog, and encouraged young readers to join his Nignog Club, a problematic name that Wise addressed gingerly in later interviews, while acknowledging the invaluable experience that he gained performing in the revues, and remaining proud of his involvement.

> The chief objects of the Nignog Club of the Children's Ring
>   will be as follow [sic]:
> 1. To create a world-wide children's friendship.
> 2. To help friendless children.
> 3. To befriend all animals [...]
> We may meet boys and girls of foreign countries who may
>   need a helping hand; we shall help them. It may be to take
>   them to a museum or a public park – what fun to take
>   them and show them round![3]

The Bradford chapter of the club put on an annual revue at the city's Alhambra Theatre, in aid of the King George Playing Fields National Memorial Fund. Ernie Wiseman made his theatre debut in the sixth revue, on Monday 30 March 1936. The first night of the week – Wiseman's first week in variety – was a sell-out and the *Bradford Observer*'s correspondent declared that:

> Individually, these little actors and actresses are accomplished
> artists – cool, confident and capable. Collectively, they are
> unique... Among these newcomers a high place must be
> given to tiny Ernest Wiseman, as the clown. His tap dancing
> and personality songs are in the best music-hall style, and he
> astonished the house with his amazing boldness.[4]

Having made such an impression, it was no surprise that Wiseman was enlisted to appear in the next revue, later in the year.

> Ernest – the 'find' of the last revue – has a Formby-Robey touch which delighted his audience last night. He is 4½ft of impish fun – a little fellow who has mastered the art of speaking by gesture, by facial expression. He beat a pretty tattoo on the floorboards in his tap-dancing, and he gave us some admirable comic songs.[5]

By the time Jack Hylton's *Secrets of the BBC* show reached Leeds Empire on Monday 25 April 1938, Ernest Wiseman was something of a local celebrity, and when it was advertised that Hylton and his associate, Bryan Michie, would be auditioning for new talent during the week, it was natural that Ernest should try his luck.

Despite being just twelve, Wiseman made his way to the audition unaccompanied, and approached the stage doorkeeper boldly. 'I found myself on the stage in front of a big plump man with curly hair sitting in the front stalls. The next thing I knew I was in London with my father – under contract to Jack Hylton.'[6]

In fact, the chain of events was not quite as rapid as Wise later made out. Hylton and Michie were certainly interested in the talented young boy, giving him a spot in the Leeds show on one of the nights, and bringing him back for the final night of the week at Bradford Alhambra three weeks later. Previewing the show, the *Bradford Observer* reported Michie as saying that Wiseman 'has a big future ahead of him in the entertainment world if he wants to take up this work as a profession. He considers him to be possessed of just the right personality and originality of style necessary for success on stage and the air.'[7]

However, the London episode did not take place for several months, when Wiseman made his West End debut at the Princes Theatre (now the Shaftesbury Theatre) in Hylton's *Band Waggon* show on Friday 7 January 1939. Despite being led by star names and based on a radio hit, the show wasn't doing well, and Hylton thought Wiseman was just the sort of novelty that could drum up publicity.

At this time, several shows were touring under the 'Jack Hylton presents' banner, and he flitted around the country making personal appearances here and there. However, his main personal involvement was with a production called *Bands May Come*, a showcase for his powerful band, with assorted variety acts for light and shade. When *Band Waggon* went out on tour, Hylton moved young Ernie over to join *Bands May Come*, so he could take care of his protégé. While Wise was thrilled to be surrounded by the cream of the profession, it will have been an extra special treat for a young jazz lover like himself when American tenor saxophone legend Coleman Hawkins joined the tour for a week at Sheffield Empire at the start of May 1939.[*]

What was Hawkins, known as 'Hawk' or 'Bean', one of the stars of the Fletcher Henderson orchestra, doing in South Yorkshire? Hawkins was coming to the end of a five-year sojourn in Europe, and Hylton had been instrumental in arranging the whole thing. 'He was talking vaguely about a European trip to a fellow musician,' wrote Humphrey Lyttelton, 'who suggested that he should get in touch with

---

[*] Evidence of Ernie's love of jazz can be found in his *Desert Island Discs* choices, both with Eric in 1966 and on his own in 1990. Sadly, the earlier show no longer exists, but the latter is available online.

Jack Hylton, then leader of the leading dance-cum-show-band in Britain. He got straight into his car, drove to the nearest Western Union office and dispatched a telegram addressed to "Jack Hylton, London, England", which read: "I am interested in coming to London, sgd Coleman Hawkins." In true fairy-tale fashion an invitation arrived the following day and, within a week, Hawkins was off.'[8]

The young Wise was very lucky to have been picked up by an impresario whose reputation had such reach. Born in Bolton in 1892, Jack Hylton had begun his performing career singing for the regulars at his father's pub. A proficient pianist, Hylton turned professional in his teens, and by the time he was twenty he was playing for the society crowd in London, with bands like Stroud Haxton's outfit at the 400 Club. After the First World War, he became a bandleader himself, and began recording extensively for the His Master's Voice label and its cheaper sibling, Zonophone.

Unlike many musicians of the era, Hylton was a skilled self-publicist and a shrewd businessman, setting up the Jack Hylton Organisation as a talent agency. When he left HMV in 1931 for the fledgling Decca label, he was given shares in the company and a seat on the board by the company's founder Edward Lewis, a move that made the chairman, Sir Sigismund Mendl, bridle. 'My grandfather was absolutely furious,' said Mendl's grandson Hugh, later a record producer of distinction, in 2002. 'He said, "You don't have that sort of man as a director." He was an artist, he wasn't a gentleman.'[9]

Hylton was certainly a player rather than a gentleman when it came to matters matrimonial. His first marriage, to fellow bandleader Ennis Parkes, foundered in the late 1920s, and Hylton's reputation as a swordsman was enough to inspire a ribald limerick:

There was a young dancer called Gloria,
Who was had by Sir Gerald du Maurier,
Jack Hylton, Jack Payne,
Jack Hylton again,
And the band at the Brixton Astoria.

Understandably, this was one that was missed out when he recorded one of his biggest hits, *Rhymes*, in 1931, with the composer Leslie Sarony singing a selection of lewd verses rendered suitable for family listening by omitting the last line of each.

As tough a businessman as he was, Hylton inspired loyalty. Once you were on the Hylton team, that tended to be it. His musicians, like Chappie D'Amato and the multi-instrumentalist E. O. 'Poggy' Pogson, stayed with him for decades. Hylton took instantly to the young Ernest Wiseman, giving him extra attention in terms of stagecraft. At first, Wiseman's act was the one he'd honed with his father in the clubs.

I came on and I told my jokes, and I sang my song and I did my clog dance... [Jack Hylton] put me into smarter clothes. He moved me upmarket. Put me into evening dress. Tap shoes instead of clogs. And he gave me my name. My name was Ernest Wiseman and he made it Ernie Wise. ... They called me 'England's Mickey Rooney'.[10]

Hylton initially wanted Harry Wiseman to stick around and look after Ernie. 'They said to him "Would you like to stay with your son and perform with him, and everything?" Or stay with him as a manager, in some way. I think he should have taken it, but looking back on it, I suppose he said to himself "Well, I don't know, I've got a regular job with the railway" and I suppose he'd got his railway pension, something like that. And so he came home, and that broke his heart, because I was no longer there to go to the clubs with him, and his life was me... It's my vulnerable... it's really my underbelly, my vulnerable side. I thought the world of him.'[11]

Although young Ernie was already a driven individual, determined to succeed, he was still a child, alone in a strange city, and his father's decision to leave him behind clearly left an impression. While he doted on Ernie, he had three other children and a wife back at home. He'd miss performing with his pal, but the money Ernie could send home would be very useful.

Hylton began to regard Ernie almost as family, taking him in at home when the show was off the road. Michie's statement that the young Wise had the right stuff to make it on the air was proven by the amount of broadcasting that the boy did in his first few months with Hylton. These even included appearing on television from Alexandra Palace on Tuesday 27 June 1939 at 9 p.m., as part of a Hylton band show. The shows were live, but if anything went wrong, only a few thousand people in the London area would see.

When a young lad from the other side of the Pennines auditioned for Hylton, Wise was practically a veteran. John Eric Bartholomew made his entrance on Earth just over six months after Wiseman, on 14 May 1926, at 42 Buxton Street, Morecambe, a typical seaside terraced house. His father, George, had married Sarah Robinson, known always as Sadie, in 1921. George was a labourer for Morecambe Corporation. Sadie did various jobs, including waitressing at the Cafe Royal and as an usherette at the Central Pier. Morecambe made a joke of the delay between their marriage and his birth: 'If my father hadn't been so shy, I could have been two years older.'[12]

George was, in his son's fond description, 'tall and easy going, with a gentle disposition... wholly content with his lot... his quiet dignity and philosophy, his simple pleasures, the respect and esteem of his work-mates and friends, and his supreme joy which he shared with my mother in watching the Turneresque sunset over Morecambe Bay'. Sadie, said Eric, 'was the opposite'. In terms of his school work at Lancaster Road Junior School and Euston Road Senior School, it seemed as though Eric was inclined to take after his father, happy to drift through.

'I wasn't just hopeless in class, I was terrible,' he later admitted.[13] Sadie wanted Eric to go to grammar school, but was told it would be a waste of time. Eric's academic failings belied the fact that he was a bright lad, and so Sadie's thoughts turned to finding her son a distracting and absorbing outlet. The answer was surrounding the Bartholomews.

Ernest Wiseman had grown up in a city with several fine variety theatres, not least the Empire, where he had auditioned for Hylton, and the City Varieties, for many years home to BBC television's *The Good Old Days*, happily still extant and thriving after a recent restoration. However, the young Eric Bartholomew had the luck to be raised in a booming, bustling seaside resort with entertainment all over town.

Modern Morecambe, even with its Wetherspoon's pub named after its most celebrated son, has a very different profile to the one it cut in its heyday. A large stretch of the West End promenade, where the Frontierland amusement park stood, is derelict. The late-1930s block housing the Empire and Arcadian theatres and the Floral Hall ballroom was bulldozed for an Aldi, which has already been rebuilt and expanded once. The four-platform railway station built on the Promenade in 1907 by the Midland Railway company to handle the influx of holidaymakers is now a pub and music venue. The trains terminate a little inland at a glorified bus shelter on a single platform.

However, one remnant of the glory days stands proud and defiant: Oliver Hill's Midland Hotel, beautifully restored and doing excellent business after years of neglect in which water leaking through the roof endangered Eric Gill's murals.

Many of those holidaymakers arriving at Morecambe Promenade came from Leeds and Bradford, among them Walter and Lilian Bennett. Their son, the playwright Alan, is convinced that he must have been conceived in Morecambe* over the August bank holiday of 1933, and maintains that the same applied two years later for the creation of his younger brother, Gordon.

In Eric Morecambe's childhood, the site of the afore-mentioned Aldi was occupied by the Arcadian Pavilion, home to Ernest Binns' Arcadian Follies concert party. Binns had originally been a theatre and cinema proprietor in Bradford, but had followed the money to Morecambe. As well as his indoor attractions, Binns also ran an al fresco troupe in an open-air theatre at the Happy Mount Park, where he staged various shows over the years, including The Happy Mountebanks and Tonics of 1939, and another Arcadian Follies show in Blackpool. When the summer was over, his lieutenant Fred Rayne would take the show out on tour as the Morecambe Follies. Meanwhile, back in Morecambe on the West End Pier, the tourists could enjoy Frank A. Terry's long-running Pierrots on Parade show.

The concert parties held sway in these days before the all-star summer seasons of the post-war era. Florrie Forde, a

---

* He admits to the possibility that it could have been Filey.

hangover from the music hall days, could often be found at the Tower, an outlandish Moorish fantasy in white stucco, which, along with Morecambe's most celebrated venue, the Winter Gardens, stayed on weekly variety throughout the summer months. Liverpool comedian Billy Matchett was a Morecambe favourite, and in his later years he would be pressed for advice by his nephew Eddie Braben, an aspiring comedy writer.

As well as the professional entertainment on offer in Morecambe, there were gigs aplenty for the enthusiastic amateur and semi-professional turn, and these were where the precocious Bartholomew began his performing career. Fundraising events made good use of acts trying to find a way in, and Eric's first public notice appears in the *Lancaster Guardian* of 19 February 1937, concerning a benefit run by the Cross Hill Ladies' Circle for a new church. The programme listing shows Eric and his partner, Molly Bunting, performing a 'Ginger Rogers and Fred Astaire' dance, alongside 'songs by Mrs A. C. Wilkinson and Mr G. Hallworth' and a 'recitation by Miss Bennett'. The evening raised £15 of the £4,000 needed for the first half of the building work, a small but welcome contribution. As Eric became more established, he graduated to the local social clubs, most notably the Ex-Servicemen's Club on Morecambe Street and the Jubilee Club at Torrisholme.

Eric's first double act had begun in Mrs Hunter's dance classes above the Plaza cinema, where Bunting was one of the star pupils. He recalled that she was 'about a year and a half older than me, with pink round cheeks, a pouting rosebud for a mouth and pert nose that always seemed to sniff the air above her whenever I went near'.[14]

He had begun attending the classes on Saturdays with his cousin Peggy Shields, a ruse by Sadie to keep him out of mischief. Sadie decided to guide him towards performing, for which he had always shown an aptitude. Eric would claim that Sadie had pushed him into show business somewhat against his will. 'She had ambitions for me beyond the average run-of-the-mill working class fellow earning, like my father, around thirty-eight shillings a week,' he later said, giving the distinct impression that such a simple life appealed to him.[15] 'At eighteen, I would get a job on the Corporation like my dad. I'd go to the cinema on Saturday nights and out in a boat fishing on Sundays. What more could a man ask?'[16] Sadie had other ideas. 'It's up to me that you are never tied to a whistle like your dad,' she told her son.

Sadie recalled it all very differently. 'Eric loved show business and performing practically from the time he could walk, which was nine months.'[17] The infant Bartholomew memorised every 78rpm record in the family's modest collection, needing little encouragement to sing and dance along.

A local newspaper notice of an Army show at the Odeon in Lancaster in December 1939 praised Eric's 'quite professional style'. Drilled by Sadie, the wayward Eric had applied himself, and by the time he auditioned for Jack Hylton, he had a polished act that consisted largely of impressions. He did the Crazy Gang's Bud Flanagan singing 'Underneath the Arches' and the 'Down and Out Blues', followed by a take-off of Fred Astaire, in which Bartholomew deployed some of the moves he'd learned at dance classes, before finishing in blackface as G. H. Elliott, 'the Chocolate-Coloured Coon'* singing 'Lily of Laguna'.

* Although blackface continued as a mainstream form of entertainment until 1978 and straggled on into the 2000s, often with a not always convincing ironic, comedic get-out, Elliott's 'bill matter' was already archaic and offensive by the 1940s. When he made his last appearance on record, in the early 1960s on an LP of music hall acts put together by TV interviewer Daniel Farson, Farson's introduction to Elliott's act puts the description in very audible quotation marks.

The one element of the act that didn't involve mimicry was a song originated by the Baltimore-born male impersonator Ella Shields,* 'I'm Not All There'. Morecambe thought the song 'ghastly', but Sadie insisted on its inclusion, and it always seemed to go down well. Many years later, Morecambe recalled the 'gormless' look he had to adopt and the comic outfit that aided the impression.

A cut-down tail-coat held together by an enormous safety pin, short evening dress trousers, black shoes, red socks held up by purple suspenders, a bootlace for a tie, a large piece of check tablecloth for a pocket handkerchief, a beret flat on my head, a kiss curl over one eye, large spectacle frames and an outsize sixpenny lollypop which was the only perk I ever got out of this act.[18]

Morecambe found the stage costume was embarrassing enough when he started performing the act at the age of twelve. As he got older, though, it became intolerable. 'I was still wearing this outfit when I was sixteen,' he said in 1981. 'My mother was quite hurt when I told her I didn't want to do it any more. I was girl-orientated when I was fifteen, but I couldn't get anyone. They'd look at me and think "Gor Blimey" and nothing happened.'[19]

The lyrics of the song concern a fellow happy to let the world think he's an idiot if it lets him get away with living life as he pleases, which seems a fairly neat summary of the comedian's lot.

* By coincidence, Shields died in Lancaster Royal Infirmary in 1952, at the age of 72, having suffered a heart attack on stage at Middleton Tower Holiday Camp in Heysham, near Morecambe.

I'm not all there,
There's something missing,
I'm not all there,
So folks declare.
They call me Looby, Looby,
Nothing but a great big booby [...]
I know they think I'm slow
But let them think, let them think. I don't care.

Sometimes I run errands for the folks up at the Grange,
With a five-pound note they trust me, perhaps you think
   that strange,
But they never fetch a policeman when I say I've lost the
   change,
'cause I'm not supposed to be all there.
[...]
All my folks are potty just like me,
They've retired and live in luxury.
Acting soft and foolish, they beat all the wise ones hollow
So their example was the only thing to follow.

Morecambe might well have hated the song, but he was
working in a long-established Lancastrian comic tradition, that
of the 'gowk' act, and Sadie knew how well 'gowks' went down
with audiences. Henpecked and put-upon, 'gowk' comedians
traded on naivety, often finding themselves in situations they
claimed not to understand. The best-known practitioners of
the form were the monologuist Tom Foy (1879–1917) and
George Formby Senior (1875–1921), the father of the much-
loved gap-toothed banjolele-strumming innuendo-monger.
   A lifelong sufferer of bronchial trouble, Formby incorp-
orated his ailment into the act, his catchphrase being 'Coughing

better tonight'. His signature song was 'John Willie Come On', in which a slow-witted Lancastrian visits London with his formidable wife. At one point, he is approached in the street:

A lady came to me and said, 'Have we not met before?'
My wife said, 'Miss, how dare you, that's me husband though be done'
Y'know, it's mine, I found it first, John Willie, come on!

Audiences would have known that the interloper was touting for business in the oldest profession, a subtlety seemingly lost on John Willie. Or is it? As with Morecambe's song, a big part of the 'gowk' act's appeal lay in the distance between perceived and actual intelligence. The apparent unworldliness is belied by a knowing wink. As Morecambe got older, the disparity between the simpleton of the song and the reality of the performer became more obvious, and throughout his career, Morecambe would tread a fine line between innocence and experience to tremendous comic effect.

Over the years, show business anecdotes become burnished, polished and improved. Timelines are lengthened or shortened for dramatic effect. The official version of how Eric and Ernie met, as laid down in their 1973 memoirs, begins in August 1939. Eric Bartholomew won a talent competition at the Kingsway cinema in Hoylake, a seaside town on the Wirral Peninsula. The cinema ran talent contests every week, offering 'three big cash prizes' and fares covered from Liverpool.[20] Normally this wouldn't have been worth Eric's while. He later said that Hoylake was so far from Morecambe that it might as well have been Australia. However, on this Saturday night, the stakes were higher, even if no cash was on offer. This contest was organised by Jack Fallon, one of Jack Hylton's right-hand men, and promoted by weekly music newspaper, the *Melody Maker*. The prize was to audition for Jack Hylton in person. Morecambe recalled:

> At the time I felt my prize was a complete swizz. A boy of thirteen likes to win something tangible... especially when he has competed, as I had, virtually under duress. Sadie, my wise and ambitious mum, certainly thought otherwise... that, who knows, this day might affect my whole life. She was right, of course. Looking up at me from the auditorium was the smug mug of Ernie Wise, his beady eyes immediately spotting a hot property... To us Ernie Wise was a big star.[21]

Sadie, Eric, Ernie and their friend Arthur Tolcher all recalled the audition as taking place at the Manchester Palace. As Morecambe told the story over thirty years later, there was a three-month hiatus between the Hoylake contest and the Manchester, then another three months of uncertainty and assumed failure before Hylton made good on his 'we'll let you know' promise, asking the young Eric to join his *Youth Takes a Bow* show at the Nottingham Empire. However, it looks likely that Eric's path from Hoylake to Hylton's star discovery was a month, not six.

Mike Craig, one of Eric and Ernie's writers in the later years at the BBC, found that the Hoylake talent contest was the back page lead story of the *Melody Maker* of 2 March 1940, not August 1939. Of the ten finalists, four had been selected to audition for Hylton at the New Cross Empire in south London, not Manchester, one of them being Bartholomew, who told the paper that his 'ambition is to become a comedian' and that he would like to follow in the footsteps of his 'hero', George Formby.[22]

The London auditions are likely to have taken place during *Band Waggon*'s week at New Cross, beginning on 18 March 1940, when Ernie was listed as being on the bill. *Youth Takes a Bow* began its week at Nottingham Empire, when Eric says he joined the company, the following Monday, 25 March 1940. Certainly, reviews show that Eric was in the show by the time it reached Portsmouth Hippodrome on 22 April 1940, and it seems that by the time the show reached Manchester in June, he was already well established.

Returning to the official version of events, Eric and Ernie are claimed to have met properly for the first time at Swansea Empire, where *Youth Takes a Bow* was the second half of a Hylton double bill. As Morecambe later told it, this was the date where Wise rejoined the company after several months back in Leeds with his family, putting Eric's nose out of joint after two months as the main comedian.

However, there is a problem. *Youth Takes a Bow* played Swansea for the week commencing 15 April 1940. Wise had joined the company at Bradford Alhambra for the week beginning 11 March, two weeks before the Nottingham engagement, where Morecambe says he joined the company. It begins to look like Morecambe changed the sequence of events for dramatic effect until it is realised that *Youth Takes a Bow* returned to the Swansea Empire in September 1940 to capitalise on its earlier success. Contemporary reports of the show after the week in Bradford mention Bartholomew but not Wise, which, given his star status, suggests he was absent.

It was decided that Sadie would go on the road with her son, leaving George at home to fend for himself. 'It was such a bizarre setup,' says Eric Morecambe's son Gary, who, with his sister, Gail, spent a lot of time with George and Sadie in childhood, when their mother accompanied their father on overseas work trips. 'She was away so much of the time, and him accepting it and being a house-husband. It was so before its time in terms of how they were living.'[23] It wasn't a situation where either or both was glad to get out of the other's hair. Sadie and George were quite a double act of their own, so the decision was a wrench. 'They'd often only have one pair of glasses. So one would be reading the paper and the other would be "Well, I'm reading a book now".'

No matter how old or successful Eric got, he always deferred to Sadie, albeit not before getting in a wisecrack, as Gary Morecambe recalls:

> Sadie would tell stories about Eric's childhood and my father would come in and say 'They're not true'. If he tried to get angry or stroppy or anything, she'd just look at him and kill him dead. He couldn't do it. You never lose that connection. She was only about 4ft 6, but she was the boss.
>
> I'll always remember Sadie saying to my father, we were walking down the street in Morecambe, and she was going on about him not spending money. He was just having a little phase. He was actually quite good at spending money. 'You can't take it with you when you go,' she said and he replied 'Well, not where you're going. It'd melt.'
>
> There's no response to that. Classic mother and son thing. It's that northern thing. Barbed, but you support and love each other.[24]

At this time, the school leaving age was fourteen, and with Eric not due to turn fourteen until May, he had to go through the formality of registering attendance at school in each town visited. 'You can imagine what we were able to learn going to a different school every week,' Wise later recalled. The war meant that education authorities weren't as punctilious in enforcing the rules as they would have been otherwise, so any progress was largely unmonitored. Given Eric's lacklustre contributions in class, when he could be bothered to turn up, it's unlikely his teachers back in Lancashire missed him much. In any case, his real education was happening on stage.

Compared to his father, who was on not quite two quid a week as a Corporation labourer, Eric's £5 a week was good money, especially as both he and Sadie had their travel costs covered by Hylton. A week's digs cost thirty shillings, a pound of it went home to George, and Eric was given five shillings a week in pocket money. However, Ernie was on £2 a week more than Eric, and even this paled into insignificance with Michie's three-figure weekly salary and first-class travel. Years later, while being grateful for the opportunity he'd been offered, an older, wiser Eric felt that he had been exploited.

Youth Takes a Bow was only half of the show. Before the interval, patrons saw a bill of seasoned variety performers like Welsh singer and comedienne 'Two Ton' Tessie O'Shea, and Adelaide Hall, the black American singer who had come to fame with Duke Ellington, another treat for young jazz lovers like Ernie and Eric. Sometimes this part of the show was billed as *Secrets of the BBC*. There was nothing salacious in the entertainment, as it was just a publicity gimmick trading on the fact that the turns had been featured on the wireless, as well as Michie's reputation as a radio personality.

If it seems bizarre that established turns should play second fiddle to kids, it was merely a large-scale version of what Harry Wiseman realised when he took Ernie to the pubs and clubs. He knew that Kid was the draw, not Bert Carson. Audiences were suckers for sentimentality. 'Children, in that age of the Shirley Temple hangover, were a big draw,' said Eric many years later, being unable to resist adding the joke that 'Ernie had a bigger hangover and bigger drawers than Shirley Temple ever had'.[25]

However, a child performer had a distinct shelf life. 'There was a regular turnover of pubescent boy sopranos whose voices tended to drop in mid-note,' said Eric. 'We saw a few run from the stage in tears.' Eric couldn't do 'I'm Not All There' forever, nor would he have wanted to, as it increasingly cramped his style with girls.

Someone who knew this better than anyone was Ernest Maxin, who would go on to be Eric and Ernie's television producer, but who began his show business career at an even younger age than Wise or Morecambe. Maxin's maternal grandmother ran a theatrical boarding house in Leeds, and his parents were good friends with many of the top variety names of the day, who would visit them in east London. One was Harry S. Pepper, sometime member of the Co-Optimists concert party and son of Will C. Pepper, the producer of a long-running minstrel show on Swansea's Mumbles Pier.

'He was going to put on a radio minstrel show at the Hackney Empire,' Maxin remembered. 'He came round at teatime. I was practising, he heard me playing a little Bach and Mozart on the piano and he said to my mother and father "You know, we'll take the kid on tour with us". My father said "No, mein boy is going to be a classical pianist", but my mother said "How much, love?".'[26]

Like Eric and Ernie, once on the road, Maxin began watching like a hawk and learning. The black American double act Scott and Whaley were on the same bill, and took the young boy under their wing, teaching him stagecraft and more than a few dance steps. However, Maxin grew up too fast.

When I was nine, I looked about thirteen – big, beefy. I wasn't cute any more and I didn't get the laughs when my feet didn't touch the floor. I was standing by the stage door of the Sheffield Empire. And Harry S. Pepper was speaking to my mum and dad on the telephone. He didn't know I was there. He said, 'I'm afraid we've got to give him two weeks' notice.' This is the expression he used, he must have been very upset at the time. 'I'm afraid he's washed up in the business.' So you're looking at the only guy who was washed up at nine without a pension.

As well as being relatively cheap labour, Michie was able to exploit the local publicity angle afforded by his young performers. For the week at Nottingham Empire, the local papers were primed with stories about singer Mary Naylor, a native of the city. When the show hit West Yorkshire, the papers would be filled with 'local boy makes good' stories about Ernie. Evidence of his local pull can be seen in the advertisement for *Youth Takes a Bow*'s week at Bradford Alhambra, where 'Ernie Wise (late of the Nignog Revue)' is billed above established adult performers like O'Shea, double act Moon and Bentley and the great sketch comedian Harry Tate. Then, whenever the show played anywhere from Liverpool to the Lake District, the big publicity draw would be Lancashire's own Eric Bartholomew.

At first, Eric was suspicious and resentful of the marginally older and significantly more experienced Ernie. 'He was taller than me at the time... [and] his mother wasn't with him... all of which gave him a debonair and, to my mind, devastating advantage with the girls,' Morecambe recalled over thirty years later. 'I remember standing in the wings... watching Ernie in his immaculate, made to measure dress suit and straw hat...

He looked so assured, a real Mickey Rooney, and I remember thinking, Bighead.'[27]

The shrewd Sadie saw Wise in a very different light. She saw a young boy putting on an act offstage as well as on, trying to survive in an adult's world. 'I little realised that under his bumptious and cocky exterior the real Ernie Wise was homesick and missed his father with whom he had done a double act practically from the moment he could stand. My mother had spotted it, though.'[28]

Young harmonica player Arthur Tolcher had noticed it too. 'Ernie was lonely and I often used to slip down to his dressing room for a chat,' he said in 1974. 'We were both kids and away from home.'

The long train journeys that were a Sunday fixture of every variety performer's life would be where Eric and Ernie's friendship truly began. If you were lucky, you'd get a brief chance to catch up with some other turns over a cup of tea at Crewe station, where so many lines converged, but most of the time you were with your own troupe. Just as the adult turns cleaved together to gossip, and the musicians stayed close-knit to gamble, it made sense for the young performers to stick together, so Ernie began travelling with Sadie and Eric.

Mature beyond his years by necessity, Ernie was still fending for himself and finding his own digs in each town, until disaster struck when *Youth Takes a Bow* played Oxford's New Theatre as part of a double bill with bandleader Maurice Winnick's *Dorchester Follies* in December 1940 and Ernie found no room at the inn. Walking around the city forlornly, he bumped into singer Doreen Stephens, later to become a television favourite with the *Billy Cotton Band Show*. Although she was fixed up, she joined him on his search, in the hope that a pretty face might prove persuasive.

At one boarding house, Stephens and Wise were overheard at the door by Sadie. Her and Eric's room had a double bed and a single, so she suggested to the landlady that she'd take the single, with Eric and Ernie sharing the double. After a suitable adjustment in fees, the plan was agreed, and that was Ernie fixed for the week. Sadie had a lot of practice in arranging digs and kept a contact book of landladies. She asked Ernie if he wanted to continue the arrangement for future dates. He leapt at the offer.

> Eric: She used to tour with me in those days, because I was only, what, thirteen, fourteen. She took Ernie under her wing as well, because my mother's a chicken, you know.
> Ernie: And we needed the eggs.[29]

It was a valuable saving for his precious bank book, his 'greatest friend' as Connie always reminded him, and being around the boy who was rapidly becoming his other best friend was no hardship either. It was an arrangement that suited everybody, not least Sadie, who was viewing Eric's mercurial temperament with disdain and saw that Ernie could be a good influence on the boy. Eric named Ernie 'Lilywhite', suggesting that he was a goody-goody, but he knew that Sadie was right in her assessment of Ernie as a basically kind, decent and fair young man. In one of the great 'what if?' moments of show business history, maybe none of this would have happened if Harry had decided to stick with his son.

Travelling and living together, Eric and Ernie never seemed to get on each other's nerves. Each recognised a kindred spirit. They spent every available moment trying to make each other laugh. Jokes they'd heard on the radio or 'borrowed' from the other acts on the bill. The flow of humour was relentless. This was less enjoyable for Sadie than it was for the boys.

'There wasn't a minute's peace for me,' she said later. 'You couldn't talk sense to either of them but they would answer you back with some cheeky gag from one of the acts... particularly Moon and Bentley.'*[30] Eric was a ball of nervous energy at the best of times, earning him the nickname of 'Jifflearse' from his mother. The matter became critical in July 1941, when instead of being stuck on a train with the hyperactive pair once a week, Sadie was lumbered with them every day for a week. The show was at Coventry Hippodrome, and Sadie had decided to keep on the digs they'd shared in Birmingham, where they had been playing the previous week, and commute. In desperation, Sadie suggested that they channel their endless in-jokes into a double act of their own. The idea appealed immediately to Eric, who was increasingly keen to bin his lollipop and beret. Ernie agreed it was well worth a go.

'At the start,' said Sadie, 'it was a question of their meeting somewhere halfway. For Ernie, it meant having to convert from his fairly slick song and dance act to comedy, and for Eric it meant a change from his gormless comedy act to something really quite subtle.'

They began by stealing liberally, with the American team of Bud Abbott and Lou Costello being the primary source of plunder. Ending with a song was traditional, and Sadie suggested adding a soft-shoe dance routine. She asked Alice and Rosie Lloyd (Marie's sisters) for advice on which song to choose, and they suggested 'By the Light of the Silvery Moon'.

The pair developed the act all through their spare time, and Eric's temper sometimes got frayed. Things came to a head when Ernie proved slightly less than word perfect and

* Moon was George Moon, while Bentley was the Australian comic Dick Bentley, later to find radio fame in *Take It From Here*.

Eric blew up at him. Sadie intervened, told her son off for speaking to Ernie so sharply and banished him from the room. Ernie told Sadie that she shouldn't have said anything. 'Don't you see? Eric is only trying to make me the best feed in the country, like Jerry Desmonde is to Sid Field... and shall I tell you something? He's going to be the best comic in the British Isles.'

The incident says much about Wise's generosity of spirit and his respect for Eric. Sadie later told Eric what had happened, and the fits of temper with his friend stopped. From that moment, they were two brains with one thought. Each learned to follow whatever the other did. There was no jealousy or attempts to undermine. The watchful and ambitious eyes of the other young performers, and the sharp elbows of their guardians, made it difficult for Bryan Michie to incorporate the new act, but when the show reached Liverpool Empire, he gave it a chance. It went down well enough to be considered whenever there was a gap, until eventually it became a regular part of the show.

The more Eric and Ernie were viewed as a double, the more Michie thought that Bartholomew and Wise was a cumbersome name for the duo. He suggested Bartlett and Wise or Barlow and Wise, neither of which met with enthusiasm from Eric or Ernie. The answer came in Nottingham when Sadie was talking to singer Adelaide Hall and her husband, Bert Hicks. It was Hicks who suggested that Eric should take the name of his home town, citing the example of his friend Eddie Anderson, who played Jack Benny's butler, Rochester, in the American comic's radio show.* However, Eric and Ernie did

---

* Anderson was, in fact, from Oakland, California, not Rochester in Minnesota, but the idea of using a place name is firmly attributable to Hicks.

not immediately become Morecambe and Wise. Instead, they were billed as 'Ernie Wise and Morecambe'.

After being on the road for most of 1940 and 1941, *Youth Takes a Bow* began to run out of steam. For a few weeks in early 1941, *Secrets of the BBC* was rested and Michie's young performers joined a bill called *Swing Is In The Air*, starring jazz trumpeter Nat Gonella and his Georgians. When it returned, *Secrets of the BBC* was renamed *Radio Roundabout*, and a new section was added where members of the audience tried their hands at acting. However, by 1942, every suitable theatre had been visited, many twice, and the gaps between the weeks of bookings became longer and more frequent. Morecambe and Wise were resting.

Attempts to join seaside concert parties came to nothing, and Ernie's contacts in the working men's clubs of Leeds and Bradford brought in a few bookings, but it was a meagre time. The uncertainty of the situation made long-term planning impossible. Ever the optimist, Ernie rationalised that it was easier to bear in a partnership. 'The wonderful thing about being a double-act is that you are never out on your own in the cold, cold world,' he said thirty years later. And there was always the unflagging support of Sadie, who instructed them both to get back to London. They took a flat in Camden, and soon heard that George Black was auditioning at the Hippodrome for a new show.

Both knew Black slightly from their time with Hylton, and they decided to go all out to impress him with their full nine-minute act, complete with props. Most auditionees got a 'thank you' at best, but as they came off, Morecambe and Wise were told that Black would like to see them. They were in the show. Ernie made the mistake of being truthful about the money they'd been getting previously, learning a valuable lesson in negotiating when Black agreed instantly to match it.

The show was *Strike a New Note*, due to open at the Prince of Wales Theatre on 18 March 1943, and it was a big deal. The boys were back in the West End, but not on their own terms. Although their energetic act clinched the gig for them at audition, there was no room for it in the show. Black told them they'd be doing 'bits and pieces'. The pair badgered Black to give their act a chance, and he told them that if the show's second comic, Alec 'Mr Funny Face' Pleon,* were ever indisposed, the double act would substitute. Unfortunately for Eric and Ernie, Pleon was one of the most reliable professionals in the business and in disgustingly rude health, so the act rarely got an outing. One day, Pleon was absent, and for two performances, Morecambe and Wise were on. However, London was not yet ready for the notes they struck, whether new, old or very obviously pilfered. 'On both occasions, the audience simply stared at us, open mouthed, aghast, wondering what was being inflicted on them and why.'[31]

As the show got into its stride, adjustments were made to the running order by producer Robert Nesbitt, and most of the 'bits and pieces' were dropped. Eric and Ernie realised they were 'glorified chorus boys'. One section of the show that would have been right up Ernie's street, bearing in mind his former bill matter, was the 'Garland-Durbin-Rooney Hit Parade', featuring Hollywood-inspired song and dance items, which *The Stage* described as 'striking'.[32]

As underused as they were, there were fringe benefits to being part of the show. It was 'a smash hit, and therefore a wonderful

---

* Although never a big star with his own radio show, Alec Pleon (1911–1985) was a solid, reliable variety performer who was rarely out of work from the 1930s to his retirement in the 1970s.

show to be in, full of new ideas and new, exciting stars', Ernie recalled. 'That whole experience of being in it opened a fantastic new world for us. We saw famous people in the audience who later came backstage – Clark Gable, James Stewart, George Raft, Deborah Kerr... Alfred Hitchcock... many, many others. The show had a certain cachet: everybody who came to London had to see it. Even *The Man Who Never Was*... In the dead body's pocket were two ticket stubs for *Strike a New Note*.'[33]

There was also valuable broadcasting experience, with a live relay of an extract from the show on Saturday 24 April, followed just over a week later by the first of a series on the Home Service called *Youth Must Have Its Swing*, featuring the cast. The need to fill six half-hour slots and the availability of two boys with a surplus of material and an eagerness to use it proved a perfect match. Noting that they were 'the youngest artistes in the programme', a Morecambe local newspaper reported that even then they were blurring the lines between straight man and comedian. 'They told jokes in the American style. Ernie was supposed to do the "feeding" and Eric complained that he took the laughs!'[34]

Also, despite living in Tooting with Sadie keeping a motherly eye on them, both Eric and Ernie were just about old enough to get a flavour of what the West End was really like. 'Girls in the show with rich daddies – and some were merely playing at show business as part of their war effort – invited us to stately homes in the country for the weekend,' Ernie remembered.[35] Meanwhile, Eric's lasting impression was of the view from their dressing room window, which faced onto the Mapleton Hotel, a favourite venue for American GIs to have afternoon assignations. 'There were days when the entire cast... would be at the window... other faces behind them desperately awaiting their turn, maddened by the applause.'[36]

Although most of the cast were youthful, not least twenty-year-old South African singer Zoe Gail, who was the musical star of the show with her husband Hubert Gregg's composition 'I'm Going to Get Lit Up When the Lights Go On in London', the comedy star of the show was pushing forty, with a long apprenticeship in the provinces behind him. It was Birmingham-born Sid Field's West End debut, and the chance to watch him at close quarters with his straight man Jerry Desmonde was a masterclass for a young double act more used to breathless American partnerships.

Ernie later said that Field was 'unknown to London audiences', becoming 'famous the day after the show opened in London'.[37] Only the latter part of this is true. While Field's main following was in the Midlands and North, he was a regular in touring revues that called at the number one halls on the London circuit, including the Trocadero at Elephant and Castle and the Stoll on Kingsway. In 1940, while playing the Kingston Empire, Field had been spotted by 'Doc' Salomon, who ran Warner Bros' British studios at nearby Teddington. Salomon put Field in his first movie, *That's the Ticket*.

Like Eric and Ernie, Field had begun performing as a child. At the age of eight, with Charlie Chaplin as his idol, he would put on clothes and a hat of his father's and walk around Birmingham emulating the Little Tramp. By the time he was eleven, he was on the stage professionally, as the understudy to the 4ft 9in Geordie comedian Wee Georgie Wood. By the time Field was thirteen, he was too tall to cover for Wood, and moved on, billing himself as a 'light comedian', building a solid reputation as he went. By 1929, he was describing himself as a 'dude comedian', playing flashily dressed characters, a prelude to his spiv character, Slasher Green.

Others would later owe a more obvious debt to Field, primarily Tony Hancock, who was also brought up in Birmingham, but an influence is there in Eric and Ernie's later work. Hancock and Graham Stark went to see Field in the 1947 West End revue *Piccadilly Hayride*, and Hancock's biographer John Fisher refers to 'a Shakespearian burlesque from the show in which Sid played King John... Taking one look at the man-at-arms standing nearby in a suit of armour, Field commented, "You wanna get a fourteen pound hammer and put a crease in them".' The whole thing could be a play what Ernie wrote, and the armour gag could easily have come from Morecambe.

Field was a sketch comedian rather than a stand-up, having honed his craft in revue for twenty years before getting the call to star in *Strike a New Note*. Just as important as his timing and delivery, his material was a cut above the usual welter of gags you'd expect in variety. One of his best-known sketches, in which he was a society photographer attempting to take a portrait of a friend who had been appointed mayor, was written for him by *Punch* humorist Basil Boothroyd, who gives his name to Field's character.

As preserved in the 1946 film *London Town*, Field is a compelling performer, and those who saw him live say that this is a pale facsimile. The flourish with which he pours Mayor Whitaker, played by Desmonde, a cup of tea, wafting the pot around the cup ('Forgive me pouring that way, I used to work on the railway.'), is a beautiful bit of business.

Sid Boothroyd: Do you know Whitaker, I've never been the same since my last operation.

Mayor Whitaker: Oh you poor soul. Was it serious?

Boothroyd: Serious? Yes, I should think it was. Fourteen

weeks on me back with me leg up.

Whitaker: Really? That's dreadful. Were you stitched?

Boothroyd (splutters tea): Well, I certainly wasn't crocheted.[38]

Strike a New Note ran for over a year, closing on Saturday 15 April 1944, before going on tour for the forces organisation ENSA.* However, by that time Ernie was no longer a 'glorified chorus boy'. The first phase of his professional career had come to an end on 27 November 1943, his eighteenth birthday, when he was called up for wartime service. He opted to join the Merchant Navy, and ended up on the coal route between the north-east of England and London, with Battersea Power Station a regular stop. One of his duties on ship was working in the cookhouse. Over forty years later, he would explain:

I used to cook for the crew, we used to be off the coast of England. The cooker was a solid fuel cooker and in heavy seas... we used to put up the rolling chocks, what we call the rolling chocks, and I used to make what they call 'Sea Pie', which was just one big saucepan, enormous saucepan, and fill it full of vegetables and meat and things like that, and put the dumplings on top to stop it [spilling over]. I burned the kitchen down once, and they said it was the first time I'd served anything hot.[39]

Eric stayed in the cast of *Strike a New Note* until the following May, when his own summons from the Crown arrived. Like Ernie, he decided to eschew a military life, signing up instead

---

* Officially an acronym for Entertainments National Service Association, set up in 1939 by the film director Basil Dean and the comic actor Leslie Henson, but dubbed 'Every night something awful' by the irreverent.

to work as a 'Bevin Boy', as conscripted mine workers were known colloquially in honour of Minister of Labour Ernest Bevin. He worked at Hargreaves Collieries in Accrington for eleven months before he was discharged with heart trouble, a baleful harbinger of things to come.

There was a perception that going down the mines was an easy option and, to many, the Bevin Boys ranked alongside conscientious objectors. However, it was hard, cold, dirty work, and Morecambe was far from the only casualty. Up in Scotland, another Bevin Boy was struggling with his health. 'My middle ear condition flared up again picking dirt out of coal in an open shed in King's Hill pit number 1 in Wishaw,' explains Stanley Baxter, who was reclassified as B1 and re-conscripted, this time into the Army.[40]

Morecambe's regrading to C3[*] spared him an immediate re-conscription, and he began work at the Souplex razor blade factory in his home town. It's tempting to assume that Morecambe's time down the mines was the origin of the heart problems that would blight his life and eventually kill him, but it's possible the groundwork was laid down in his school days, when he admitted to spending most of his time in the lavatories 'smoking anything I could ignite'.

His time out of show business must have been brief, because he turns up in August 1944 at the Royal County Theatre in Bedford, on a bill headed by Tommy Trinder. Morecambe was working as the straight man to comedian Gus Morris, the lesser-known brother of the northern radio favourite Dave

---

* An A classification meant fit for general service at home and overseas, B meant unfit for general service, but fit for base or garrison service at home and overseas, while C indicated fit for home service only. D was temporarily unfit and E was permanently unfit. The numbered sub-groupings referred to vision, mobility and other health issues.

Morris. Morris had numerous First World War injuries that limited his physical capabilities, but Morecambe never forgot his kindness, and learned a lot from the older man.[*]

The influence of the other Morris was particularly obvious with Morecambe later, when it came to the way he treated guests. Nobody, regardless of how grand they were, was safe from being knocked. John Ammonds had also been Morris's radio producer in the early 1950s: 'He did a show called *Club Night*. It was a real sawdust on the floor thing, not like the star clubs – Batley. Humble working men's clubs. It was very popular on the Northern Home Service and Alick Hayes used to produce it. I think they did it live and they were always overrunning. Dave was furious that they were fading him out all the time. The great thing was to try and get it on the network, on the Light Programme, which eventually we did. The head of the Light at the time was a fellow called [George] Camacho. He came to visit us in Blackpool where we doing the show. I knew Dave would say something outrageous when I introduced him, and I wasn't disappointed. When I said "Dave, this is Mr Camacho, controller of the Light Programme", Dave said "Ah yes, I've seen your picture in the *Police Gazette*". Luckily Camacho had a sense of humour.'[41]

By July 1945, Morecambe had begun working as the straight man to a comic called Billy Revell in a touring revue called 'Revel In Fun'. As ill-suited as a natural comedian such as Morecambe was to being a straight man, it took him into that first postwar autumn with regular work. Sadie knew that Eric needed to be based in London, and found him some digs

---

[*] Cheekily, Gus Morris had a later stooge who took the stage name 'Ricky Morecambe', who later went on to become a stage director for the Howard and Wyndham circuit.

with a Mrs Nell Duer at 13 Clifton Gardens, Chiswick, just around the corner from the Empire, one of the number one dates on the London variety circuit.

Meanwhile, Ernie – who had kept his hand in with brief engagements for Bryan Michie between tours of duty on the coal boats – was also in London, lodging in Brixton and looking at resuming his performing career fully. Each seems to have been unaware of the other's proximity. It seems bizarre in this ultra-connected age that two close friends should fall out of touch with each other, but this was the case. It was only a matter of time before their paths would cross once again.

2

'We ARE a tatty music hall act'

The reunion happened by chance. If Ernie hadn't spotted Sadie and Eric walking along the other side of Regent Street and dashed across to greet them, the history of British comedy might have been very different. Ernie might have become the song and dance man he was always cut out to be, Eric might have become a solo stand-up act.

Catching up, Eric mentioned that Mrs Duer charged thirty shillings a week 'all in'. Ernie was paying more in Brixton. If he could be around his friend and pay less, it was a win-win situation. Sadie rationalised that they 'might as well be out of work together as separately',[1] and Ernie moved in. This was no joke on Sadie's part. These were lean times for a young variety performer trying to establish themselves, and possibly even harder for child performers trying to make a name as adults.

Fortunately, Sadie had chosen well in Mrs Duer, in Eric's words, 'a tall, strong, angular woman... [who] was always smiling – I don't remember an unpleasant word or incident in all the time we stayed with her'.[2] She virtually adopted Eric and Ernie, telling them to pay her when they could, and sheltering them through months where they couldn't get arrested. Sadie had taken such a liking to her that she felt able to return to Morecambe, leaving Eric in her and Ernie's care. If, during a lull, their room was needed by a paying guest, Eric and Ernie would bunk in with the Duers.

Over on Strutton Ground, off Victoria Street, a group of recently demobbed servicemen were congregating around a pub called Grafton's with new ideas about comedy. Even though Eric and Ernie were younger men, they were from a different, older, more traditional world of entertainment. It would be some years before they met Spike Milligan, Peter Sellers, Harry Secombe, Michael Bentine and Dick Emery.

Sadie was always on the lookout for opportunities for Eric, so she was thrilled to learn of a touring show in need of a comic. Even better, the show was being put together by Edward Sanger, an old associate of Bryan Michie's. However, there were to be no theatres on this tour, no gilt cherubs or fancy Frank Matcham plasterwork. It was Lord John Sanger's circus, reconstituted for the 1947 season with a variety show clamped on. The laudable idea was to take a variety bill to places that had no theatres of their own.

Although Sadie was leaning on a half-open door when she approached Sanger, proffering her son, she was most perturbed to learn that the position of comic had already been filled, and that Sanger was now only looking for a feed, earning £10 a week, £2 less than the funny man. The money wasn't the issue; Sadie took exception to the idea of her brilliant boy as being only a sidekick, setting up someone else's laughs. When she learned the identity of the comedian, her apoplexy was absolute. Eric would be 'feeding' Ernie Wise, a reversal of what she saw as the natural order of things. However, that was the offer, and as nothing else was on the horizon, the engagement was accepted.

Screaming 'It's new! It's novel! It's Sanger's!', the billings promised a 'first class presentation', with 'the best of circus, stage and radio on a full-size stage' and called it 'the show that is different'.[3] Different it was, but first class it most certainly wasn't. The band consisted of a piano, a banjo and a drummer. While chief jester and wire-walker 'Speedy' was undoubtedly a master of the clowning craft, being a member of the Yelding family, a genuine circus dynasty, there might have been some exception taken to his billing as 'England's greatest clown' from, say, Charlie Cairoli. It was even more of a stretch to describe singer Molly Seddon as 'your broadcasting favourite' when an extensive search of the *Radio Times* fails to bring up her name even once.

The breathless advertising for the show barks up the presence of 'ponies, cowboys and cowgirls, dogs, the Pearl Moss girls, wire-walkers, pigeons, daring trapezists, black-faced minstrels, the Electrical Fantasia',[4] while describing Ernie as 'Star of the Forces' and 'England's Mickey Rooney'. Poor Eric fails to rate a mention by name, having to make do with being one of the '20 star acts' promised for the price of entry, which varied between two shillings and six shillings, depending on where you sat.

Opening in Crowborough on Monday 31 March 1947, this tatty affair visited a new town or village daily, save for days off and the odd two-night stand. As well as performing two shows, at 4.45 p.m. and 7 p.m., the turns were expected to muck in with setting up and striking the tent, and to partake in publicity stunts during the day. Everyone lived in RAF surplus trailers and used latrine trenches, the whole thing making Eric and Ernie long for the draughtiest dressing rooms and the dingiest digs of their bricks and mortar touring. Ernie bemoaned the lack of laundry facilities, particularly when performing in muddy fields required them to set off their evening dress with a pair of Wellington boots.*

The amount of effort put in was not matched in audience appreciation. The advertisements claimed there was capacity in the tent for 1,500 patrons, 1,000 of them seated. 'One night we went through the whole performance for six kids who came in at half-price and were shown up to the cheapest seats at the back,' Eric recalled ruefully over thirty years later.[5] Eventually, the turns were asked to take a 50 per cent pay cut to keep the show on the road. In lieu of any better offers, they pressed on until a final three-day stand at Nottingham Goose Fair in October. For this engagement, the seats were abandoned, and the audience were hustled through the tent while the company gave a continuous performance.

'On the first day, the Thursday, we did seventeen shows, on the second twenty-four shows, and on the Saturday we hit the record with thirty-two shows,' Ernie remembered. Sadly, the local press recorded none of this extreme effort, merely reporting the presence of the Sanger company and noting that the 1947 fair was the first where geese would actually be on sale since 1936. It turned out to be the end of the road for Lord John Sanger's Circus and Variety.

Two good things, however, emerged from this benighted adventure. It gave Morecambe and Wise a fund of stories that they retold part ruefully, part gleefully, for the rest of their career. And it was where Ernie Wise met a young dancer from Peterborough called Doreen Blythe. Ernie was twenty-two when they met and Blythe, one of four dancers in the show, was fifteen. He liked the look of her instantly and set out to impress her with his wit, but this plan backfired spectacularly when the

* A clear thirty years before Jimmy Cricket had the same idea.

company broke for lunch one day on the tour. Wise launched into comic observations about the ways different people ate their soup, and the noises that issued forth. Blythe became very self-conscious, and when her next mouthful was not perfectly silent, both Eric and Ernie laughed. 'Doreen considered me far too loud and pushy for her taste,' said Wise.[6]

After the tour came crashing to an ignominious halt in Nottingham, Ernie and Doreen embarked on a long-distance relationship, writing to each other and stealing the occasional hour on railway platforms when their travel arrangements to their respective shows coincided. That, with occasional visits to Doreen's family home in Peterborough, was it for the young couple for several years. Meanwhile, Ernie was on the road with Eric, and the pair were either too busy or too poor to go on dates with anyone.

Eventually, Sadie asked Ernie why he hadn't proposed to Doreen, and he replied that he couldn't consider it until Eric was married. This was partly out of loyalty to the partnership and his awareness of the duty of care that Sadie had passed on to him years before, and partly because he didn't want to split his money with any woman until Eric did because he knew he'd be unbearable about it.

Childhood stardom counted for nothing in the post-war era. *Youth Takes a Bow* could very easily have been the brightest that Eric and Ernie's stars ever shone. However, the pair seemed driven. Their love for the business, for better or worse, was obvious. In trying to re-establish themselves, though, they found themselves hitting a massive snag. To get gigs, you needed an agent, most of whom were based in offices along London's Charing Cross Road. Cast from your mind all thoughts of big desks, sharp suits and cigars. The most a turn usually saw of their agent's office was a hatch in the door of a festering rathole, through which they would enquire plaintively once a week about the availability of work. And that was for artists successful enough to have an agent already. If you didn't have one, you were caught in a vicious circle, as Eric recalled many years later.

A hatch would open. A secretary's face would appear.
'Yes?'
'We're a double act. We'd like Mr So and So to handle our bookings.'
'Where can we see you? Where are you working?'
'That's why we've come to you. We would like you to get us work.'
'We can't do that until we see you.'
It was ridiculous and heartbreaking.[7]

The most effective way out of the impasse was to get booked for a week at one of the London halls where agents were known to congregate on the lookout for new acts. One of these was Collins' Music Hall on Islington Green. 'The agents used to stand in the bar and listen to the show from the bar,' recalls ventriloquist John Bouchier, who began his career in the mid-1950s as a fourteen-year-old and would later become part of Eric and Ernie's entourage. 'One of them came round afterwards and said "Have you left school yet, son?" and I said, "Yeah, I left last week." He said, "Well, I'm looking for a front cloth act in my show. My name's Snuffy Tracey, my wife's a star." I said, "Oh who's your wife?" and he said "Phyllis Dixey." The show's called Peek-A-Boo, and of course I thought I'd died and gone to heaven, all those chicks with no bloody clothes on. In paradise I was.'[8]

The other main showcase venue for up-and-comers was the

Metropolitan, Edgware Road. The 'Met', now best known for the LP Max Miller recorded there in 1958, was one of the small Syndicate Halls circuit, along with the Brixton Empress, the Chelsea Palace, the East Ham Palace and the Walthamstow Palace.

Ernie, always the more businesslike of the duo, managed to secure a week at Walthamstow in March 1948, at the bottom of a bill headed by Harry Parry and his BBC Radio Rhythm Club Sextet, with a view to getting a week at the Met. Also on the bill were comic duo Vic Wise and Nita Lane. Having made his London variety debut in 1932, after a decade or more working in South Africa, Australia and the US, Wise was very much the senior act. As a result, he was able to pull rank and get the young up-and-comers to change their name, if only for the week. So it was that Eric and Ernie appeared on the bills as 'Morecambe and Wisdom'. Whatever they were called, they, in Eric's words, 'made virtually no impression on audiences' and when the show transferred to the Met the following week, Miss Florence Leddington, the feared and respected booker for the Syndicate venues, denied them the opportunity of hawking their wares.

It was a thin time for the boys. Ernie would come up with the odd Masonic dance or a week in the provinces, but there were yawning gaps in the diary. It was almost back to the days of the 'pies and peas', those early charity shows for the elderly where both Eric and Ernie had learned their craft with the meal in question being their payment, but with the added challenge of rationing. During these stretches of unemployment, which Eric later estimated to be between fourteen and eighteen weeks long at a time, they were reliant on the kindness of Mrs Duer.

Through this dark period, there was a faint flicker of hope from Aeolian Hall on Bond Street, home of the BBC radio variety department. Morecambe and Wise made their first broadcast as a fully fledged double act in the Light Programme series *Beginners Please* on 6 December 1947, with a return booking on 20 March 1948, a couple of weeks after the disappointing stint at Walthamstow. Ernie had his eyes on the prize of a booking on *Variety Bandbox*, one of the top-rating shows of the day. Internal memoranda show that *Beginners Please* producer Roy Speer regarded them as a 'reasonably good comedy double', and felt that their two programmes of broadcast experience stood them in good stead in lieu of a formal audition. Unfortunately, no *Bandbox* date was forthcoming, but Speer did find them a berth in an August 1948 edition of *Show Time*, alongside a recently demobbed Peter Sellers. Although the legwork in getting these gigs was done by Ernie, BBC paperwork lists the pair as c/o Cyril Naylor, the father of Mary Naylor, a singer they knew from the *Youth Takes a Bow* days. After this brief flurry, though, the BBC connection goes quiet for a couple of years.

With dogged persistence and the kindness of Mrs Duer, things began to pick up slowly. After a brief period being represented by former comic turn Gordon Norval, Morecambe and Wise finally, in 1949, came into the care of the National Theatrical Variety Agency of 35 Panton Street in London's West End. This grandly named organisation, run by a gentleman called Frank Pope, was not merely wishful thinking on an embossed letterhead. While not quite at the level of Joe Collins, Joan and Jackie's father, or the Winogradsky boys, Lew, Bernie and Leslie, Pope had a fair amount of clout. A veteran with thirty years' experience in variety, Pope had worked for the Michael Lyon Universal Variety Agency and the Hyman Zahl Vaudeville Agency – UK representatives for Sophie Tucker* – before striking out on his own.

Pope placed acts at all of the major venues, but he was also the exclusive booking agent for the F. J. Butterworth circuit. The Moss Empires and the Stoll Theatres were the 'number one' halls, the dates that every artist aspired to. The Butterworth halls, which included the Norwich Hippodrome, the Aston Hippodrome in Birmingham and the Bristol Empire, were among the best regarded of the 'number two' venues. Pope, then, was an agent who could take them places.

Unfortunately, he had a disturbing habit of getting the names of influential figures slightly wrong in correspondence. Getting people's names deliberately wrong has long been used in business as a disorientating technique. However, in Pope's case, it seems likely to have been simple ineptitude.

Although they'd already been professionals for over a decade and a double act for much of the time, the boys were always learning their craft and developing from their early efforts, which even they admitted had been coarse and derivative. Reviewing an April 1950 performance at the old Metropolitan, Edgware Road, one of the top 'number two' halls, and a favourite of Max Miller, *The Stage* noted that the 'lively' Morecambe and the 'lackadaisical' Wise had 'developed a great style of humour and... improved tremendously during the last year or so'.[9]

They were also adding to their store of experience with theatre managements and proprietors of theatrical digs.

---

* Sophie Tucker (1886–1966) was born in Russia just 18 months before her family emigrated to the United States of America. Her big, brash style earned her the nickname 'the Last of the Red Hot Mamas'. She popularised the songs 'Some of These Days' and 'My Yiddishe Momme'.

'Funnily enough, the worse the digs, the stricter the rules and the dirtier and nastier the landlady,' Morecambe observed in 1973, recalling one boarding house in Wigan where bedbugs were rife and the landlady claimed that Morecambe and his family had been the source of the infestation.[10]

Each guest house maintained a visitors' book, displayed with pride, with some being a who's who of the variety business assembled over many years. It was customary to leaf through it on arrival at digs. Alongside each name was a comment, invariably complimentary, but Eric and Ernie had long since learned the convention in such matters. One apparently innocent line, if it appeared, instructed browsers to seek alternative arrangements.

'You could write all the eulogies you liked in a visitors' book,' Eric explained, 'but if you did not intend them to be taken seriously, you merely added, "And I shall certainly tell my friends." That was the thumbs-down signal. Whenever we saw those words we groaned. They were never wrong.'[11]

The horror shows were outweighed by the decent digs, and Eric and Ernie admitted that the landladies worked hard for their £3 10/- a week. 'What every pro looked for,' Ernie noted, 'was a place where the landlady was just starting out and doing her best to please. Beginners were always good – more attentive and more generous... They served you with large plates, not small plates to make the helpings look big, and they piled your plate high and not just with potatoes.'[12]

Once established, the portions tended to decrease, but still some landladies shone through. The pair remembered with great fondness a Mrs Davies in Swansea, who, in panto season, was happy to provide a Christmas dinner that Ernie described as 'out of this world' to any waifs and strays in the cast, regardless of whether they were staying with her.

Then there was Mrs McKay in Manchester. 'She charged a little more than most of the others, but she was five-star,' said Eric.* The only point counting against Mrs McKay was her rigorously enforced apartheid between variety artists and 'legitimate' actors. She owned two adjacent houses, one for each category, and she was most put out when Flora Robson went next door to talk to Eric and Ernie after seeing them in a show at the Hulme Hippodrome. Quite what Mrs McKay would have made of Robson, by then a Dame, sending herself up on Eric and Ernie's television show twenty years later is unknown.

Just as there were favourite landladies, there were also favourite venues and managements. The Swansea Empire was always a happy spot, and not just because of its significance in their early story. Others were less so. Alan Grahame, the vibraphone player with the Jerry Allen Trio, recalls one date where a pompous manager took exception to Eric's personal grooming regime.

It was somewhere like Hanley, which was awful. In the Potteries, somewhere. Eric was standing on a chair in his dressing room, putting his electric razor in the light fitting. There was a sign that said 'No electrical appliances to be used', and by chance, the manager walked past and said 'You do anything like that and you'll never work in a theatre again'. Eric just laughed.[13]

* Mrs McKay's walls were bedecked with signed photographs of past guests. She was also an avid royalist, and kept a picture of the Queen and the Duke of Edinburgh on the mantelpiece. In his memoirs, George Melly recorded that an unknown hand had autographed the picture as per the other pictures in the house, with the irreverent inscription 'Lovely digs, Liz and Phil'.

Pope managed to get them on the bill of a show that looked to be a full year's work. Spending that long touring with the same show is likely to have given them a chance to develop in a way that might not have been possible if they'd been doing a week here and a week there with differing bills. The feeling of being part of a company gave a sense of security and camaraderie.

The show was called *Front Page Personalities*, and it opened at the Savoy in Scunthorpe on 28 February 1949. With a couple of minor changes in the cast, the show remained firmly on the road until a week in Hereford in early December, and only then came off because the pantomime season was about to begin.

In assembling the bill, Australian multi-instrumentalist and impresario Reggie Dennis, a close associate of Frank Pope, had chosen acts who had all made the news somehow. The top of the bill, the east-London-born mentalist Maurice 'the Amazing' Fogel, was a regular in the papers with his bullet-catching illusion, and when escapologist Alan Alan was asked by locksmiths to test their wares, Fleet Street reported it dutifully.

Eric and Ernie had both been objects of interest to journalists in their days as child stars, but their presence on a bill of curiosities touring the number two halls indicated that those days were past. Nonetheless, reviewers praised their 'deft fooling'.[14] Observing a performance at the Queen's on east London's Poplar High Street, *The Stage*'s reviewer commented that 'Mr Morecambe combines gags with a mirthful appearance and manner, and Mr Wise, as well as being a sound feed, has a nice singing voice and also tap dances'.[15]

Like so many comedians making their way in the immediate post-war era, Morecambe and Wise did a stint at the Windmill Theatre in Soho, where comic talent and scantily clad but motionless lovelies combined to create what the theatre's owner Vivian Van Damm called 'Revuedeville'. The Windmill performers certainly earned their money, putting on six shows a day between 12.15 p.m. and 10.30 p.m. The comedians' main purpose was to give the scene hands time to change the tableaux. Their reward for such a thankless task was the possibility of being seen by an agent.

Eric and Ernie were engaged for a week with an option on a further five weeks, at a shared weekly fee of £25. They lasted the week, but by the Wednesday they had been told by Vivian Van Damm that the option was not being taken up. Their act hadn't gone down well, but very few of the comic acts that appeared at the Windmill did. Years later, Eric admitted to Barry Cryer that he had been to blame for losing the gig.

'The great Van Damm, VD, whatever he said, Eric had a smart reply and he didn't like that. Eric overdid it one day and came back at him with some remark and he dropped them. Eric couldn't switch off. He owned up later and said "It's my fault".'[16]

Eric's romantic situation changed at the Edinburgh Empire on the morning of Monday 14 July 1952. It was the band call, where the turns put their sheet music on the stage ready for rehearsal. If two acts wanted to do the same song, whoever put their dots down first took precedence. It was also, for a young man with an eye for the ladies, the first chance to check out the chorus girls. Casual flirtation was normally the order of the day, but when Eric saw Joan Bartlett, the previous year's Miss Margate, that was it. 'I saw this tall girl, very beautiful with wonderful eyes and a sort of sweetness that makes your knees buckle, and I knew immediately she was the one for me for life.'

Bartlett shouldn't really have been there. She was trying to establish herself as a solo singer, but the work hadn't come along, despite having the support of Lew and Leslie Grade. The Edinburgh week was a last-minute fill-in for a walk-on part. It wasn't the sort of work she was after, but it was work. Bartlett was attached at the time, but Morecambe was so smitten, he even agreed to go shopping with her for her boyfriend's birthday present.

After that week, Morecambe and Bartlett seemed to keep ending up on the same bill, and getting to like each other. When Eric and Ernie worked in Margate, they stayed at the digs run by Joan's mother. When Joan had a week in Morecambe, she stayed with Sadie and George. Very soon, the boyfriend was out of the picture, and Eric and Joan were an item. Within five months of meeting, a wedding was arranged, crammed in at the end of a week in the north and before a broadcast with Tessie O'Shea. Eric spent his wedding night going over the script.

Although Eric's whirlwind romance took Ernie by surprise, he soon realised that he could marry Doreen with a clear conscience. The ceremony was to take place in her home town of Peterborough, but coming in the midst of the panto season in Sheffield, it meant a mad dash down on a Sunday, then back up again.

Eric and Joan wasted very little time in starting a family, their first child, Gail, arriving on Sunday 13 September 1953, ten months after the wedding, while the proud father and Ernie were nearing the end of a mammoth summer run at the Winter Gardens in Blackpool with American singer Allan Jones. Taking his responsibilities seriously, Eric learned to drive, having previously let Ernie take care of the transport. All of his life, he regarded it as a necessary evil, and as soon as finances allowed, he employed drivers to take him to work engagements so he could arrive as unstressed as it was possible for someone as naturally stress-stricken as him to be.

Ernie and Doreen took a decision early on not to follow the same path as Eric and Joan. Family life was not to be for them. After Wise's death, Doreen explained it had been a question of fidelity. If she travelled with him and they kept up their sex life, he'd never be tempted to stray.

Some variety stars took full advantage of the opportunities offered by their adoring fans, not least of whom was David Whitfield, 'The Singing Bricklayer', a labourer from Hull who had come to pop stardom in the early 1950s with a string of hits on Decca, including 'Cara Mia'. An 'untrained but powerful tenor', in the words of Bob Monkhouse, his voice wasn't his only appealing feature. 'Along with the looks of a Greek god, life had handed him access to all its carnal delights and he had the appetite, strength and energy to exploit them as prodigally as… Priapus,' explained Monkhouse, himself no stranger to stage door liaisons.

During the 1955 summer season, Whitfield was at the Winter Gardens Pavilion in 'Sing a Happy Song' with Semprini (yet to be declared an obscenity by Monty Python), while Morecambe and Wise were at the Central Pier in 'Let's Have Fun', and tales were legion about the sort of fun Whitfield was getting up to. Eric Morecambe decided to pop over and see the singer, reporting what he saw to Monkhouse years later.

'I didn't believe all the stories so I called round to have a look for myself and, bless my soul, it was like a non-stop orgy going on there. Girls were hanging around the stage door but I didn't realise why. I'm innocent about things like that. I was pushing my way up the stairway, wondered what these giggling girls were queuing up for. I thought they just wanted autographed photos or at most a kiss! When I got to the doorway and looked inside, David and three of his mates were hard at it with about six half-naked teenagers. I suppose I'm easily shocked because I've never gone in for that sort of thing, more's the pity. Anyway, David spotted me and shouted for me to come inside and help myself. I said thanks very much but I'd already had some that day at the vicar's coffee morning.'[17]

Just as the romantic outlook brightened, so did the professional side of things, with Eric and Ernie becoming radio regulars. Like so many northern comedy acts emerging in the 1940s and 1950s, including Ken Dodd, Ken Platt and Dave Morris, Eric and Ernie got their first big chance at broadcasting thanks to Ronnie Taylor, variety producer at the BBC in Manchester. The senior variety staff at the BBC in London tended to be career BBC men – the infamous 'suits' – or those who'd come up through the dance band side of broadcasting.

Taylor had performed regularly on the radio before moving over to become a writer, co-writing the scripts for the 'Old Mother Riley' radio shows with Kitty McShane. His connection with the Manchester end of the Corporation began in 1949 when he started contributing scripts and songs to the *Variety Fanfare* series. When the show's producer, Bowker Andrews, died suddenly in 1951, Taylor took over and began subtly shaping the whole of the north region's entertainment output.

'Ronnie Taylor was my favourite as a boss because he was such a clever bloke,' said producer Johnny Ammonds, one of Taylor's protégés, in 2005. 'He could do anything really. He was marvellous. I have no hesitation in saying that he was the nicest and cleverest boss I ever worked for at the BBC.'[18]

Comedy was very much his strength. He left the musical side to the experts, with good reason, as studio manager Peter Pilbeam recalls.

I was doing a *Music While You Work* broadcast from the old Studio 1 in Piccadilly, and Ronnie was producing it. Being Ronnie, he wasn't all that worried about rehearsals and balance. He left that to the studio manager always. He was a great one for delegating in that way. He came down at the end of rehearsal and said, 'How's it going, Pete?' I said, 'Not bad, but the saxes seem to think that they've got to play so loudly they don't need microphones.' He said, 'Ah, I'll go and see.' This band came from Rawtenstall, I think it was, way up in the valleys, and the bandleader was one of the local butchers. Ronnie went in and he said, 'How is it, Ronnie?' Ronnie said, 'It's going fine, thanks very much, but Pete says that the saxes are a bit overblowing, a bit loud.' He turned round to the saxes and said, 'Take it all down a semitone, chaps.'[19]

Between May 1952 and March 1953, Taylor gave Morecambe and Wise fourteen *Variety Fanfare* bookings, turning them into semi-regulars. It was quite a gesture of faith, given their paucity of broadcast credits before this, but such a leap was characteristic of Taylor's willingness to back talent. When Ammonds went for his 'board', as the BBC referred to job interviews, Taylor all but guaranteed him the job with a generous endorsement.

'I'd met him once, at Aeolian Hall,' Ammonds recalled, 'and it was typical of Ronnie that when I went up for the appointment board, the chairman turned to Ronnie and said "Are there any questions you'd like to ask Mr Ammonds?", and Ronnie said, "No, I know John's work terribly well." I'd met him once, and that was fairly typical, as I found out later.'

Billed as 'high-speed variety from the north of England', with at least six acts per show separated by musical links, the *Variety Fanfare* run was great experience and exposure for a young turn, bringing them into the same orbit as Austrian piano duo Rawicz and Landauer, basking in the success of their hit recording of Richard Addinsell's Warsaw Concerto, and veterans like Arthur Askey, as well as up-and-coming acts including Bob Monkhouse, Barry Took and singer Jimmy Young.

The shows came from the Hippodrome theatre in the Manchester suburb of Hulme, a great place for generating the right atmosphere for the broadcasts. Capturing that atmosphere was another matter, as Peter Pilbeam explains. 'We had a permanent outside broadcast control room in the circle, which was in fact a garden shed. No sound insulation whatsoever, it was an impossible place get a decent balance out of anything. We heard more through the walls than we did from the loudspeaker. We did some good stuff there, though.'

When the *Variety Fanfare* commitment came to an end, Taylor's thoughts turned to giving Eric and Ernie their own radio show, at first only on the north region Home Service. *You're Only Young Once* was to be the title, the show was to run for six weeks on Mondays from 9 November 1953, the stars were to receive 20 guineas a show, and Blackpool-based writer Frank Roscoe, who was a regular at Broadcasting House on Manchester's Piccadilly, was brought in to write the scripts.

The shows were recorded on Sunday nights at the Hippodrome, requiring a mad dash from wherever they'd been performing on the Saturday before haring off to the following week's engagement. For the first recording, they had to travel from Stockton to Manchester, then back off to Newcastle.*

---

* In contrast, in August 1954, a one-off *Goon Show* special called *The Starlings* was recorded at the BBC studios in Newcastle because Harry Secombe and Peter Sellers were at the Empire with former Goon Michael Bentine.

For the second week, it was Newcastle–Manchester–Hull. The plan was to record two shows on the second session, and give Eric and Ernie a week off yo-yoing to and from Manchester, but a special session had to be scheduled for the 'off' week after a recording fault at the previous session.

The downside to Frank Roscoe's prodigious talent was that he was in high demand and ended up spreading himself a little too thinly. 'Frank Roscoe was our writer,' Eric explained in 1973, 'it would be more accurate to say we had a share of him. For oft were the times he'd be working on three scripts, one for us, another for Ken Platt, and a third for Al Read. Oft too were the nights we went to the microphone with mimeographed pages of scripts that were still wet.'[20]

If this sounds like a fanciful tale, it is backed up by Johnny Ammonds, who remembers the scripts being assembled largely at rehearsal. 'Eric and Ernie used to bring their gag books to Piccadilly on a Sunday. Ronnie Taylor, shortly after I got the radio job, said to me, "Can you work a Roneo machine? That's one of the main qualifications for the job." Because on Sunday nobody was in.'

However haphazardly the show was assembled, it proved to be an instant hit with northern audiences, and the decision was taken to extend the run by three shows, taking the series into the new year. Becoming a successful headline act meant an increase in their earning potential. For their first broadcast in 1947, they had received a mere 8 guineas, which rose to 15 guineas for their second appearance just four months later. However, there they stuck until September 1952, when they were given a rise to 20 guineas.

In November 1953, with YOYO well underway, Ronnie Taylor wrote to the booking manager of the radio variety department, Pat Newman, to argue for an increase. 'Certainly their value has risen considerably in recent weeks, and I felt that the decision to extend their series, taken here in Manchester, would justify this suggestion for more money.'[21] Newman, who showed dangerous signs of possessing a sense of humour, a quality not normally encouraged in BBC administrators, replied, 'Yes indeed, they shall have another fiver towards the rent.'[22]

Even when they had the services of Frank Pope to deal with the vulgar financial details, Ernie Wise still liked to negotiate directly with the BBC, getting the fee up to 30 guineas just five months after Taylor engineered an increase. Wise's manner and tone give an insight into the sort of man he was, his letters tending to be forthright but sweetly polite and appealing to Newman's sense of fun. He aims high, but always seems happy to compromise. 'If you don't ask, you don't get' seems to have been Wise's maxim.

'We would be happy with £45-0-0, would you be happy with paying it to us?' he asked in September 1955.[23] Newman was, at first, unwilling to go higher than 40 guineas, also arguing against a higher fee for shows where Morecambe and Wise were the star turn. He said it was a matter of swings and roundabouts, and that on shows like *You're Only Young Once*, the duo didn't have to give any of their fee to writers. However, within a week, Newman had changed his mind and decided that Eric and Ernie were worth not £45 as requested, but 45 guineas, two pounds and five shillings more than Ernie had requested.

A further rise, to 50 guineas, followed in 1959, but by the summer of 1961, Ernie decided a significant hike would be justified. One hundred pounds was the figure he had in mind. Newman had a little fun with his reply.

Double. A big jump indeed… surely only Gagarin* has jumped further. Still, it's two years, I agree. I have discussed this with the staff here and, in our scale of fees, we seemed to think that you would fit at 60 guineas. But then someone said 'Well, that's only 5 guineas each, isn't it?', which seemed a bit mouldy. Right then, we will spring 70 guineas, but not I think more… if you think you could lower your sights a little and find this acceptable?[24]

Wise joined in the fun with *his* reply.

It's quite remarkable that's the amount we had in mind. If you had offered us 60 guineas we would have replied 'Well, that's only 5 guineas each, isn't it?' which seemed a bit mouldy. I have discussed this with my staff, my staff being my wife, Eric's wife, two children and two dogs, oh I did mention it to Eric and he lowered his sights a little and nodded his head.[25]

The drive that Sadie saw in Ernie served the partnership well over the years. An illustration of Eric's less ambitious approach can be seen in a conversation he had in the 1950s with Alan Grahame, vibraphone player with the Jerry Allen Trio, regulars on ATV's magazine programme *Lunchbox*.

It might have been Glasgow Empire, which was hard. Between doing our act, we used to sit in the dressing rooms and chat. They used to have American singers, usually, to close the show, like Guy Mitchell. They loved singers and they liked our act because it was fast and jazzy with comedy

---

* Yuri Gagarin (1934–1968) was a Russian cosmonaut who became the first human being to travel into outer space.

vocals. Eric and Ernie were dying a bit. They closed the first half. We used to chat in the interval and Eric said, 'I'm so glad we're not top of the bill, you know, because we'll never have to worry about pulling an audience. We're never going to be responsible for putting bums on seats.' Little did they know. The next thing is they are top of the bill and everybody wanted to see them.[26]

This wasn't just Eric rationalising his and Ernie's place in the variety pecking order. Years later, a conversation with Barry Cryer made it clear he enjoyed these early days when they were establishing themselves and getting riotous responses without having to carry a show. A Leeds boy like Ernie, Cryer was a regular at the Empire and the Grand, witnessing the men for whom he would later write Christmas spectaculars. 'I'd been to their shows. I was a fan, obviously. Eric said to me once, "Happiest time of my life. We weren't top of the bill." He said people kept saying, "You stole it tonight." He said that was wonderful.'

The aforementioned Glasgow Empire was one place where they never quite stole it, although the audience liked them enough to let them live. 'Glasgow was definitely the grave,' said Morecambe in 1969. 'Comics' graveyard. Oh, I used to be ill when the telegram came in, "Go to Glasgow". Oh we did well there. We always did well there. Walked off to our own footsteps, but we always did well. The fireman once said "They're getting to like you here". And we'd died. "They're getting to like you." "What do you mean?" "They never shouted."'[27]

Other English comedians weren't so lucky. Mike and Bernie Winters were greeted with a cry of 'Fuck, there's two of them', Des O'Connor faked a faint rather than continue with his act, and Roy Castle's trumpet playing, singing and tap-dancing were rewarded with a withering shout from the gods of 'Is there no end to this cunt's versatility?' James Casey, son of Jimmy James and one of Eric and Ernie's early radio producers, was shocked when he learned that even Liverpudlian monologue comedian and wartime radio mainstay Robb Wilton went down badly at the Empire. 'He was my favourite and my father's favourite. We met once and he asked where my dad was. I said Glasgow Empire. He said, "Oh God, I've given that up, Jim. Thirty years I've been waiting for a laugh." I said, "If they can't laugh at you, Robb, this is where they should test the atom bomb."'[28]

Twenty years later, Eric joked to Marty Feldman what it took to survive in front of a Glasgow Empire audience. The Scots liked local talent, Americans and black singers. 'We used to go on with black make-up on, in a kilt and talk with an American accent. It was the only way you could get away with it.'

However, Eric did not lack drive. In rehearsal and performance, Morecambe was relentless. He was a worrier, whereas Ernie tended to be more easy-going, if no less hard-working. 'He always had to have a worry,' says Gary Morecambe. 'If he didn't have a worry, he'd be worried he hadn't got a worry.'[29] Indeed, he was almost never 'off'. He was always looking for the joke. Michael Aspel, a guest on numerous Morecambe and Wise shows, observed in his autobiography *Polly Wants a Zebra* that 'Eric, like Harry Secombe, gives away thousands of pounds of free entertainment every week'. Joyously, he could just not stop being Eric Morecambe. Barry Cryer recalls one instructive incident. 'I was with Eric once and a man buttonholed him and started pronouncing about showbusiness. To Eric Morecambe. Eric, sucking on his pipe, just listened very politely, and this man worked himself up to a climax and said, "I think in showbusiness you need three things." Eric said, "If you've got three things you should be in a circus."'

While David Whitfield's feats of stamina and endurance were reserved for the dressing room, the Blackpool season where Eric witnessed an orgy saw Morecambe and Wise sharing the bill with a young comedian who became known for his relentless pounding of audiences on stage. Although he was roughly the same age as Eric and Ernie, Ken Dodd was only three years into his professional career, and his rapid rise must have caused the double act to wonder if they weren't at risk of being left behind after the debacle of *Running Wild*, their first television series as headliners, of which more in the next chapter. Eric and Ernie were topping the bill, Dodd was second spot comic, but already he was stealing shows and making it hard for anyone to follow him. He was also, even then, beginning the tendency to overrun his allotted time, to the delight of the punters, but not necessarily of his co-stars or theatre management. By 1959, Dodd would have his own networked BBC television show, while Eric and Ernie were doing TV guest spots left right and centre, but it looked like they'd already blown their chance of small screen stardom with their first series.

3

Television: the box in which they almost buried Morecambe and Wise

Television had reached the north of England with the opening of the Holme Moss transmitter in October 1951. There wouldn't be a northern television studio capable of staging variety shows until the acquisition in 1954 of the converted Methodist church that was the former Mancunian Films studios. However, Barney Colehan, who had produced the Wilfred Pickles game show *Have a Go* for radio, had transferred to television and made good use of the outside broadcast units to establish northern television light entertainment, and he made a point of televising the big names from the Blackpool summer season shows.

It was an appearance on one of Colehan's spectaculars, *Stars at Blackpool*, in August 1953, that brought Morecambe and Wise fully to the attention of Ronnie Waldman, BBC TV's head of light entertainment. They were appearing at the Pavilion Theatre in the Winter Gardens complex in the summer season show *Something to Sing About* with Ken Platt ('I'll not take my coat off, I'm not stopping.') and Harry Worth, neither of whom, oddly, were selected for the show. The broadcast was promoted with a two-page spread in the trailblazing weekly illustrated magazine *Picture Post*, with Eric and Ernie getting half a page to themselves pictured eating oysters on the beach in front of Blackpool Tower. Lest either of them should get too big-headed, the picture caption got their names the wrong way round.

The show went out on the Friday night, and by the following Wednesday, Frank Pope was in telephone discussions with Waldman about a Morecambe and Wise TV series. Pope followed this up later the same day with a letter confirming that the duo would be free to concentrate on a television series between April and June 1954. Before then, they had a guaranteed eight weeks at the Lyceum, Sheffield, in *Babes in the Wood*, with an option to extend past the end of February if successful, and after June, they were contracted exclusively to do summer shows across the British Isles for George and Alfred Black.

Waldman took three weeks to respond to Pope, but did so full of enthusiasm, noting that two television spots had been offered before the Sheffield season, and giving what looked (and transpired) to be a firm commitment to a series. Waldman promised a meeting when he returned from a business trip in mid-November. In the event, the meeting took place at 11.30 a.m. on 25 November 1953 in Waldman's office at Television Centre, still in the early stages of construction and being used for offices several years before it opened as a studio.

However, before that could occur, an article on 9 November by the London *Evening Standard*'s television correspondent George Campey caused Pope a degree of discomfort. It spoke in glowing terms and argued that the BBC simply had to snap Morecambe and Wise up. 'I count these two men the white hopes of television humour... and television badly needs a new comedy series,' wrote Campey. He quoted Morecambe as saying that 'there is nobody making a mark on television now... we would like to try – especially after the fan mail we received after our last television appearances.' Campey went on to note that the boys were currently earning £150 a week in variety, and that television would need to match this to entice them.[1]

The article reads very much like Campey was primed by Pope or Morecambe and Wise themselves, but in its effusiveness, Pope feared it had gone too far. Pope was worried that Waldman would think Campey was trying to take the credit for the BBC picking up on Eric and Ernie. In a letter to Waldman, the agent explained that he had indeed put Campey in touch with Morecambe when he was approached for a quote and that he was 'unaware of what he was going to put in the write-up'.[2]

In the event, it didn't queer the pitch too much. Indeed, Campey's BBC contacts were so good he was most likely independently aware of the negotiations already. The 25 November meeting was a success, and a further meeting followed on 8 December. It was at this point that discussions hit a snag, with the financial side falling considerably short of what Pope had hoped for and Campey had suggested would be the bare minimum. The assistant television booking manager, Bush Bailey, had opened the batting at 80 guineas a show, quite an increase on the 25 guineas they usually got for television. After some haggling, Bailey went to 100 guineas.

However, in a letter to Waldman, throughout which Pope referred to Bailey as 'Mr Daly', Pope reasoned that with the show being fortnightly and no stage work being possible in the off-weeks, even if the BBC offered £150 a show, it would effectively be a halving of their pay. In truth, there was some overlap between the transmission of *Running Wild* and the recording dates for the second series of *You're Only Young Once*, so that was another 30 guineas per show for just a day's work. Bailey had fallen silent for a few days and Pope asked Waldman if the series was off.

The letter galvanised Waldman to renew the commitment, but there was to be no movement on the pay. What Pope wanted was viewed in the contracts department as too much for an act in its first starring series. Jimmy Jewel and Ben Warriss were on 200 guineas a show, but they were proven. Even the well-established and beloved Jimmy James was only getting 140 guineas a show, out of which he had to pay his stooges, Bretton Woods and Hutton Conyers. The television booking manager, Holland Bennett, noted in a memo to Waldman that he knew the head of light entertainment was 'desperately anxious' to get Eric and Ernie, but indicated that if they went as high as 125 guineas, then everybody else would want a 25 per cent rise and it would bankrupt the department. Bennett had consulted with Pat Newman, and so knew that, whatever Pope said, Eric and Ernie themselves were unlikely to refuse the chance. So it proved and the contract was issued on 21 December at 100 guineas per show for six shows, totalling £630, compared to £1,800 for twelve weeks in variety. Their keenness to make it in television won out.

Ostensibly, the outlook was excellent as the new year hove into view, with *Picture Post* predicting Eric and Ernie to be among the 'bright stars of television in 1954' in the first issue of the year, alongside Benny Hill, Billie Whitelaw, Laurence Harvey and Malcolm Muggeridge. The article quoted Graeme Muir, producer of Henry Hall's show *Face the Music*, on which they had appeared just before Christmas, as saying that they 'seem to have that rare thing – a television sense of comedy timing'.[3]

Behind the scenes, however, there were already grounds for concern. Pope wrote to Waldman on 8 January, explaining that the writers suggested by Waldman had been in touch with Eric and Ernie, but 'do not seem to have submitted anything useful'.⁴ Pope also wondered if a producer had yet been allocated to the show. Waldman replied that Bryan Sears would be producing the show and that Bob Monkhouse and Denis Goodwin, one of the hottest young scriptwriting teams of the time, were 'very interested' in being involved.⁵

The interest was theoretical. The partnership was already fully stretched, writing material for Monkhouse's many TV appearances, and a weekly radio series for Arthur Askey. When Monkhouse's own TV series, *Fast and Loose*, began in May, Monkhouse faked a collapse from exhaustion moments after coming off air, convincing enough to get the rest of the series postponed until the autumn. However, when Sears went up to Sheffield to meet his charges and see them in pantomime, Monkhouse and Goodwin were maintaining the illusion.

Unusually for a BBC light entertainment production of the time, Sears was not slated to direct his own show. At this stage, each production office consisted of a producer and his secretary. Production assistants were a couple of years away. In the case of *Running Wild*, it was to be directed by a promising young man called Ernest Maxin, who had begun his showbusiness career as a child prodigy in a minstrel show and had later been one of the 'Windmill boys', the deft and debonair (clothed) male song and dance men who complemented the glamorous girls at Vivian Van Damm's house of tasteful nudity.

Even if nobody had any idea who would be writing the show, it needed a title. Morecambe and Wise's own suggestion was 'Here's Looking At You', while other titles under consideration included 'Hey There!' (presaging the song from the musical *The*

Pajama Game by a couple of months), 'Side by Side!', 'Running Riot', 'Stand Well Back', 'Look Who's Here', 'Easy Does It' and 'These Foolish Things'. In the end, *Running Wild* was chosen.

The first script was ready by 16 March, just over a month before the series was due to start on Wednesday 21 April. When the first show went out, all of the concerns raised by Pope and his clients turned out to be well founded. The series went out live and no recordings were made, but the reviews give a flavour of the product. In the *Daily Mirror*, Clifford Davis called it 'sick characters in search of an author' and declared that singer Alma Cogan was 'much too good to be mixed up with such stuff'.[6] In the *People*, Kenneth Baily was even less in favour, reviewing the show in just fifteen words: 'Definition of the week: TV set – the box in which they buried Morecambe and Wise.'[7] Morecambe was so stung by the line that he carried the cutting in his wallet for the rest of this life.

The *Sunderland Daily Echo*'s anonymous reviewer noted that Morecambe and Wise 'worked tremendously hard' and suggested they could be stars 'given the right material',[8] but Emery Pearce of the *Daily Herald* pronounced it 'TV's worst effort for months'.[9] It seems that only the *Shields Daily News* had anything nice to say about the show, noting with approval that Morecambe mentioning Whitley Bay in a sketch was publicity for the resort that money couldn't buy.

What is notable about these stinking reviews of the first show is that none of the critics seek to blame Morecambe and Wise themselves. All identify the script as the problem, and their comments seem reasonable, judging by the example quoted by Davis:

First comic: I've got a fear of being locked up. It's a complex.
Second comic: The magistrate calls it six months.

Waldman found himself apologising to controller of programmes Cecil McGivern, promising 'we will do all we can to improve it (and I think it <u>will</u> improve)', and putting it into the context of the wider problem of half-hour comedy shows failing to hit the mark generally. 'We can't just go back to 1949 and rely on little variety bills... but trying to force a solution with only second-rate artists and fourth-rate writers at our disposal is pretty heartbreaking.'

This assessment is at odds with Waldman's noted enthusiasm for Eric and Ernie and his encouragement for them throughout the whole sorry business. It was only inexperience in television that made them 'second-rate' at this stage.

Who were the fourth-rate writers? The *Radio Times* billings for the show are notable for their lack of a writing credit, but Len Fincham and Laurie Wyman were involved, and as the series went on, Ronnie Hanbury, who had been working with Jewel and Warriss and on *Life with the Lyons*, was drafted in.

The hoped-for improvement was not evident by the time of the second show, if a review in *Picture Post* by *What's My Line?* panellist Gilbert Harding is any indicator. 'This half-hour of horror fascinated me – as a rabbit is paralysed by a weasel... I find that there is actually a script for *Running Wild*! It is only fair to Morecambe and Wise to say that they don't write it.'[10]

By the fifth show of the run, on Wednesday 16 June, Eric and Ernie had become thoroughly miserable about the whole situation. The morning after transmission, Frank Pope wrote to Ronnie Waldman requesting that the last show of the run be pulled. 'They can only perform as good as the material and production around them, and I am sorry to state that outside of the fourth Television broadcast, the material and production, etc. they have been given has been impossible.'[11]

Waldman replied that he was 'at a complete loss' to understand Pope's letter and request. He pointed to audience research showing consistent increases in approval throughout the run, and a national newspaper review stating that the show had improved. Waldman said that the involvement of Ronnie Hanbury made it 'difficult to uphold your statement... that the Corporation have provided your clients with poor material'. He hinted heavily that pulling out of the final show would be a breach of contract, calling Pope's request 'hasty and unwise'.[12] Pope took the hint, and the final show went ahead.

On *Running Wild*, Morecambe and Wise had the benefit of Sears and Maxin, two of the most capable individuals in the light entertainment department. Maxin had only joined BBC Television as a producer in 1952, but he had made a big impression quickly, along with another young producer who had joined on the same intake, Brian Tesler. Both were ferociously bright young men from East London Jewish families. Tesler had honed his craft in revue at Oxford University, while Maxin had spent most of his life on the boards.

Both made their reputations by learning the technology thoroughly and striving to make variety television rather than televised variety. When Tesler left to join Lew Grade and Val Parnell's ATV in 1957, Waldman knew that Maxin was one of the producers he could ill afford to lose. His assistant head of light entertainment, Tom Sloan, divided the producers into groups A, B and C. A could handle any programme, B had limitations, and C were only useful for very specific types of programme. Sears and Maxin were both group A material. So what went wrong?

One obvious factor was that Sears was the wrong producer. A former repertory actor at the Sheffield Playhouse, he had joined BBC radio in 1939, moving into television after the

Second World War. He was more comfortable with genteel revue than red-nosed variety, and it seems as though he put a minimal level of effort into keeping *Running Wild* from living up to its title. He remained with the BBC until 1970 and, by the end, the nature of the productions he undertook suggested that he had been overtaken by the development of the medium and become a B or a C. Although young and relatively inexperienced, it might well have been better to let Maxin take complete charge.

Then there was the material. Ronnie Hanbury might have been doing good business for Jewel and Warriss, but was he just writing more of the same for Eric and Ernie, rather than tailoring the material to the turn? Laurie Wyman would go on to create the long-running radio sitcom *The Navy Lark*, so his pedigree is not in doubt, but again, was he the right writer for Morecambe and Wise?

And perhaps some of the blame must fall on Eric and Ernie themselves. As Eric had said to Alan Grahame, it was always harder for the act that had to carry the show, and maybe when they got the offer to make *Running Wild*, they simply weren't ready. Throughout the history of the BBC, there has been a not-always-friendly rivalry between London and the regions, and the poaching of acts was a regular source of resentment. In the case of Morecambe and Wise, there was a feeling that London had taken over a good thing and botched it. 'We'd done a lot of work with them, [then] they go to London, do the television series with Bryan Sears who didn't understand them at all,' said John Ammonds, 'We'd been grooming them and been pretty successful with them.'[13]

Aside from the infamous Kenneth Baily review, there was one other possible lasting legacy for Morecambe and Wise. Sears was a flamboyant theatrical gay man. Once, when in a relationship with a young floor manager, a lover's tiff spilled over into the studio. Sears gave his lover an unwelcome instruction. Thinking he couldn't be heard on talkback, the floor manager cursed Sears as 'a ludicrous old queen'. Immediately, he and the whole studio realised that Sears had heard everything. There was a shocked silence before Sears replied, 'I am not a ludicrous old queen. I am a beautiful young princess. Now can we please get on with this?' Ever after, the camp, fruity television producer was a running joke in Eric and Ernie's shows.

The *Running Wild* experience is often depicted as nearly fatal for Eric and Ernie's career, but their exclusive contract with George and Alfred Black meant that they had a full date sheet into 1955. They returned to the fray with a week at the Ardwick Hippodrome in Manchester in mid-July on a bill with singer David Hughes, and two relics of ancient music hall, Billy Danvers and G. H. Elliott, whom Eric had begun his life as an entertainer impersonating. A month later, they found themselves reunited with Hughes at the Birmingham Hippodrome, also sharing the bill with a young comedian and singer who would later come to figure heavily in their career, one Desmond Bernard O'Connor. Through the autumn, the pair were doing the rounds as part of a package with the Ray Ellington Quartet – then at the height of their *Goon Show* fame – and Hungarian-born singer Eve Boswell, still a year or so away from having a hit single with 'Pickin' a Chicken'.

They were also welcomed back by their friends in the BBC radio variety department in Manchester. There was a third series of *You're Only Young Once* in the winter of 1954. Then in the spring of 1955, they began a regular booking for Geoffrey Wheeler and Ronnie Taylor, hosting and doing a comedy spot in *The Show Goes On*, which again promised 'variety at high speed'. It might have been that the pace of the delivery was needed to cover the quality of the material. Eric and Ernie were still a few years away from scripts that matched their talents. Wise was still very much the 'and what did he/she say?' straight man, in the mould of George Burns or Bud Abbott. In this exchange from the show that went out on 24 May 1955, Eric's character is the priapic innocent, full of lust and smart lines, but who'd probably run a mile or miss all the signs if faced with a real woman.

WISE: And now ladies and gentlemen, it's my pleasure to introduce a young man whose name is rapidly becoming a household word. Too bad you can't say it in front of the children. Eric Morecambe.

MORECAMBE: Thank you. Hey, I've only been in Manchester a few hours and I've met Milly Laura and Doris and Fido.

WISE: Wait a minute, Fido sounds like a dog.

MORECAMBE: You think Fido is a dog. You should see Milly Laura and Doris. Really I'm looking for a girl who does not drink, smoke, swear or go out with other men.

WISE: Why?

MORECAMBE: I don't know. Mind you I met a lovely girl here recently.

WISE: Did you really? How old was she?

MORECAMBE: I asked her that. I said 'How old are you love?' She said 'That's my business.' Believe me I think she'd been in business a long time. I said 'Watch out kid, I'm a go getter.'

WISE: And what did she say?

MORECAMBE: She said 'Go away, I'm looking for an already gotter.'

WISE: Did you buy her a present?

MORECAMBE: I bought her a fur coat.

WISE: A fur coat?

MORECAMBE: Before I realized what had happened, she snatched it from me hand, threw it in the wardrobe, locked it and said 'Oh you shouldn't have bothered'. Then I bought her some roses for ten shillings a dozen. The florist said he raised them himself. I think he raised them from six shillings a dozen.[14]

Nonetheless, they had become something of an industry in-joke, as evidenced by a reference in *The Greenslade Story*, a December 1955 edition of *The Goon Show*, where announcer Wallace Greenslade is poached to become a star on the halls performing nothing more than the weather forecast. His stardom is, however, short-lived when the idiot Eccles steals his audience.

Greenslade: This means ruin? No more luxury? I'll have to stop eating in the canteen? Give up my subscription to the Nursing Mother?

Seagoon: And so we became vagrants.

[...]

FX: Coin dropping into cup.

Seagoon: Oh thank you kind sir.

John Snagge: It's nothing. I've plenty more buttons. Aren't you Jewel and Warriss? Or Morecambe and Wise?

Seagoon: No, it's Seagoon and Greenslade.

Snagge: Oh horrors. How the mighty have fallen.[15]

During this period when television wasn't showing Eric and Ernie much love, they managed to keep their names in the public eye with random appearances in the newspapers. They were among the many variety artistes to enlist the services of a Birmingham-based press relations man called George Bartram. Bartram coached his clients in the art of writing humorous letters on topical matters to local newspapers immediately before they were due to appear in a town, and he also knew a good bandwagon when he saw one. Morecambe and Wise's interest in 'tegestology' – or, in simple English, beer mat collecting – had all the hallmarks of a Bartram wheeze.

The term first crops up in a November 1956 correspondence in the *Daily Mirror*'s long-running 'Live Letters' column, 'conducted by the Old Codgers'. A Corporal Lebor, serving with the RAF on the Rhine, wrote in to ask if his collection of 200 beer mats was the biggest, only to be outboxed by H. J. Adams, the landlord of the Traveller's Rest in Mapperley, Nottinghamshire, with 700, who supplied the Latin name for the hobby. During their season in Blackpool the following summer, Morecambe and Wise outed themselves as practising tegestologists, picking up numerous examples on their travels around the country, and the arcane enthusiasm was mentioned regularly in interviews for the following decade. When Coventry man Christopher Walsh founded the British Beermat Collectors Society, it was natural that Eric and Ernie should be approached to become joint presidents of the organisation, a duty they discharged for several years.

Their return to the small screen came via ATV, the ITV contractor for weekends in London and weekdays in the Midlands. Following a couple of successful appearances on *Sunday Night at the London Palladium* in November 1955 and February 1956, Eric and Ernie were offered a residency on an upcoming ten-week series starring the Trinidadian pianist

Winifred Atwell,* to begin in April 1956. Lack of suitable material had been one of the biggest problems on *Running Wild*, but this time, Eric and Ernie knew they couldn't settle for any old tripe. Thankfully, they were in luck. The main writers on the show – billed as 'script supervisors' – were to be Glaswegian former journalists Bill Craig and John Law, but it was a junior member of the team, a former dance band drummer called Johnny Speight, who would make the difference for the boys.

Speight was the first writer to see Eric and Ernie as personalities rather than gag men, and he had an inspiration that presaged Eddie Braben's realisation twelve years later.

> They were then purely and simply... like Abbot and Costello. Straight man slapping the comic's face and all that kind of thing. I had said 'It's not an original idea, why don't you be more like Laurel and Hardy? Both be funny men, and have the straight man as even dafter than the daft one, so you integrate that way?'. They tried it and loved it, and went on always doing that. In fact, towards the end, it was Ernie who was more the idiot. It gave them more flexibility.'[16]

Eric and Ernie knew that there was a lot riding on this booking. They had to be impressive, and as important as a good script was, their success would ultimately be down to their skill as performers. The *Running Wild* experience had taught them a lot about television, in particular what to avoid.

---

* Atwell (1914–1983) was the first black artist to have a number one in the UK singles chart. Classically trained at the Royal Academy of Music in London, she became most famous for her 'other piano', a battered upright perfectly suited to the honky-tonk sound of hits like the 'Black and White Rag'.

They'd thought about the needs of the medium and how they had to balance working to the cameras and working to the studio audience. Eric, however, was a worrier, and no amount of thought and planning could remove the element of the unknown. Joan was in the late stages of expecting their second child, Gary, and the two events had Eric on the hop.

'Imagine the state of my nerves,' he recalled in 1973. 'I would sit rigid, staring at an object like a "fool gun-dog" until somebody snapped a finger in front of my face.' The show's producer – cited by Morecambe as Dicky Leeman, although the first show of the series was produced by Bill Lyon-Shaw – tried to calm the comedian down by telling him it was only a TV series, not awaiting execution on death row. Morecambe replied 'If I'm going to "die", let it be on a stage', to which the hard-bitten veteran producer (both Leeman and Lyon-Shaw were old BBC hands from the Alexandra Palace days) replied: 'As long as it gets a laugh on my show.'[17]

Like *Running Wild*, the shows were transmitted live from a former variety theatre that had been converted to television studio usage, in this case the Wood Green Empire. Videotape recording was a couple of years away, and when things went wrong, millions knew. During the first show on Saturday 21 April 1956, things went wrong. One of the sketches was a somewhat elaborate quickie involving a real-life London taxi, with Ernie in the driving seat. Eric was to hail the cab, get in one door then straight out the other, ask Ernie how much, and, on paying, tell him 'OK, but next time don't drive so fast', at which the taxi would zoom off.

Except it didn't. The engine was off, to avoid asphyxiating the audience and crew, and the cab was to be hauled on and off by scene hands pulling ropes. For the illusion to work, the car needed to be in neutral, but when it came to the exit, Ernie, a keen driver with a penchant for sporty cars, absent-mindedly put the car into gear and it wouldn't budge. Eric and Ernie both ad-libbed to cover, while they tried to work out what was wrong. Soon enough, one of the scene hands noticed the gear stick and invisibly reached in to rectify the fault. After the show, the producer told the boys how impressed he was with the way they'd handled the cock-up. It was decided, to the comedians' dismay, to put further tests in future shows. Eventually, they had to beg Leeman to stop because Eric was getting so worried each week about what the deliberate mistake was going to be, but one of the staged cock-ups was a prop door that wouldn't open, a simple gag to which the pair would return very fruitfully later on.

Ten weeks of live television on a Saturday night had the effect of taking an act out of circulation for variety bookings, and Morecambe and Wise were acutely aware of the effect that several weeks' bad exposure could have had. It also ruled them out of taking on a summer season, as the Atwell series finished on 23 June, by which time all of the big seaside shows were in the final stages of rehearsal or already underway. However, a good run of TV work was an excellent shop window, and would pay dividends. So it proved, with a full date sheet for the rest of the year, beginning with a week at the Regal in Great Yarmouth with Pearl Carr and Teddy Johnson.

The night before the Yarmouth booking began, Eric and Ernie were back on BBC television, as part of *Variety Cavalcade*, a special to mark the golden jubilee of the Variety Artistes' Federation. Their turn was noted by *The Stage* as the 'best of the modern type entertainment', although the reviewer felt that the show was a grim affair overall, with 'the music hall profession... doing everything it can to drive the final nail into its own coffin. Groaning about unwantedness, gloomily publicising the fact that "things aren't what they used to be", blaming this that and the other... [and refusing] to jerk itself out of its present condition of lethargy and self-pity... in front of the largest audience in the country'.[18] As much as they loved the profession they'd grown up in, Eric and Ernie sensed the way the wind was blowing earlier than most and knew they would be wise to adapt.

Then the following year, they were topping the bill in *Double Six*, broadcast live on Sunday evenings from the stage of the Playhouse theatre in Hulme, just next door to the Hippodrome, where they had made their radio shows. In the absence of any surviving recordings, the show, again produced by Ronnie Taylor, seems to have carried over the 'variety at high speed' element of *The Show Goes On*. While they were the stars of the show, they weren't expected to carry it as they had with *Running Wild*, with contemporary reports referring to 'the pattern of the show... [being] derived from the teamwork of the old Co-Optimists'. 'None of the acts will last more than about four and a half minutes,' Taylor told the *Radio Times*, promising 'singing, comedy sketches and dancing'.[19] Indeed, Sunday was the only day they had free to make the show, being in summer season at the Central Pier in Blackpool for the rest of the week.

As well as the lighter workload, Eric and Ernie were in safer hands with Taylor and his colleagues from Broadcasting House, over the National Provincial Bank on Piccadilly Gardens. The booking seemed a sure sign that the pair hadn't been rendered unsuitable for television by the *Running Wild* debacle.

However, apart from some spots for the ever-loyal Barney Colehan on *The Good Old Days* and his usual Blackpool round-ups, after *Double Six* the BBC seemed to lose interest in Eric and Ernie. It had filled five half-hours pleasantly enough, but was to be a one-series wonder. Through 1958 and 1959, Frank Pope wrote dutifully to producers to announce the boys' availability, to no avail.

The reason becomes clear in a memo sent in February 1959 by Eric Miller, a Manchester radio variety producer on attachment to television light entertainment in London, to the head of north region programmes, Bryan Cave-Browne-Cave. Miller had put together a script for a possible Morecambe and Wise television show with Edward Taylor, later to create the long-running radio sitcom *The Men from the Ministry*. Miller explained that Tom Sloan, assistant head of television light entertainment under Eric Maschwitz, had 'seen it and although he liked the script very much, has not a great deal of personal admiration for the abilities of Morecambe and Wise as television performers'. Taylor admitted that he felt they were 'at their worst on stage, as no doubt they control their own material and production',[20] but suggested that with the right script and production they would 'come up quite well'. Miller suggested circumventing Sloan by doing the show as a north region only opt-out.[21]

Cave-Browne-Cave read the script and declared he had 'got a lot of laughs out of it... some of it is very promising', but added that 'the motor car sequences and the faulty sets going from programme to programme, were not so good'. Cave-Browne-Cave indicated that at a planning meeting shortly before, 'we decided we would go ahead to try and find a satisfactory formula for Morecambe and Wise'.[22]

While this correspondence was ongoing, Eric and Ernie were several thousand miles away in Australia, working with Winifred Atwell in a show called *Rocking the Town*. The opportunity to work while seeing the world, in particular avoiding the British winter, was too good to pass up. The boys decided to treat the experience as a working holiday, taking their wives. They meandered out in stages to Australia, where it would be the height of summer, flying out via New York, San Francisco and Hawaii, with a similarly leisurely return via New Zealand, Fiji and Los Angeles. Lew and Leslie Grade were the bookers for the Tivoli theatres in Melbourne and Sydney, and the show was booked in at each for two months apiece.

Spending six months away from England at such a critical stage in their re-establishment programme seemed to be a risk. Would they come back to find that they had been forgotten and supplanted? At least they had some insurance. Frank Pope had booked them in for the 1959 summer season in Blackpool, working for Peter Webster, again at the Central Pier.

Initially, Joan had not known whether to stay at home with Gail and Gary or accompany Eric on tour. The answer, as with so much in Eric's life, came from Sadie, who said she and George would love to look after their grandchildren. Gary was not yet of school age, and Gail could go to Eric's old school. Sadie would write every week, and if Joan was feeling the wrench, she could come home and pick them up at any time. Ernie and Doreen had no family commitments, but on arrival in Australia, Doreen remembered a Peterborough butcher who had known her parents before emigrating. She made contact with him, and he and his family became native guides, as well as giving the Wises and the Morecambes a traditional Christmas.

The show was a big hit in both cities. It helped, Eric said, that the previous show in Melbourne – a revue called 'Femmes and Furs' – had been a disappointment, leaving the punters hungry for entertainment. They also realised that even their most well-worn material was falling on fresh ears and getting a new lease of life.

On their return, though, Pope told them in no uncertain terms that they had lost ground during their absence. The summer season was all that he had in the date book for them. Perhaps as penance, one of the first dates they picked up on their return was a week at Glasgow Empire. However, as they were back on *Sunday Night at the London Palladium* almost as soon as they had returned from Australia, it was clear that they had good friends in the Delfont/Grade axis. The world of variety theatres that Pope knew best was on the way out. They gave Pope the required notice and began looking around for new representation.

When the news got out, numerous big-time agents were interested, but the obvious choice, Billy Marsh of the Bernard Delfont Agency, didn't put himself forward. A child of a Russian emigré family, Bernard Winogradsky had adopted the stage name Delfont when he was a young dancer, following in the hoofsteps of his elder brother, Lew, who had anglicised the family name to Grade for his own professional purposes. With younger brother Leslie, the Winogradsky boys became the top agents in the country, and Lew had been early into commercial television as co-managing director with Val Parnell of Associated Television.

Billy Marsh was Bernard's protégé, the son of a Kentish farmer who abandoned agriculture for show business. As a stagestruck teenager, he cycled miles to shows in Dover and Folkestone, and became well known to the stage doorkeepers. One of the touring shows that visited the Dover Hippodrome was looking for a secretary. Marsh could type and do shorthand, so off he went on tour.

Being represented by the Delfont firm wouldn't harm Eric and Ernie's chances of getting regular television work, and they had already worked with Delfont and Marsh, who had packaged the Winifred Atwell shows. Ernie wrote to Marsh and arranged a meeting.

At the meeting, Marsh agreed that Eric and Ernie should be doing better than they were, topping bills rather than supporting, but that it was television that made the difference. He picked up the telephone to ATV's head booker, Alec Fyne, and got them a spot straight away. With his connections, that was the easy part. If you were good enough for Billy Marsh, that was it. Once the phone was back on the cradle, he explained that the difficult part was up to them. Many of the biggest names in music hall had toured for decades with the same act. Television was different. Acts needed a constant supply of fresh material to survive and thrive. Marsh said that if Eric and Ernie could come up with the goods every time, he could get them the bookings.

Marsh was unusual among agents, because he would refuse work if he didn't think it was right for his clients, no matter how much money was on offer. Others were about the percentage. Marsh was about building careers and keeping his talent at the top. Gary Morecambe went to work for Marsh and saw Marsh hard at work and then relaxing afterwards.

Eric and Ernie would have jumped at anything, but he stopped them. He stopped Ernie taking loads of work after Eric died. Constantly, just 'No'. Amazing, astute man. Come 6 o'clock, the office would vacate, and just as I was getting my coat, the intercom would go and it would be Billy. 'Gary, come to my office. Go to the bar, get a whisky, pour one for yourself.' And I was thinking, 'There's the train gone. Next one.' And the drinks cabinet was hidden. You had to lean on the wall and out came the whisky. Then the phone would ring and he'd throw it in the bin. And then he'd say to me

'How's your da... hang on. Yeah yeah yeah', back in the
bin. Extraordinary character, larger than life. You don't get
them any more. They'd be fired now. They ran the business
brilliantly by being eccentric.[23]

Not that Marsh was refusing approaches from the BBC,
though. One Manchester-based producer who knew the duo
well expressed reservations in a letter to Edward Taylor,
concluding rather damningly that the reason Eric and Ernie
hadn't taken off wasn't script quality or misguided direction,
but Eric and Ernie themselves. 'I like the ideas in the script but
after seeing Morecambe and Wise the other week in their show
from the Central Pier, Blackpool, I am not at all sure as to their
strength on a TV programme,' he explained.

It seems to me that they have learnt very little over the
past five years or so – still working the old gags and, in my
opinion, frequently working the wrong type of material...
They are quite a disappointment to me because when I first
worked with them in this region on sound I thought they had
a great future but quite frankly I don't think they will ever
be in the Number One class. It is even more depressing that
it seems they are quite happy to jog along as they are doing
at the moment. I have always thought Eric Morecambe to
be a naturally funny man and I still think he could be very
successful on vision, but only if he could be detached from
Ernie whom I think is the big weakness.

The producer in question rounds off this harsh assessment
by telling Taylor that 'I am sorry to be so pessimistic but I
really cannot see them making the grade in a TV series'. The
producer who wrote the letter could have had no idea that ten

years later, Eric and Ernie would be the BBC's biggest comedy stars, and still less of an idea that he would be the one who put them there. The producer who wrote the letter was Johnny Ammonds.[24]

Perhaps sensing Sloan's antipathy, Eric and Ernie wrote personally to Eric Maschwitz on 25 November 1959 indicating their desire to do more television, knowing it was the future, and got a polite but brief reply on 3 December saying that he would inform all of his producers. However, their only BBC TV bookings in this period came from Barney Colehan in Leeds, who used them on a *Good Old Days* over Christmas.

Eric and Ernie hadn't had a sniff of television since the summer, but viewers got three chances to catch them over the Christmas period, indeed twice on the same day. On 19 December, Eric and Ernie turned up in a *Val Parnell's Saturday Spectacular* showcasing the singer Alma Cogan, 'the girl with the laugh in her voice'.

Their spot was a routine with Eric as a black belt in judo, being interviewed by Ernie, who consistently outwits and overpowers him. The pay-off was Morecambe being stretchered off. The most interesting thing about the routine is Morecambe trapping Wise by holding a hand under his chin and saying 'Get out of that'. Shorn of context, this would become a regular callback for Eric and Ernie, with very few viewers recalling the sketch from which it came. Somehow, dropped in randomly over the years, it became funnier and funnier. In this performance, it's over-egged by the insistence of adding a percussive sound effect on a woodblock every time Eric gets Ernie in the hold.

Then on Boxing Day they could be found at 7.30 p.m. on ITV in *This Particular Show*, a starring vehicle for singer Tommy Steele, transmitted under the *Val Parnell's Saturday*

Spectacular umbrella, sharing a bill with The Three Monarchs, a comedy harmonica troupe featuring Les Henry, a fellow Bryan Michie discovery. At 10.45 p.m. on the same day, they could be seen on the BBC in mock-Victorian garb of bowler hats and checked suits on *The Good Old Days*.

Their first appearance in the Steele effort involves them singing Cole Porter's 'Be a Clown' with the star. Curiously, when doing a solo verse, Eric gets out of step with the orchestral backing, while Ernie's time is rock solid. Later in the show, they return without Steele to sing 'Back in the Old Routine'. Just as they're starting the number, there is a noise off-screen, with something being dropped or knocked over. They continue undeterred, acknowledging the mishap with a smile. They break off in mid-song to do a bit of crosstalk, and Eric addresses the noise directly, as well as letting light in on magic with a reference to reading lyrics from cue cards:

Ernie: You know, Eric, how long have we been doing this song now?

Eric: About five seconds. Just before that bang.

Ernie: No, I mean how many years have we been singing it?

Eric: About fifteen?

Ernie: Fifteen years? It's a long time, isn't it? Don't you think it's about time that we changed it?

Eric: Change it? I've only just learned the words of this. What are you talking about? Using cards now. Lost my place.

Ernie: You know I used to come to this theatre and see a lot of great performers.

Eric: Did you really?

Ernie: Some wonderful performers.

Eric: You come from Leeds, don't you?

Ernie: Yes. Harry Champion.

Eric: I liked him.

Ernie: Vesta Tilley.

Eric: Who?

Ernie: Vesta Tilley.

Eric: I liked him as well.

Ernie: Hey, wait a minute, Vesta Tilley was a woman.

Eric: Was he? I never knew that. Funny that. You learn, don't you?[25]

While it's nice to see them, they seem curiously underused. Any up-and-coming double act of the time could have done two spots of this length. However, what comes across is their assured manner, even in the face of adversity.

In *The Good Old Days*, they top the bill, and we see them starting to come into their own. Despite the archaic trappings of the performance, there was nothing dated about the material. In 1954, civil aviation rules on charter flights changed, ushering in the era of the package holiday. Three years later, British European Airways began flights to what the ad men dubbed the 'Costa Blanca'. The package boom was some years off, but an overseas holiday was within reach of many people for the first time. Indeed, Steele had capitalised on the interest by starring in a film called *Tommy the Toreador*, which begat the hit single 'Little White Bull'.

In their new routine, Ernie talks of how he wants to make Eric 'the greatest bullfighter in the world'. It was one they had worked up for a summer run of *Let's Have Fun* at the Central Pier in Blackpool – ironically, given that the package trip was what would ultimately kill the British seaside holiday. The idea had been planted by their former *Front Page Personalities* colleague Bobby Dennis when he met them on a train between engagements. Dennis gave them the structure and various ideas for gags, and the pair could see the potential, but had to work on it to make it right for them.

'The original routine Bobby Dennis gave us was a lot more suggestive,' Ernie recalled. 'We cleaned it up a bit and wowed the audience with it in the opening spot… Peter Webster, who owned the theatre, came running backstage, saying he had never known anyone to get laughs like that so early in the show.' Even toned down, it was still a bit too 'blue' for the boys, who already had a rock-solid sense of what their manner was and who their audience were. So, they kept working on it, making it cleaner, without forsaking the laughs. By the time it reached the BBC television audience on Boxing Day 1959, it was honed to perfection, and met with the predicted response.

The true art is to conceal the art, and this is a very early example of Morecambe and Wise doing exactly that. The routine had long since been locked in place, but Eric and Ernie still made it feel spontaneous. Cleverly, Colehan went in for two-shots, where both Eric and Ernie filled the screen, and what comes across is their shared glee. Ernie seems perpetually on the verge of corpsing, Eric leading him on cheekily. Was Ernie faking the glee, or was he simply enjoying his work, and the mechanics of conspiring to make the nation laugh with his best mate? Evidence suggests that it was the latter.

Colehan would use the boys in *Little Miss Music*, a one-off show for Sheila Buxton, the singer with the BBC Northern Dance Orchestra, in March 1960, but increasingly, their TV dates were coming from the other side. Sometimes these bookings involved playing second fiddle to someone who hadn't their breadth and depth of experience. Tommy Steele was ten years younger than Eric and Ernie, but was already the established headline act just three years after his first hit single, 'Rock with the Caveman'. The world of show business was changing. Suddenly, pop singers like Steele, Adam Faith and Cliff Richard were the big names. Morecambe and Wise ran the risk of being cast aside as relics of a bygone age, despite their relative youth. The rock and rollers had suave managers, like Steele's mentor Larry Parnes, to guide their careers. Even with Billy Marsh and the Delfont office behind them, there was the possibility that Eric and Ernie had got as far as they possibly could.

4

The Comeback Kids

By the spring of 1960, Eric and Ernie felt they had served their penance and improved massively. The guest bookings from ATV were coming in thick and fast through Marsh, as they kept up their side of the bargain with fresh material every time. They felt they were ready to be top of the bill on television.

Perhaps surprisingly, given Jack Hylton's close involvement on the light entertainment side, they had never worked for Associated-Rediffusion.* This, however, was a blessing in disguise, given the poor reputation of Hylton's productions. Although ATV was their bread and butter, they persevered with the BBC, even though Ronnie Waldman had moved on, and while Eric Maschwitz was head of light entertainment, the day-to-day running of the department was down to his assistant head, their nemesis Tom Sloan. In March, they sent a

---

* Associated-Rediffusion, rebranded on-screen in 1964 as Rediffusion London, was the ITV contractor providing London and the South East with commercial television from 1955 to 1968.

storyline for a half-hour show to Sloan for his consideration, even including a stamped addressed envelope for its return. Sloan replied that although the idea was 'good value', he would have to decline.

Sloan's antipathy was an obstacle, but it wasn't fatal. Morecambe and Wise had allies at Television Centre in the form of another well-established partnership, writers Frank Muir and Denis Norden, who were advisors to the BBC comedy department.* They were developing a 'flat-out fast broad-comedy laugh show' with 'new ideas in presentation and construction',[1] called *Four Aces and a King*. They were keen to get Eric and Ernie on board, and the interest was reciprocated, but they told Muir and Norden that they were busy with commercial television and panto until March. The writers were willing to delay the show's launch to fit accordingly.

With resounding support from such expert figures, Sloan had to swallow his pride and enquire with Billy Marsh as to Morecambe and Wise's availability, but found the agent curiously difficult to pin down. In January, after several unanswered telephone calls, Sloan wrote to Marsh for a final answer. Marsh took his time in replying, only to tell Sloan that it would have to be a no because they were now under contract to ATV, and that he had been 'completely unaware that the BBC were interested in these artistes'.[2]

At this stage, the ATV agreement contained no firm commitment to give Eric and Ernie their own show. The summer of 1961 found Eric and Ernie at the newly built Princess Theatre in Torquay on a bill with singers Joan Regan and Edmund Hockridge, to say nothing of Tommy Cooper.

---

* In organisational terms at the BBC, Light Entertainment was a group of two departments, comedy and variety.

During the run came the word that there could be an autumn slot that ATV needed to fill.

The *Running Wild* experience had made two things clear. They needed the right material and the right production. Meanwhile, at the Pavilion, the headliners were Jimmy Jewel and Ben Warriss. Warriss had taken the flat above Ernie and Doreen, and one night, Wise and Warriss had a drink and a chat about the ATV offer. Warriss said that he and Jewel had been lucky to land good writers in Dick Hills and Sid Green and a brilliant producer in Colin Clews. Warriss's advice made Eric and Ernie adamant. They would need Hills, Green and Clews. The answer came back that the trio were not available. Eric and Ernie insisted. Without Hills, Green and Clews, the deal was off.

It was a risky strategy. If ATV refused, they had two choices. Back down and do the series with whoever was allotted, or stand their ground and risk losing their second big chance. At this time, ATV was the ITV network's main provider of light entertainment programming, churning out hours of variety and comedy from the Wood Green Empire, the Hackney Empire and the new Elstree studios.[*] An idea of the production throughout can be gained from a comment made by Jack Parnell, big band drummer turned musical director, and nephew of Val Parnell, the co-chairman.

> At one time, we were doing five live television shows a week, and the pressure was unbelievable. LIVE television shows. We had a huge team – we had four rehearsal pianists doing a show each, a whole bunch of arrangers. It became much easier when we could record. The pressure came off a bit. That live business was terrifying – you couldn't make a mistake.[3]

* Like most studios named Elstree, they are in fact in Borehamwood.

Playing hard to get could backfire, but they had Marsh on their side, and his insistence on quality control meant that he couldn't countenance a bad series. Marsh believed in career development. Not all publicity was good publicity and not all money was good money.

Someone who knew this better than anyone was Bruce Forsyth, who, in 1958, had been propelled from summer season obscurity in Babbacombe* to hosting ATV's big prestige variety show *Sunday Night at the London Palladium*. In 1953, Forsyth had signed a five-year contract with an agent called Miff Ferrie, who also represented Tommy Cooper. Not long into the contract, however, Forsyth fell out with Ferrie. 'I soon realized,' said Forsyth, 'that, essentially, he was a musician who, although he thought he was put on this earth to produce great comedians, knew nothing about comedy.'[4] Ferrie would turn up at rehearsals and tell the performers and producers they were doing it all wrong.

When Forsyth's big television break came, it was the work of Marsh, even though he wasn't Forsyth's agent. He had seen Brucie performing, liked him and put him up for an ATV series called *New Look*, featuring new talent like Roy Castle and Lionel Blair. Forsyth moved on swiftly to the Palladium, with Ferrie – who had done nothing to lift Forsyth from obscurity – taking the commission. To add insult to injury, Ferrie's cut was 15 per cent rather than the industry standard 10 per cent. Val Parnell, like just about everyone else, found Ferrie hard to deal with, and had begun to deal directly with Forsyth.

---

* Babbacombe Theatre, in the northern suburbs of Torquay, had been the home to Hedley Claxton's 'Gaytime' summer shows since the end of the Second World War, and had become known as a training ground for future stars, including magician David Nixon.

Eventually, Forsyth decided to sack his pointless agent, but discovered that the five-year contract renewed on a rolling basis, and was effectively a life sentence. Forsyth took Ferrie to court to get free, and the buyout cost him £27,000, plus all the legal bills. He signed immediately with Marsh, who took the standard 10 per cent and managed to get Forsyth's fees upped, so the expense of freedom was soon recouped. 'It was the best deal I ever did,' Forsyth recalled.

Morecambe and Wise had been very lucky to fall in with Marsh. They stood firm. For a while, it looked very much like the show would not go on. However, with October approaching and thirteen half-hour slots still to fill, ATV bosses acceded to the demands. There was also the prospect of an Equity strike making ATV keen to get contracts signed all round.

After a sticky start in the mid-1950s, the ITV companies were making handsome profits. When Scottish Television chairman Roy Thomson said that an ITV franchise was a 'licence to print money', it gave commercial television's critics a stick with which to beat ITV.

At the April 1961 Equity AGM, André Morell, best known as Professor Bernard Quatermass in the BBC's *Quatermass and the Pit*, complained in his commanding voice that actors were getting 'the crumbs from the television boardroom tables', with fees being whatever they'd been 'bamboozled' into accepting.[5] There needed to be a clear structure, with fees related to the size of audience. Eric and Ernie were members of the rival trade union, the Variety Artistes' Federation, whose endeavours were looked down upon by Equity, so would be unaffected by any action.[*]

---

[*] The VAF did begin its own parallel action against the TV companies, with the result that *Sunday Night at the London Palladium* was forced off air for a few weeks, but artists with long-term contracts were allowed to keep working.

Hills and Green were both former schoolmasters, and so far their biggest achievement in television had been the surreal, brilliant, knowing sitcom *The Strange World of Gurney Slade*, written with singer and actor Anthony Newley. The latter episodes of this six-part series involve Slade standing trial for the crime of being unfunny on television. Any idea that this had been a response to falling audiences can be dismissed by the fact that the whole series, made at considerable expense on 35mm film, was in the can before the first episode went out. However, the writers did seem to have anticipated the response, as the show moved from prime time to late night.

The first ATV Morecambe and Wise show, entitled *Two of a Kind,* after the Bobby Darin and Johnny Mercer song* that had been adopted as the signature tune, went out at 8 p.m. on Thursday 12 October 1961, live from the Wood Green Empire, with Chris Barber's Jazz Band and singer Janie Marden as guests. It was an uncomfortable experience for the stars. A sketch with Eric and Ernie as spies used so many additional actors that they felt they were getting lost in their own show. Hills and Green insisted it was funny, but the response was muted. Eric and Ernie asked them to pare it back for the second show, but they persisted. 'The jokes were there,' said Ernie years later. 'We had some very funny lines, but again we were sure it was wrong for us.'[6]

Hills, Green and Clews were making the sort of show that had worked for Jewel and Warriss. As disconcerting as it must have been to find themselves overruled as they had been on *Running Wild,* history was not quite repeating itself. There were issues, but it wasn't a disaster. Sections of the press

---

* The number was absolutely fresh, having had its first outing in April 1961, when the Darin and Mercer LP of the same name was released.

appeared to have forgotten their earlier show had happened. Indeed, the *Daily Herald*'s correspondent expressed surprise that Eric and Ernie should have had to wait so long for their own vehicle.

By the third week, the show was being watched in 5.24 million homes, tying for thirteenth place in the Television Audience Measurement (TAM) ratings with Granada's drab drama series *Family Solicitor*, which followed it at 8.30 p.m. Then, forty-eight hours before the fourth show was due to go out, talks between the ITV companies and Equity broke down, and the strike began the next day, Wednesday 1 November.

The union was allowing members to honour long-term contracts, so shows like *Coronation Street* were able to continue. However, booking actors week by week for comedy sketches was out of the question. At first, Hills and Green thought it was over, but Morecambe and Wise saw the chance to prove what they'd been saying all along. With simpler sketches and quick costume changes, they could do everything themselves. Then came the idea of putting the writers on screen as well. S. C. Green and R. M. Hills became Sid and Dick, or Sick and Did, if Eric was feeling playful. The fourth show went out in this new streamlined form, and found instant approval. Even the dour Aberdeen *Evening Express*, which had called the second show of the run 'dull as ditchwater', was prepared to admit that 'as variety programmes go' it was 'no worse and no better than most others'.[7]

The show was originally set to run for six weeks with an option for three more, and between the fourth and fifth shows, ATV took up the option. It's unclear how much of this was the result of the improvement of the product and how much was insulation against the strike, but it gave Eric, Ernie, Sid and Dick time to explore ideas further and gain confidence. By the sixth week, the show had risen to ninth in the ratings. By the end of the run on 7 December, they were up to seventh place, while their BBC counterpart *The Seven Faces of Jim*, starring Jimmy Edwards, wasn't even making the top twenty. Morecambe and Wise had exhumed the box, and themselves.

In time, the stars and their writers settled into a working pattern, consisting of improvising around a theme together. 'We only need an idea,' Eric said in 1966. 'That's all we need, you see, and the four of us build from that.'[8] When the dynamic was fully established, Hills would bring a single sheet of paper to rehearsals bearing his and Green's ideas for the week. The quartet would flesh out the bare bones 'by collectively ad-libbing around it while a girl took the gags down'[9] to create a draft script, which was then edited.

Clews had come up through the technical rather than the theatrical ranks, and the writers liked his willingness to let them get on with it, concentrating on how to capture the comedy on screen. Before wartime service in the Royal Navy, he had been an outside broadcast sound engineer in BBC radio. Rejoining the Corporation after demob, he had gone up to Alexandra Palace to join the camera crews re-establishing the television service. He quickly became one of the BBC's top studio cameramen, and when producer Bill Ward left to join Lew Grade and Val Parnell's fledgling ATV in 1955, he took Clews with him to run the camera department. Through a combination of necessity and his ability to learn quickly, Clews was promoted to direct programmes within six months.

With 'comedians like Morecambe and Wise', said Clews modestly in 1964, 'all you have to do is have one camera on the two of them and another camera ready to go on to whichever of them is saying a funny line – and you don't necessarily know when they are going to say it! The only skill you need is to be able to react quickly when they go off the script and go into one of their ad libs.'[10]

Eric and Ernie's first ATV series had coincided with the ascendance of traditional jazz as a dominant force in popular music. Acker Bilk was booked as a guest on the third show, with Monty Sunshine's group, Micky Ashman's Ragtime Jazz Band and Alex Welsh following later in the run. When the duo took part in the 1961 Royal Variety Performance at the Prince of Wales Theatre, they shared the bill with a 'trad' session, featuring Bilk, the Temperance Seven and Kenny Ball and his Jazzmen. Ball was one of the musical guests when the second series got underway in the summer of 1962, and while pop tastes would soon leave trad jazz behind, it was the beginning of a long association between the trumpeter and the double act.

Although Marsh had counselled the use of fresh material at all times, they went with a trusted routine for their royal debut. 'Morecambe and Wise kept the flag of British humour flying high with their very fine act... a bullfighting sequence... they must have been delighted with the response it received from the audience.'[11] The sketch is absent from the surviving ATV recording of the show, possibly because it was already so well worn. Their only appearance on the televised show is a bit of business with Arthur Haynes and compère Bruce Forsyth, with all parties confused as to who was due to appear next, and Morecambe and Wise announcing that it couldn't be them because they'd been on already.

After that first live series, Eric and Ernie's growing cachet meant that ATV was more likely to fit with their plans than expect them to fit with whatever slots were available. As a result, the shows were recorded on videotape in blocks whenever

Morecambe and Wise were free. The second series, which went out in the summer of 1962, was recorded in the lull between finishing panto – *Sleeping Beauty* in Leeds – and starting a summer run at the London Palladium with Bruce Forsyth. Their third series, for summer 1963, was stockpiled at Wood Green Empire in the autumn of 1962 and in April–May 1963, some of the very last TV shows to be made there. For the 1964 series, the show moved to the ATV studios at Borehamwood, being recorded in two blocks before and after Eric and Ernie's pantomime commitment at Bristol Hippodrome. When it came to the fifth series, in the spring of 1966, Eric and Ernie were available to record the shows the night before they were due to be transmitted, which didn't allow Clews the luxury of switching the order around to maximum effect.

The success of *Two of a Kind* led to an offer from Wally Ridley at His Master's Voice to make records. First came a single, a version of 'Me and My Shadow'. This was to be followed by a comedy album. The result, *Mr. Morecambe Meets Mr. Wise*, consists of audience-free remakes of some of the most successful TV sketches, including the Pilbroch Bla (a Scottish folk tune send-up), the Grieg Piano Concerto and a sketch in which Eric tries to reinvent himself as a rock and roll singer. In the original television version, he begins singing Elvis Presley's 'Are You Lonesome Tonight', before Ernie suggests that he, Sid and Dick join in on backing vocals. Through a series of nefarious manoeuvres, Ernie takes over the lead singing, and Eric is muscled out altogether. For the record version, which was also released as a single, Hills, Green and Ridley wrote a new pastiche song around which the sketch was reassembled.

Going with Ridley was a curious choice, as the comedy records for EMI tended to be handled by George Martin. When

Martin took over the Parlophone label in the early 1950s, it was very much the poor relation of EMI's imprints, with a mouldering artist roster and no access to American recordings. The Scottish country dance band leader Jimmy Shand was about as racy as it got for Parlophone. Ridley at HMV and Norrie Paramor at Columbia guarded their popular hit turf jealously, so with his label under constant threat of merger or closure, Martin cast around for ways to refresh and update without treading on his senior colleagues' toes.

The answer was comedy, and he made numerous innovative discs with Peter Ustinov, Peter Sellers, Spike Milligan, Michael Bentine and Bernard Cribbins, pushing the then limited studio resources to their limits and beyond. It might have been that Martin was too busy to take on another comedy act, or it might be that Ridley was setting his tanks on Martin's lawn. Ridley, a former music publisher's plugger, was more of an old-style artists and repertoire man than a hands-on producer like Martin, regarding his job as finding the material and getting a performance down on tape. Consequently, Eric and Ernie's debut LP is a much plainer and flatter effort than a George Martin production would have been.

The pop world was changing considerably, and Martin was at the centre of it. The trad fad had passed, and although that sort of jazz would continue to pop up on Eric and Ernie's shows, the guest bookings began to favour pop groups. In the third show of their fourth series, Eric and Ernie were visited by the biggest group of all, signed by Martin in 1962, but only after Paramor and Ridley had both rejected them.

The Beatles' appearance on the show is different to that of most of the musical guests, who got a 'this is/that was' and were otherwise left alone to do their number. It was obvious from their interviews that here were four funny young men.

Indeed, George Martin had signed them more because they made him laugh than for their music. Also, they'd held their own with comics on television before. When they appeared with Ken Dodd on a regional programme in Granadaland, the comedian said he was thinking of changing his name to something more rock and roll, like Cliff or Rock. Something earthy, he said. 'Sod?' ad-libbed George Harrison.

So after they'd played 'This Boy', 'All My Loving' and 'I Want to Hold Your Hand', Eric and Ernie joined them for a comedy routine. This was unusual. Eric mistakes them for the Kaye Sisters, and calls Ringo 'Bongo', then 'Bonzo'. There's an obviously scripted exchange ('We're the ones with the big fat hairy heads', declares George Harrison), but this soon gives way to what appear to be genuine ad libs. When John Lennon tries to suggest that Eric and Ernie are old-timers ('What's it like being famous?' 'Well, it's not like in your day, you know.'), Eric acts hurt and turns to Ernie, saying, 'You didn't expect that, did you?' Morecambe asks what Lennon means. Lennon replies, 'Well, my dad used to tell me about you', holding his hand to indicate 'when I was so high'. Eric pounces. 'Have you only got a little dad, then?' Lennon begins laughing, his hard man image gone instantly. Eric gives as good as he gets and, throughout, Paul McCartney is in raptures of laughter. This is one of the few occasions in the ATV series where Eric is allowed to get the upper hand.

Eric disappears briefly and it is agreed that they will sing an old-fashioned song, with Lennon suggesting 'Moonlight Bay', for which The Beatles and Ernie don striped blazers and straw boaters. Eric reappears in one of the Pierre Cardin jackets that the group had made famous, wearing a deluxe Merseybeat wig, shouting 'Twist and Shout', 'Wooooooo' and 'I like it' – a hit for Gerry and the Pacemakers – over the lyrics of the veteran number.

During the fourth series, the running gag that closed each show involved Eric filling time by telling a joke about two old men in deckchairs, only for Ernie to stop him each time, knowing that the punchline is unsuitable for television.* As the credits rolled, the question of how to fill the time comes up. Lennon volunteers to tell the joke, but manages to make its unsuitability blatantly obvious, much to everyone's delight, by phrasing it: 'There were two old men sitting in a dirty deckchair.' Throughout the whole sequence, there is a sense that everybody on that studio floor is having enormous, infectious fun.

Although The Beatles' first appearance on *The Ed Sullivan Show* on 9 February 1964 blew America wide open for British music acts, Eric and Ernie had got there first, albeit to less acclaim. Every act has an off night, even Morecambe and Wise. Sometimes, it can be an off-week or, if you're really unlucky, an off-season. This was the case with *Every Night at the London Palladium*, which ran through the summer of 1962 at the nation's showplace. Packaged by Bernard Delfont and hosted by Bruce Forsyth, it was very clearly a spin-off from the Sunday night TV show, and as semi-regulars with links to the Grade agency and ATV, Eric and Ernie were an obvious choice. For some reason, though, they just weren't getting the response they wanted.

One afternoon, they were having an idle chat with Forsyth in his dressing room, and he remembered a Blackpool summer season when he'd been ill for the first week, and the great success he'd had rescuing the show after the 'load of rubbish'

---

* In full, the joke runs: 'There were two old men sat in deckchairs. One says to the other "It's nice out, isn't it?", and the other replies "Yes, I think I'll take mine out as well".'

who'd filled in for him. Forsyth blushed to the tip of his chin when Eric and Ernie reminded him gently that they and Tommy Cooper had been the 'load of rubbish' in question. The ribbing raised their spirits and they went out on stage in a better mood than they had for most of the season. Just as well, because in the audience was Ed Sullivan, and he liked what he saw.

Sullivan had a face that was almost set in granite and betrayed no signs of a sense of humour,* and his on-screen manner had all the wit and easy charm of decking. However, he was a massive fan of vaudeville comedy acts, and he'd seen plenty in his years as a journalist and broadcaster. He had a particular fondness for British acts. 'Two Ton' Tessie O'Shea was one of Sullivan's favourites, and Tommy Cooper was another who appeared on the show several times. He knew precisely how good these two Englishmen were.

'There was one thing that really attracted him,' Eric recalled in a 1971 radio interview with Barry Took. 'I don't know if you remember it. We did a thing on TV with a paper bag. I used to throw nothing up and catch something where there's a visual catch thing that we had and he saw that because we used to do it in the act at the Palladium, and that was really what he bought. We went over there and we based, because we only did about four or five minutes, we based the act around that paper bag, which was very very funny for them.'[12]

Just as they had on the Australian trip, Eric, Ernie, Joan and Doreen made the most of the opportunity by setting out a few days early and building in a stay in the Bahamas on the way out and returning to London via Miami. The mini-break did little to calm Eric's nerves about taking on a whole new

---

* He could have passed for the cousin of Bill Herbert, Billy Cotton's deadpan banjo player. One for the teenagers, there.

audience. They'd failed before and come back from disaster, but if this went wrong, it would be a very visible failure.

They arrived at Studio 50, the former Hammerstein Theatre at 1669 Broadway in New York, on 16 March for rehearsals. This would give them an indication of how things were likely to go. Sullivan was known to ditch acts before air time if their rehearsals went badly. They survived the test, and prepared to come back the next day for the show, all live across America.

They had illustrious comedic company on the bill. Sid Caesar, who virtually invented American television comedy in the 1950s with *Your Show of Shows*,* was on, performing a number from *Little Me*, the Broadway musical in which he was then starring. Then there was the black comedian Dewey 'Pigmeat' Markham, a broadcasting favourite since the late 1940s, with one of his 'Here Comes the Judge' courtroom burlesques.

Eric and Ernie decided to stick with proven material for their two spots in the show. In the first segment, the Swiss slapping dance was the main item, preceded by some crosstalk. Watching the performance some sixty years later, they seem to get off to a slightly uneasy start. Even a trusty old gag like the one about the three-foot-tall man swallowing a four-foot sword, which was still getting appreciative chuckles back home a decade or more later, gets a muted response. The physical comedy of the slapping dance goes down a little better, but the overall impression is of playing to a hung jury.

For the second spot, they plumped for their rendition of 'Me and My Shadow', with Eric getting out of step with Ernie. As they left the stage, there was cause for cautious optimism. Sullivan

---

* A show that gave Mel Brooks, Carl Reiner, Neil Simon and Woody Allen their first breaks as scriptwriters.

called Eric and Ernie over to shake their hands, something he never did with acts who had, in his estimation, bombed.

Soon after the show came confirmation that Sullivan had been pleased with their performance. He asked them if they could stay around and come back the following week, doing one live appearance and pre-recording a piece for a later show. The Morecambes and the Wises, now joined by Hills and Green, took the chance to spend a few days sightseeing in New York.

The judo routine – 'Get out of that. You can't.' – that they had been doing on UK television since the Winifred Atwell days was the one for the next show. On the first appearance, Sullivan got their name slightly wrong. In interviews afterwards, both Eric and Ernie insisted that Sullivan had introduced them as 'Morry, Cambie and Wise', but on the recording, Sullivan merely divides Morecambe into two words. Second time out, Sullivan gets their names right.

The dialogue seems to fall on deaf ears again, but the audience responded enthusiastically to Eric throwing himself around. The pre-recorded item involved Eric and Ernie attempting a xylophone duet. There are flying mallets, dead notes on the xylophone and the routine ends with the pair of them playing tunes on each other, miming to the house band's percussionist. Once again, the American audience responds best to some fairly physical comedy.

Their next visit to Studio 50 was in November, and its timing hints at how highly Sullivan rated them. Their appearance was in the week when the ratings sweeps were being done, and it was traditional to stuff shows with only the best guests. For this appearance, they dusted off Eric's attempt to become a pop singer, which had been a hit on TV and a minor success on a single record – 'Boom Oo Yatta-Ta-Ta'. In the original, the vocal quartet had been completed by Sid and Dick, but here the positions were filled by Sullivan himself and musical director Raymond Bloch. Sullivan appears to revel in sending himself up, possibly a little too much, as Eric appears a little uncomfortable with his overenthusiastic 'Boom'-ing. The gusto with which Sullivan threw himself into the sketch was the clearest visible evidence of his hidden love of comedy.

Eric and Ernie, quick on the uptake as ever, tuned their act for American audiences. A lot of the character dialogue that got the warmest response in their shows at home fell flat, but broad physical comedy went down well. They also followed advice from the host, as Eric recalled:

> Sullivan always said to me, 'For Pete's sake, will you do me a favour? Will you slow down?'... I think we had a better chance over there because we have a slight American accent with being Northern. The a is a little flatter or harder, and that helped... They're much slower than what we give them credit for... We always think that the American image is rather fast talking... There's only somebody like [Bob] Hope, and he was English, and maybe a couple of others that really work at that speed.[13]

When they did an established routine involving Eric buying three Louis XIV crystal goblets, the various ways the valuable antiques met their end – one thrown to the ground by Ernie when giving a toast, another shattered by sound waves and the third knocked off the table by a slamming door – got the biggest laughs. The original preamble for English audiences was cut. There is a brash assertiveness about Eric in the American version.

When British bands began to establish their dominance of the pop music industry, Sullivan was among the first to capitalise, as he had with rock and roll and Elvis Presley. Like Eric and Ernie, The Beatles were invited back the week after their first appearance, although this was by popular demand rather than the host's personal preference. They were back again the week after that, with Eric and Ernie's goblet routine in the same show, although this time The Beatles were on tape, having returned home a week earlier. Then, on 2 May 1965, Sullivan summoned Eric and Ernie back to bolster a true British Invasion musical line-up of Dusty Springfield, Tom Jones and the Rolling Stones.

Despite never getting the wild responses they were used to back home, Eric and Ernie would appear on the Sullivan show twelve times between 1963 and 1968, largely as an indulgence for the host. Ernie praised his perseverance:

> This is where he was very clever, Ed Sullivan. I don't know, he had an insight. It's one thing having talent, it's another thing being able to see talent, and he could see it obviously... Ed Sullivan liked us. His son-in-law, who used to present the show, Bob Precht, liked us very much and the American audiences wanted to like us. They looked at us. They knew we were funny. They couldn't quite understand why, what or where, but they knew we had it, whatever it was.[14]

They would probably have notched up a couple more appearances before Sullivan retired in 1971 had it not been for Eric's first heart attack, which seemed to draw a line in his mind under trying to break America, because of the travel and stress involved. Trying to make fresh shows for the fans at home was strain enough.

Although the variety circuit had dwindled, in the mid-1960s a top-line act could be guaranteed work all year round if they wanted to do it. Pantomime would start on Christmas Eve or Boxing Day and run through potentially to March in the big cities. Then the summer season, with seaside shows all round the country, began in June and ran through to late September, or even longer in Blackpool, which had the Illuminations extending the holiday season into October.

Even before they became TV stars, Eric and Ernie were summer season and panto regulars. Between 1957 and 1967, they never missed out on a summer season, doing the two biggest resorts – Blackpool and Great Yarmouth – twice each. By 1967, they were on £3,000 a week between them for the season at the Yarmouth ABC* – £39,000 for the whole run. The seasons almost qualified as a working holiday, with Joan, Gail and Gary joining Eric in the school summer break at the house he'd rented for the season.

Eric and Ernie always tried to keep their stage shows free of material that the paying public might be overfamiliar with from their television appearances, and one routine reserved for the summer season audiences was their turn as Marvo and Dolores, an inept magician and his assistant. The characters had been created by Hills and Green for a 1963 revue at the Adelphi Theatre called *Six of One*, where they had been played by John Hewer† and Amanda Barrie. Never ones to waste a good idea by using it only once, the writers passed the sketch on to Eric as Marvo and Ernie dragged up as Dolores. Doves were merely handfuls of feathers, and the climax of the act, with Dolores standing in a box while Marvo plunged swords through it, ended as badly as you might imagine.

---

* A former cinema with a circle like the north face of the Eiger, as I can testify from childhood holidays.
† Later to become a familiar face, if not a name, when he starred as Captain Birdseye in the frozen food commercials.

No clue was given in the programmes or publicity, as Marvo and Dolores were billed as an act in their own right. Even the local press played along. It was only when the act began that audiences realised who they were really watching, and how much of a bonus they were getting. The industry was in on the joke, as Eric and Ernie took out the traditional advertisements in *The Stage* that jobbing turns used to remind the world of their existence, accompanied by a long-distance shot of the pair on stage and the information that their agent was Billy Marsh. In August 1965, they announced their availability for 1966, being vacant for every month except June, when they were on holiday.

The viewers at home were let in on the secret at the 1966 Royal Variety Performance, and they repeated the act to great effect on *The Ed Sullivan Show* in 1967. Indeed, in 1966, there were two royal shows – the standard benefit for the Variety Artistes' Benevolent Fund, and a gala at the Palladium a fortnight later, in aid of the Cinema and Television Benevolent Fund. At the start of their spot in the second show, Ern brushes some feathers from Eric's collar, a callback to Marvo and Dolores' attempts to make doves disappear, which gets a knowing laugh from the audience, and an acknowledgement from Eric: 'Just in case anybody didn't see it two weeks ago.'

Pantomime was regarded as more optional, with Eric and Ernie happy to miss a year if they were anticipating a better offer or just wanted a break. All of their pantomime appearances between 1961 and 1966 were productions of *Sleeping Beauty*, which they'd first performed at Leeds Grand and could probably have done in their sleep by the time it reached Birmingham Hippodrome five years later. For most of these, the cast remained remarkably similar, not least Wise's friend and Peterborough neighbour, the Canadian baritone Edmund Hockridge.

In 1967, they were offered the London Palladium panto at £4,000 a week guaranteed, or £3,000 plus a percentage of the ticket sales, but they felt able to turn down this enormous deal because there was a prospect of being asked to go to America to appear on *The Ed Sullivan Show* again. While all of this television and stage success had been happening, Eric and Ernie had been trying to conquer another medium.

5

'We're making a film at the moment. It's called the ABC shall not have them. It's written by Lew Grade.'

By the start of 1964, Morecambe and Wise were topping the bill at the theatre and topping the ratings on television. Film was an obvious next step, and they registered their intention in a striking way by making a bid for British Lion Films when the company came on the market. British Lion had been in and out of financial trouble since the 1950s, when it was run by the lavish Alexander Korda. It had been bailed out by the government in 1954, and a 50 per cent interest was held by the state through the National Film Finance Corporation. After a successful run in the late 1950s and early 1960s, with Frank Launder and Sidney Gilliat's St Trinian's films and the Boulting Brothers making films like *I'm All Right Jack*, the government bought the other 50 per cent in December 1963, in order to sell the whole company.

With a price tag of £1.6 million, bids came in from expected sources like the film producer Sydney Box, and then, in mid-February, Eric and Ernie staked their claim from their dressing room at the Bristol Hippodrome, where they were in panto. 'Very few British comics have a chance to appear in films nowadays with the present state of the film industry,' Ernie told the *Daily Mirror*,[1] adding in an interview with the BBC's regional news programme *Points West* that he saw their plan as like United Artists.[2] The tone of the interview is jokey, with Eric pretending to confuse the trade minister Edward Heath with bandleader Ted Heath, but when the BBC interviewer, Jeremy Carrad, asks if it's a publicity stunt, Eric replies, 'No, it's quite serious… Basically, the idea is sound.'

Despite suggesting that they'd be getting 'Ken Dodd, Harry Worth, Harry Secombe, Max Bygraves and other entertainers' to invest, the bid was unsuccessful, and when a consortium led by Ealing founder Sir Michael Balcon prevailed, Eric and Ernie sent him a telegram of congratulations, suggesting he'd outbid them by a million.

A few months later, it was announced that Eric and Ernie would be going into films, albeit not as studio bosses, but working for the Rank Organisation in the first of three comedy movies, to be written by Hills and Green. The producer behind the deal was Hugh Stewart, who had been riding high on the success of Norman Wisdom's slapstick films, and for the first film Wisdom's director, Robert Asher, came in.

Stewart told the press that he had 'looked around at all the leading stage and television comedians and tried to decide which had got the capacity and talent to break through to film stardom. My instinct tells me that Morecambe and Wise stand the best chance of all because of their style of comedy, which is strictly contemporary and appeals to so many tastes… Their personalities are endearing, and they have a great freshness and spontaneity.'[3]

Shooting of *The Intelligence Men* began at Pinewood in October and continued into November. On one of the days, Morecambe got up at 5.30 a.m. and drove from his home in

Harpenden to the studio, only to be bundled straight back into a car and driven off to the day's location, five minutes from his house. He told the press that it was a lesson in reading the call sheet properly.

Morecambe's character was not dignified with a surname, merely being a barista in an apparently Mexican-themed coffee bar, who becomes involved in a plot when a Russian spy sings the 'swan theme' from *Swan Lake* to him as a code. Amusingly, the Gaggia machine in Eric's coffee bar fails to work, resulting in him serving under-the-counter Nescafé. Wise plays Ernie Sage, an office junior in military intelligence trying to impress his bosses and gain a promotion. Over his lunchtime coffee, he realises that Eric is being mistaken for a now-dead double agent, Major Cavendish, and persuades him to pose as the Major. The climax of the film involves an assassination attempt on a Russian ballerina, which Eric and Ernie foil more by luck than judgement.

The script is credited to Hills and Green, with experienced playwright and screenwriter Peter Blackmore getting a credit for the story. Having talked up the freshness and spontaneity he saw in the act, the end result shows both Eric and Ernie at their most stilted and uncomfortable. Any fun in the film comes from Eric and Ernie doing bits of business, and in compiling the script to Blackmore's blueprint, Sid and Dick were environmentally friendly. The 'Get out of that – you can't' judo routine is reprised, and is one of the few highlights of the film, being observed as it is by an impassive Francis Matthews. Matthews, like William Franklyn, who plays the head of military intelligence, was a so-called 'legitimate' actor with a huge sense of fun and very fine comic timing, which he later got to display fully in Alan Plater's *Trinity Tales* and *Middlemen*, both roles playing against his suave image as detective Paul Temple. The inclusion of the judo routine is justified by the final denouement, where Eric tries it on the ballerina's thwarted stalker.

The Intelligence Men premiered in Manchester on 25 March 1965. This was a tough week for a new film, as it was competing with *The Sound of Music*, which was sweeping all in its wake. The reviews were lukewarm at best. The *Daily Mirror* said: 'Though they haven't won a coconut with their first shot, they rate a consolation prize for effort.' The reviewer chose to blame the writers and the director rather than the stars, who he 'prefer[red] in smaller doses', and suggested charitably that 'their next film should really click'.[4] The *People*, which had entombed Eric and Ernie in a television set eleven years earlier, said it was 'a good deal less funny than you'd expect from two such masters of lunacy'.[5]

Despite the reviews, the film did well at the box office, being the thirteenth most successful film of the year in terms of takings in the UK. However, this was not such an impressive achievement as it sounds. Films with a British TV comedy connection were almost guaranteed to fill seats wherever the shows had been sold. As the *Sunday Mirror*'s review had said, Eric and Ernie 'lose none of their TV reputation'.[6] This reputation was what Rank was buying. It was a no-risk punt on the part of producer Hugh Stewart. 'The other market for these films was the seaside resorts in the summer,' explained TV and film director William G. Stewart. 'Because you could be sure of a wet afternoon, they all made money. They didn't make a fortune, but they all made their money back, either abroad or at the seaside.'[7]

Eric and Ernie took a year out from pantomime to work on their next film, *That Riviera Touch*. *The Intelligence Men* had followed the Rank formula for comedy films, including the *Carry On* series: keep them studio-bound for reasons of economy, with locations as local as possible. Stewart threw a little more money at *That Riviera Touch*, enabling a stint of location shooting in the south of France, which must have been welcome given the time of year.

This time Eric is given a surname, Simpson, while Ernie becomes a Clarke. They play traffic wardens who decide to escape to the south of France in their vintage car after Eric attempts to give the Queen a ticket. On arrival, they are identified by Le Pirate, a notorious master jewel thief played by Paul Stassino, as ideal unwitting mules for stolen emeralds, with Claudette, played by Canadian actress Suzanne Lloyd, luring them in. They are given the free use of a villa, which sounds wonderful until they realise how spooky the place is. Eric keeps seeing bodies, which disappear before he can show them to Ernie, who thinks his partner is going mad. In fact, they're rival jewel thieves on the hunt for the sparklers, and the kitchen of the villa is equipped with a trap door leading to a chute that carries the corpses out to sea.

On a night out on the town, Eric unwittingly wins a fortune at the casino, and becomes Champagne Charlie, over-tipping everyone he meets, with Ernie clawing the money back ingeniously each time. Eventually, they realise that Claudette is not all she seems, and they find out they're up to their necks in something sinister and dangerous. Back at the villa, they save her life by unwittingly outwitting the rival thieves, and draw the police into catching Le Pirate. At the end, Eric, Ernie and Claudette emerge from a church after a wedding ceremony. Eric's closing line, addressed directly to the camera, 'We'll cross that bridge when we come to it', has shades of Joe E. Brown's 'Nobody's perfect' at the end of *Some Like It Hot*.

This time the script is billed as being by Hills and Green

'with Peter Blackmore', suggesting that the more experienced screenwriter had more of a hand in the process. Also, Eric and Ernie seem to be getting better at film acting, although still lacking the ease and confidence that they displayed on television. It looks like Rank saw the success of *The Pink Panther* (1963) and its sequel *A Shot in the Dark* (1964), and attempted to get a piece of the jewel heist comedy action themselves. However, *That Riviera Touch* lacks Peter Sellers as Inspector Clouseau, a subsidiary character in the first film whom director Blake Edwards had the sense to make the pivotal figure in the sequels, after he saw the reaction Sellers got from audiences.

Again, it's the bits of business that make *That Riviera Touch* watchable, rather than its own intrinsic quality. There's a lovely running joke where Eric is knocked out by one of the criminals every time he drinks some of the wine in the villa, blaming his incapacitation on the strength of the booze. Meanwhile, the final sequence, where Eric and Ernie chase Le Pirate, and Eric ends up being dragged around the harbour on the back of the master criminal's speedboat, is spectacular in scale and very funny.

The *Daily Mirror* wished it could all have been as good as the end. 'If only the rest of *That Riviera Touch* had the same pace and slapstick gusto of the finale, then the second film attempt by Morecambe and Wise could have been marked up as a winner... Though a marked improvement on... *The Intelligence Men* this one is still sluggish and lacks that vital spark which has made the comedians a likeable and popular pair on television.'[8]

The *Times* took a similar view, noting the improvement on the previous effort, but also noticing the lack of pace, calling it 'slow and cumbersome'. 'The plot... is serviceable enough, and some of the individual gags are funny. But the spontaneity, the instant rapport with an audience, which bring their television shows immediately to life, are sadly lacking.'⁹

The Rank contract was for three pictures, and Eric and Ernie returned to Pinewood in September 1966 after a shorter-than-usual summer season in Bournemouth. This time, Hills, Green and Blackmore had been joined by Michael Pertwee, who was credited with the story for *The Magnificent Two*. Eric and Ernie find themselves in Parazuellia, a politically unstable South American republic. They're only travelling toy salesmen, but Eric's marked resemblance to a notorious revolutionary called Torres propels them into hot water. When Torres dies in an accident – he falls out of a moving train after Eric opens the door trying to get to the lavatory – his followers pay Eric to impersonate their dead leader and oust the country's ruler, President Diaz, and Eric is duly installed as the new leader of Parazuellia. The revolutionary army assume he's too stupid to do anything radical, but when he announces popular policies that make wildly undeliverable promises, they realise that he must go.

The perks of *That Riviera Touch* shot partly on location in the south of France were absent this time. They were back in the studio with the Buckinghamshire countryside in autumn being expected to pass for South America, and Longmoor Military Railway in Hampshire being used for the train scenes, including Eric clinging to the outside of a moving train, part of the effort on this film that won him and Ernie honorary membership of the Film Stuntmen's Guild. This was, however, its primary achievement for the pair.

By this time, they had given up on the standard practice of watching the 'rushes' from the previous day's filming as soon as they were available. Eric said he was 'frightened to death of them… they petrify you',[10] and Ernie added that 'even then you can't tell in rushes. You can't tell. We can't.' The 'we' is telling. It could be read as an admission by Wise that he and Morecambe hadn't gained enough of an understanding to be able to tell, but it can also be read in the spirit of Hollywood screenwriter William Goldman's famous assertion about the film industry that 'nobody knows anything' and that everybody is guessing.

This stood in contrast to Morecambe and Wise's sure-footedness on stage and in television. With an audience, they could tell straight away. 'I get nervous, and you can't correct it, you see,' said Wise. 'When it's up there, and the audience see it, and they laugh at it, you probably could have, if you'd have been doing it live, you could have adjusted it quickly to get even a bigger laugh, but you can't. It's there, it's done.'

'It has long dull patches of plot exposition and only a few good jokes,' wrote John Russell Taylor of *The Magnificent Two* in *The Times*, noting perceptively that 'the twosome still seem sadly in need of an audience as sounding board'.[11] Meanwhile, the *Daily Mirror* said it was 'their third and best film, but it still isn't good enough', consisting of 'a rag-bag of gags and situations which create a number of cheerful laughs but too many dull patches. On TV, [they are] allowed to spark. In films they become separate entities and neither is funny enough on his own.'[12]

One of the biggest problems with the three films Eric and Ernie made for Rank was that anybody could have done them. While they were competent comedy films, there was nothing distinctively Eric and Ernie about them. To Rank, it didn't matter. They had a name draw for films that would do good business regardless of their quality. Like *Running Wild*, it was a rare example of Eric and Ernie overcoming their better judgement and listening to the supposed experts.

The film-making experience left both Eric and Ernie slightly bruised. A couple of years after *The Magnificent Two*, Eric spoke to Marty Feldman for a documentary on comedy in BBC2's *One Pair of Eyes* strand.

> We have a spontaneity, Ernie and I, that is not allowed to come over in films. I couldn't, for argument's sake, move over there if I felt like it. You can't walk off the set, obviously. You've got to go to marks and finish on such and such a line, and do it six or eight times. What I feel that they go wrong with a lot of comedy in films, is they don't allow you to work long enough. It's a minute bit, instead of, say, a well-rehearsed seven-minute bit which they can then cut up. Also, I think they've got too many close-ups, it's all this all the time. You do the gag then you get a close-up. The biggest example of that was W. C. Fields. You never saw him in a close-up. It was always either three-quarters or full length.

Morecambe said that he almost felt superfluous to the film-making process. 'You're in the way of them.' Feldman suggested that maybe the only way it can work is for the comic to have artistic control, but Morecambe admitted that 'I must be honest, I don't think I could direct a film'.[13]

The conversation is notable both for what Morecambe says and his manner. In interviews, he was inclined to go into an act. He felt the need to give value, do jokes and bits of business. This also had the handy effect of deflecting any deep questions, something many comedians are wont to do in discussions. Very few people got Morecambe to be serious and to answer questions straight. Feldman was one of them. During the encounter, there's an obvious respect and warmth between them. Perhaps it helped that Feldman was a fellow old pro. While he'd come to be associated with younger university-educated comics like John Cleese and Tim Brooke-Taylor, Feldman had served his apprenticeship on the halls, as part of the act Morris, Marty and Mitch.

Making it in movies would persist as an ambition to the end of Eric and Ernie's career. Interviewed six years after his partner's death, Ernie said that Eric 'wanted to be a film star... I think he would have been much happier as the smart sort of debonair type... he was always very self-conscious about being the dopey one'.[14] Maybe they would have stood a better chance of success with a director like Dick Lester. The gritty black and white of *A Hard Day's Night* contrasted with the wit and whimsy of Alun Owen's script. Years later, Eddie Braben said he'd happily write a film for Eric and Ernie, but it would be set entirely in the flat. The Rank films lacked that knowledge of what worked for them. The missed opportunity would rankle forever.

6

Top of the tree

As successful as they became, one thing that both Eric and Ernie shied away from was talking about comedy or their skills in any great depth. Interviewers were liable to get a polite brush-off if they seemed to be overanalysing. This was very much in evidence when they were interviewed for BBC2's *Late Night Line-Up* on the night of the Royal Variety Performance.*

There is an outright anti-intellectualism bordering on hostility at the start of the encounter, as though Eric and Ernie are suspicious of the interviewer, Michael Dean, and his motives. The network had a double act in the form of Peter Cook and Dudley Moore, so these northern chaps from ITV seemed to wonder if BBC2 were treating them more as the subjects of a wildlife documentary. At this early stage, just over two years after going on air, BBC2 was often on the receiving end of inverted snobbery. It was available only to those who could afford a new dual-standard television, and

* It was filmed on the night and transmitted a week later.

it was viewed by some as the home of the obscure and high-minded, an impression that lasted for a couple of decades at least.

Ernie sets his stall out before Dean can even ask a question. 'Are you going to ask intelligent questions?' he asks jokingly, adding 'We're going to be in trouble here.' He suggests that they 'find it difficult to examine things intellectually... we just do it'. Eric is steadfastly unromantic about why he went into show business. It all 'began as a way of making money, quite honestly'. Interestingly, throughout the chat, Eric makes jokes about Ernie's financial acumen, but he shows himself to be just as obsessed with money. Asked when he knows whether a film performance has gone well, he answers, 'When the cheque comes in.' Saying that the partnership works so well because each knows what the other is thinking, Eric tags it with 'We're both thinking the same thing now. Where's the cheque?'*

Part of the evasion is an attempt to preserve a mystique about the process. In interview situations, comedians are inclined to keep telling gags, and Morecambe was particularly vigorous in this regard. For all of his protestations, Wise at least tries to answer Dean's questions seriously. Part of it is fighting shy of pretension. This down-to-earth manner was a big part of their appeal and they didn't want to ruin it by appearing grand or haughty. No matter how much they were earning, and no matter who they were starring alongside, both of them still viewed themselves as working-class northern comedians, and it was important for them to convey the sense to their audience that they hadn't forgotten who they were.

---

* The fee for the interview was £40 split between them.

This interview was the occasion when Eric, when asked what they would have been if they hadn't been comedians, answered 'Mike and Bernie Winters' before checking himself with 'Very cruel, shouldn't have said that'. He then suggested he'd have become a Morecambe Corporation labourer like his father, while Ernie says that he'd have joined his father on the railways, starting as a fireman and eventually being promoted to be a driver. That Wise held to a stereotypical young boy's idea of what he wanted to be is because he had never had to consider an alternative career seriously. It was also, perhaps, because neither he nor Eric ever really grew up.

Part of Dean's original question contains the suggestion that it was 'impossible to imagine' them as anything other than comedians, and this seems a fair summary. Could these two men have reasonably done anything else? That the only other jobs they could think of were their fathers' suggests that they knew what they wanted to be all along. Wise was driven from an early age, and, for all of his protestations of laziness, Morecambe seems to have regarded giving up on a show business career at any point after Sadie first pushed him into the limelight as an impossibility. He liked to make out he hated it, but he needed it. Show business was hard work, but it brought joy and it had the only passport out of a lifetime of hard, joyless work for two poor northern teenagers.

While Eric and Ernie avoided overtly political comedy, they were – like many working-class northern comedians, including Ken Dodd, Jimmy Tarbuck and Les Dawson – Conservative voters. Canvassed by the *Daily Mirror* at the time of the 1979 general election, Ernie said that while he was sticking with the Tories, he was 'a bit worried about Margaret Thatcher. I'd prefer a male Prime Minister.' He balanced his old-fashioned outlook by admitting that Doreen was 'shouting that I'm a chauvinist'.[1]

They described themselves cheerfully as capitalists to Vanessa Redgrave when she tried to interest them in some Workers Revolutionary Party literature. Perhaps it was a reflection of the hard times in which they'd grown up and the years of struggle, but Morecambe in particular seemed to believe that he had to keep on working and earning, although he admitted to John Bouchier that there was a limit to this. 'Eric did say to me on a couple of occasions, "Well, if we earn more, we give it straight to the taxman, so there's not a lot of point."'[2] Until that 1979 election, the top rate of income tax had been 83 per cent. In Thatcher's first budget, it was reduced to 60 per cent. For top earners like Eric and Ernie, this amounted to a significant pay increase, and after Eric's second heart attack, it meant that easing up on work was more of a realistic possibility.

The slight edginess of the *Late Night Line-Up* interview is in contrast to whenever Eric and Ernie found themselves being asked questions on children's television shows like *Ask Aspel* and *Val Meets the VIPs*. There's an obvious sincerity and honesty from both of them, answering seriously and treating the children asking them as equals.

They made an appearance in the first series of *Jim'll Fix It*, fulfilling the wishes of Nicola Perry, who wanted to give Eric the trademark double slap, and Juliet Smith, who wanted to be Janet Webb, one of Eric and Ernie's regular accomplices in the BBC years. Getting them was quite a coup for producer Roger Ordish, who explains: 'It gave the programme a boost, causing other celebs to think "If it's OK for Morecambe and Wise, it'll be OK for me."'[3]

Both men were still doing the jobs they'd been doing at thirteen into their fifties. Eric's affinity with younger people was particularly notable to the friends of Gail and Gary. If the younger Morecambes were unavailable, their friends would ask if Mr Morecambe could come out to play, and he'd happily climb trees with them and bomb around on bikes when his health allowed. Morecambe's long-running association with Luton Town FC began when he wanted to find a local team whose games he could attend with Gary. In the 1970s, conscious that he had missed elements of Gail and Gary's childhood, Eric and Joan adopted a son, Steven.

To the end, Eric remained the fidgeting teenager his mother nicknamed 'Jifflearse'. He and Ernie were contrasting and complementary personalities. Ernie was placid, calm and generally unflustered. Eric was hyperactive, his nervous tension being visible in every performance. His eyes darting all over the place, losing interest in what's going on, turning to mug at the camera, interrupting his partner. He was well aware of these traits. When the pair appeared on *Parkinson* in 1972, he started telling a story but then suggested it would be better coming from Ernie, so that he can 'interrupt and get a couple of good laughs'.[4]

Ernie found it easy to switch off. His main hobby was messing about on the river near his home in Maidenhead, in his boat, *Lady Doreen*. He kept fit, mainly by playing squash. Eric's hobbies – fishing and birdwatching, often shared with his son Steven – were characterised by absolute stillness and quiet. It was almost as if he had to find a situation where sudden movements and exclamations were actively discouraged, if not forbidden, in order to reach a state of calm.

'I think he should have pursued those more,' says Gary Morecambe. 'He should have had them as passions rather than interests. He'd have a day's fishing, love it, a day's birdwatching, him and Bill Oddie, both fanatics, they'd talk about it. He had his European bird books and he'd take them on holiday. Great, soon as it ended, put those away now, back to work.'[5]

Eric was perhaps acutely conscious of the preciousness of time after his first heart attack, but he had been unwilling to waste it even before. One of the most frustrating aspects of the film-making process had been the unfavourable ratio between the long days with hideously early calls and the amount of usable footage – sometimes only one or two minutes a day. Even at their most painstaking, a day in the television studio could yield at least ten minutes of screen time.

None of this is to say that Ernie was uncomplicated. Both of them performed out of a sense of neediness, but in Wise's case, this only became transparently obvious after his partner's death. While Eric was alive, he knew they had an appreciative audience whatever – each other. Sometimes, at the height of their fame, they remembered the days when they'd been the only ones who found each other funny. Ernie was always more open about his drive to perform. Eric claimed to hate performing, just as he insisted that Sadie had forced him into show business, and yet he seemed irresistibly drawn to it throughout his life.

Also interesting is the way that in their comic universe, Ernie was a money-obsessed skinflint. In real life, Eric was always stressing that his partner was the business brain of the outfit, and this is undoubtedly true. When Eddie Braben was working on a film script for Ned Sherrin, Wise intervened and got the writer's fee upped from £1,000 to £4,000. However, it's obvious from interviews that Eric was just as interested in the loot as Ernie, with his joking but not joking references to the fee. 'Is it cash?' he asks Michael

Parkinson at the end of their first encounter in 1972. For all of his claims that the comedy was the thing, Eric, like Ernie a self-proclaimed capitalist, knew his professional value to the last farthing.

7

'Keep going, you fool.'

The official line on why Morecambe and Wise moved from ATV to the BBC in 1968 was that the Corporation were offering to make and transmit the shows in colour immediately on BBC2. 'Lew Grade wouldn't compromise on that,' Ernie recalled. 'He said, "You'll have colour when I say you have colour."' In truth, Grade could only offer colour when the Independent Television Authority told him he could, and that wasn't due until November 1969. ATV had already been producing colour shows for the American market since 1966, and had made the 1967 Morecambe and Wise series in colour for export.

There was also a matter of scheduling, as Grade was at the mercy of the ITV network system, and repeat runs couldn't be guaranteed. However, Bill Cotton Jr, who as Tom Sloan's assistant head of light entertainment was running the variety side of BBC TV output, remembered the situation somewhat differently in 2004.

'Well, it was money,' he explained. 'He [Grade] wouldn't meet their demand, and they used colour exactly the same with coming to me, as they used making a film when they went to Thames.'[1] Cotton was keen to bring the boys over to Television Centre, and went in as high as he possibly could. 'They'd done very well for ATV, but they weren't enormous stars,' he said. 'I made an offer that was right at the top of the BBC's scale.' Although the bean counters quailed at the offer, Cotton pointed out that it was a long-term contract and that if his hunch was right, by the third year the £3,500 a show he was offering would be the biggest bargain in show business.

Many show business performers tend towards insecurity. Eric was one of them. As important as money is the feeling of being wanted. Harry Worth had a habit of calling Billy Marsh to ask him to line up summer and panto commitments. He didn't want to spend weeks away from home. He just wanted to know the work was there. Marsh would just tell Worth he'd fixed the gigs, knowing that the star would ring back half an hour later to say he'd had second thoughts. With Morecambe, this manifested itself in a constant need to keep people laughing, with the result that he was, in the show business phrase, 'never off'.

Lawley: He was the insecure one?

Wise: Yeah, I think so... *Running Wild*... was a critical time of our career and he was very upset over that. I was always the... I won't give up, you know that. I'm tenacious.

Lawley: So you kept him going?

Wise: I'm thick-skinned and I kept him going.

Lawley: Yes, but it did always seem with Eric, I mean off-screen, this constant need to make people laugh.

Wise: Yes. Yes, he couldn't understand it. It was what one might call a neurosis. If you were in company, he would be the life and soul of the party. People used to say to him "You know, why don't you switch off some time?

You know, take the batteries out" because he was always
ebullient and full of life.

Lawley: Why couldn't he switch off?

Wise: Insecurity. I think he felt that they would stop laughing.

Lawley: He was frightened that suddenly he wouldn't be
able to make people laugh any more?

Wise: I think yes, when we came on if they didn't laugh, it
frightened him to death.[2]

Michael Palin observed the tendency at the BBC light
entertainment Christmas party in 1972. Morecambe 'never
dropped his comic persona all evening. If one talked to him,
or if one heard him talking to anyone else, he was always
doing a routine. He has a very disconcerting habit of suddenly
shouting at the top of his voice at someone only a foot away.'
Morecambe knew his place, though, as *Parkinson* producer
John Fisher recalled of an incident in 'hostility' after Eric and
Ernie had appeared on the show. 'Everybody was gathered
around Eric, listening, and he said, "You're listening to me now,
but if Tommy [Cooper] came in, everybody would go." He had
this magnetism.'[3] Cameraman Stuart Lindley, who worked on
most of the BBC shows,* supports Ernie's assertion. 'You could
talk to Ernie better than you could to Eric. Eric had to hold

---

* While BBC camera crews worked across all genres of programming,
some became known as particularly adept at certain shows. Producers/
directors would have their favourites, who they would request for all
of their programmes. John Ammonds and Ernest Maxin both preferred
working with Crew 16, under senior cameraman Ken Major, with
Lindley as Major's second-in-command. Lindley gained a reputation
in rehearsals for being an audience substitute, with Morecambe once
commenting that he knew a gag would go well that night because it had
kept Lindley laughing all day.

court. You could see that. That is him. If there were a group of you waiting around because something else was going on, or they were making decisions up in the gallery, Eric would come past and join you, but he would have to dominate. Whereas Ernie would come in and be part of you. Being paid to be entertained was wonderful, and being able to talk to these people as friends. I always enjoyed doing the work, whatever it was, but to work with them was just a bonus.'[4]

Eric's public persona and private face began to merge, as his son Gary observed:

My father, when I was 3, 4, 5, 6, maybe, he wasn't the Eric Morecambe that we all know and love, but he became that character, even at home. Over about fifteen years, he changed into this other person, both of which were very nice in their own ways, but the Eric Morecambe one was so much larger than life. He'd still sign cheques in the old days as Bartholomew, John Eric Bartholomew, it was normal to do that, but once he became Eric Morecambe, Superstar, the rest just went.[5]

Eric and Ernie had started to wonder whether ATV really wanted them or knew what to do with them. Being made in colour for America, the *Piccadilly Palace* series contained remounts of a number of hit sketches from previous shows, including the Grieg's Piano Concerto sketch from 1963. Eric and Ernie had stipulated in their contract that they would have a degree of input over how the shows would be edited for UK transmission. Both knew that the critics would pounce if there was too much old material. ATV didn't care. 'It's strange really how the Grade Organisation are quite willing to let the shows go out as they are, which proves they are not really interested in us,' wrote Eric in his diary. 'It's a damn good job we had so much put in the contract, otherwise they would crucify us.'[6]

Shortly before leaving ATV, Eric and Ernie had met ABC's light entertainment boss Philip Jones when he visited Great Yarmouth. Eric wanted to get him to offer them a series at Teddington via the Grade Organisation, to see if serious approaches would get through or if they'd be screened out to keep them at ATV. Bill Cotton's offer showed that there was no connivance between Marsh and the television arm of the family. Cotton's obvious care and attention when it came to the product was also exactly what Eric and Ernie wanted. They'd worked on the halls with the senior Billy Cotton[*] and they knew the younger man well.

Not that Cotton's keenness to get Morecambe and Wise meant he was a pushover. It was in Eric and Ernie's new BBC contract that they had to have Hills and Green as writers. Cotton managed to negotiate this with their agent, Roger Hancock. They had Sick and Did, but they didn't have 'Clewsie', who would remain at ATV and its successor, Central, until his retirement. Cotton knew exactly who to call in: their old radio producer, Johnny Ammonds, now working in London.

'He'd done the Val Doonican show, and he'd done the Harry Worth show when he was still in Manchester,' Cotton recalled. 'So I knew he was rock solid at organising a show. I also knew that was what the two boys required. They'd been rubbished a bit at ATV. It's not unfair to say that.'

The son of a theatrically inclined watchmaker, Ammonds had begun his BBC career during the war as a sound effects operator. 'I joined the BBC on 10 February 1941,' he said in

---

[*] To his dying day, Cotton Jr was known to many BBC hands as 'Young Bill'.

2004. 'I wasn't seventeen, because my seventeenth birthday wasn't until the May.'[7] A month's posting to the Variety department in Bristol, where it had been evacuated, turned into a permanent attachment, and when bombing raids made Bristol as dangerous as London, the whole operation moved up to Bangor in North Wales.

> I spent an incredible two and a half years learning show business. What better way to learn it? No university could give me the instruction I had in that time. I was working with Jack Buchanan, Evelyn Laye, Robb Wilton and all these big stars of the time. And of course *ITMA** with Tommy Handley. We did that live. It makes me shudder to think of that now. Most of the effects were done at the mic because we couldn't time it on disc. That was an incredible experience with all the teamwork.

Called up for military service at nineteen, Ammonds joined the Royal Signals and found his way into forces broadcasting. Upon demob, he returned to the BBC as an engineer and then a studio manager and eventually a producer. He wanted to work in comedy, but saw limited opportunities to establish himself. 'I didn't want to do dance bands and *Music While You Work*, and the chance of a scripted show coming up was a bit remote.' When an internal advertisement for a variety producer at the North region in Manchester came up, Ammonds applied, knowing the department's pedigree for solid comedy under Ronnie Taylor.

---

* *ITMA*, or *It's That Man Again*, to give its full original title, ran on BBC radio from 1939 to 1949, and made a star of Liverpudlian comedian Tommy Handley.

In 1958, Ammonds moved from radio to television, and in 1965 returned to London. Cotton's approach to Ammonds with the Eric and Ernie job offer was gloriously informal and indicative of the way the BBC worked then. 'I was in the bar at lunchtime. Bill Cotton came up to me and said "How do you fancy producing Morecambe and Wise?" I said "Can a duck swim? But Lew Grade's got them." He said, "No, I have."'

When it came to planning the shows, Ammonds began to see the weaknesses of Hills and Green. At ATV, they'd been writing ITV half-hours, which ran to twenty-five minutes allowing for adverts. At the BBC, the shows were between thirty and thirty-five minutes. 'They thought they could do anything,' he explained. 'That was the trouble. They did write some good stuff, but they didn't write all the time good stuff. When they repeated shows, you could see it was a bit thin. Also they were doing half-hour shows on commercial with two guest stars. So they didn't have much left to write.'

The boys had to leave their ATV musical director, Jack Parnell, with whom they'd first worked at the Glasgow Empire in the big band days, back at Elstree. Parnell had been with the company from the start. While some might smell nepotism from the fact that his uncle, Val Parnell, had been the co-chairman of the company, his musical credentials were beyond reproach. Parnell had been the UK's top poll-winning jazz drummer in his years with Ted Heath and his Music, and later had been the leader of the hardest swinging big band in the country. He left the arranging to other hands, but had often popped up in the ATV shows, either as the musical director being bearded by Eric, or having fun behind the drums. The last show of the second ATV series in 1962 had featured Parnell and his 'Debonaires', a selection of the studio band, including trombonist Don Lusher and trumpeter Tommy McQuater, playing trad jazz in flat caps and mufflers.

Fortunately, the BBC was able to offer superb musical support in the form of Alyn Ainsworth.* Then, for the second series, Peter Knight took over. Raised in Plymouth, he had cut his teeth playing piano with and arranging for local dance bands. By the early 1950s, he was in London, and worked with Eric and Ernie on a Henry Hall TV show in 1953. At the end of the decade, he was virtually a fixture at Pye Records, while working extensively for Granada Television at its London studio in the former Chelsea Palace theatre. Unlike Parnell, most of the dots conducted by Knight had been his own scoring, and the pace was relentless, but Knight was a pioneer of multitasking. 'A wonderful musician. Brilliant. He had this nice bungalow type house out in the country near Rickmansworth. He had his bureau, the desk looking over the garden to the swimming pool, with this little stubby pencil in his hand. He'd be watching football on the television and coming up with wonderful arrangements,' says producer Terry Henebery.[8]

Only three full shows – two of them recovered, amazingly, from a cinema in Sierra Leone – and some excerpts exist from that first BBC series, and they illustrate Ammonds' concerns amply. They follow a similar pattern to the ATV shows, with a guest singer and Kenny Ball's Jazzmen putting musical grouting in between the sketches. Unfortunately, the sketches seem, at best, to drag on aimlessly, and at worst are the sort of deeply problematic material not generally associated with the boys.

---

* Alyn Ainsworth (1924–1990) came to prominence as the chief arranger and conductor of the BBC Northern Variety Orchestra, which became the Northern Dance Orchestra. A flamboyant gay man with a penchant in later life for astounding wigs, he was known affectionately if irreverently to fellow musicians as 'Eileen'.

The seventh show of the series features a jarring sketch where Hills, Green and Wise conspire to con Morecambe out of his football pools winnings, but is redeemed by a closing item where Wise and Michael Aspel try to exclude Morecambe from a big dance number with an unsurprising lack of success.

It's the fifth show that harbours the most troublesome elements, though. It opens with Eric walking on stage brandishing an instant camera. He explains to Ernie that it's 'for those pictures that you can't send away, because if you do, you're sent away with them'. Ernie suggests that Eric should take some compromising pictures of supporting actress Jenny Lee-Wright, as she changes costume in the wings. The sketch ends with Eric being punched by Lee-Wright's supposed boyfriend, a boxer.

This item makes clear that we are very much dealing with the same Eric and Ernie we'd seen at ATV. Ernie is the clever one, Eric is the easily led fool. It makes for a contrast with the way their characters were later to develop. Both of them are full of lecherous intent, rather than overgrown innocence. The later Eric and Ernie would not have spied on women with a camera. Also, curiously, Eric says the word 'knob' a lot while explaining how the camera works, but there are no knowing laughs from the audience. The word had seemingly not yet ascended to the pantheon of innuendo.

However, it's the overlong and underwritten sketch in the middle of the show, with Morecambe, Wise, Green, Hills and guest Ronnie Carroll as Irish republicans, that jars most heavily. First Ernie introduces it, with shades of *Macbeth*, as 'the Irish sketch', but later calls it 'the IRA sketch'. All concerned are dressed in caricature Irish outfits, and attempting Irish accents, with the exception of Eric, who offers an impersonation of Robert Newton in *Treasure Island*, apart from when he lapses into an Asian accent, claiming to be from 'County Curry'. The punishment for not getting the accent right is to be 'clobbered' by Carroll with a shillelagh.

The idea that as resolutely apolitical an act as Eric and Ernie could be doing this material with Irish nationalist tensions already increasing and just months before the Provisional IRA began a thirty-year campaign of using bombs, not shillelaghs, is baffling. Quite apart from the issues of taste and judgement, the material is woefully thin.

Eric and Ernie's lucrative transfer to the BBC was just one part of what looked to be their most successful year yet. There was a booking in New York in the offing and Bernard Delfont asked them to fill four spots at the 1968 Royal Variety Performance. They even turned down a chance to star in a West End show. Meanwhile, they were increasingly in demand in clubland. Many of the variety theatres where they'd learned their trade had been closed and demolished for office blocks. However, the appetite for live entertainment remained strong, and in the north of England cabaret clubs sprang up to fill the void.

In a sense, these were a return to the 'song and supper rooms' that had been the birth of music hall, usually built onto the backs of pubs by enterprising Victorian landlords who fancied themselves as showmen. By popular demand, these showmen demolished and rebuilt bigger, the results looking more like legitimate theatres. The great and the good saw music halls as vulgar or worse, and strove to make the proprietors' lives difficult. One element of uneasy compromise was an end to serving drinks in the auditorium, with bars being segregated and used only in the intervals.

The big northern clubs moved forward by going back. Drinks and meals were served in the auditorium. In many cases, the clubs were established with generous loans on highly favourable terms from local breweries. Stockton-on-Tees had the Club Fiesta, Wakefield had the Theatre Club, Rotherham had Greasbrough Social Club, but the top of the shop was Jimmy Corrigan's Batley Variety Club, which had opened on Easter Sunday 1967.

Although Corrigan got the big names because he offered the best money, there was another element that made Batley irresistible to performers. The 1,500-strong audience were arranged in a semicircle around a large stage that jutted out into the centre of the room. It soon gained a reputation for being somewhere that an act could 'get across' perfectly. 'There have been two great stages,' says Con Cluskey of the Bachelors, who were on the club's opening bill. 'One is the Palladium, the other was Batley Variety Club, because you felt that you could just reach out and touch the audience.'[9]

Morecambe and Wise were booked by Corrigan to do a fortnight at Batley from Sunday 3 November 1968. Comedy writer Mike Craig was there for the opening night, having seen them there on their debut season a year before. '[I] can honestly say I have seldom heard a volume of laughter like it,' he recalled. 'Eric... ad-libbed with people at the ring-side tables as only he could.'[10] Craig returned a couple of nights later, to talk about a sketch idea for the BBC shows, and found Morecambe to be decidedly off-form: 'He kept holding his left arm with his right hand and disappearing for half a minute or so into the adjoining dressing room... His timing, normally so immaculate, was fractionally out.'[11]

After the performance, Eric asked Ernie if he'd be willing to do the expected autographs solo, so he could get back to his hotel in Selby and sleep. Eric was known to his partner as a hypochondriac, and Doreen Wise assured her husband that there was nothing to worry about, but Morecambe had been noticing a slight pain in the arm since the Monday of the engagement. It had sharpened on the Thursday evening, and increased in intensity during their seventy-five-minute show. Every time he felt he was flagging, another laugh would come and he felt boosted.

By the time Morecambe was driving through the deserted streets of Leeds, the pain had become intolerable. As soon as he spotted a human form, he stopped the car and asked for directions to Leeds General Infirmary. The gentleman he'd accosted, Walter Butterworth, struggled to explain clearly, and Morecambe asked him if he could drive him there. Butterworth explained he'd only driven a tank before. Morecambe assured him that his Jensen Interceptor effectively drove itself.

Morecambe was admitted to casualty and Joan was called in Harpenden. She should come as soon as possible, the nurse advised, apparently convinced that the end was nigh. By the time she arrived, Eric's condition had stabilised.

The press reports in the evening newspapers on Friday and the morning newspapers on Saturday were to the effect that Morecambe had suffered 'a slight heart attack'. In fact, it had been a serious one, and the comedian had been lucky to survive. He had arrived at the hospital just in time. The understatement of the public announcement was largely to avoid worrying Morecambe himself, at the orders of Billy Marsh.

The hospital had also called Wise, who arrived to visit the next morning. After seeing his friend, Wise headed off to Morecambe's hotel to collect his belongings and settle the bill. Always the sober, practical one, Wise got on with taking care of business while deeply affected by the news. Joan Morecambe saw him fighting back tears as he left his partner's bedside.

As the news travelled, friends from show business all wanted to visit, but the excitement was proving too much for the patient. 'The intensive care team watching Eric had noted that the moment he saw anybody he knew, especially in show business, his electrocardiograph went mad. He is built that way.'[12]

Years later, when producing their shows, Ernest Maxin knew this better than anyone. During rehearsals he would see Morecambe tense up if something wasn't going right, or if there was any concern about whether there would be enough material for a show. On one show, they were five minutes short. 'This was on the Monday morning read-through and we were going to start rehearsing immediately after lunch. I told him a lie. I said, "Don't worry, I've got something special for you." I had to, to calm him down. He was a worrier and that was why he was so good, I think.'[13]

At the time of the first heart attack, Wise knew his partner's tendency towards worry, but was unaware of what had been clear to Joan Morecambe, who saw him chain-smoking. 'He was smoking between sixty and a hundred cigarettes a day and living on his nerves,' Ernie observed in 1973. 'None of those who worked with him, including myself, quite appreciated the pressures he was under.'

'The lifestyle for British comics was rubbish,' says comedy writer Gail Renard. 'It was a terrible lifestyle. They played the clubs, they played theatres, it was a hard life, and very often, they were playing two, three or more theatres at once. They'd do their seven minutes in a theatre, finish their act, run across the street to the next theatre, do their act, run down to another theatre, and it was a hard life, and by the time they finished, late night, and they came off. They were living in digs having fry-ups and they would come out at eleven o'clock or something, the only thing to do to unwind was drink.'[14] Eric Morecambe was just 42 at the time of his first cardiac arrest.

Despite Morecambe's illness, Eric and Ernie played a major part in the Christmas Day schedules of their first year at the BBC in *Christmas Night with the Stars*, a smorgasbord of light entertainment output that had been running since 1958. As well as featuring sketches from the casts of *Dad's Army* and other sitcoms, there was a variety show element hosted by Eric and Ernie and produced by Stewart Morris, with Louis Armstrong and Cliff Richard, which had been recorded on 27 October.

The seriousness of Eric's heart attack cast doubt on the future of the partnership. Ernie was uncertain that Eric would ever be fit to pick up where they left off. Moreover, if his recuperation took too long, the world of show business might have moved on, and there would be no room for them to re-establish themselves. Perhaps worse, Wise feared Morecambe getting back to peak condition, then relapsing. Peter Boita, a drummer who would go on to work extensively in television, recalls an encounter with Ernie at a gig in Peterborough with Bob Miller's Millermen.

'It was in a gym hall, so the acoustics were all horrible. In the interval, Ernie came into the dressing room, which was a changing room, and it was just after Eric had had his heart attack. He said "He's not too good. I don't know how long we can keep going."'

During Eric's convalescence came some news that might have risked setting him back. While he had been convalescing, negotiations continued for the second series. Bill Cotton went to lunch with Sid and Dick's agent, Roger Hancock,* to ensure

---

* Tony Hancock's brother.

that they'd be willing and ready to spring into action as soon as Eric was fit to perform again.

Hancock had a surprise for Cotton:

He came in and said they wanted to be executive producers, etc. The fact of the matter was that Eric and Ernie had in their contract that I had to secure Hills and Green to do the show. They thought that was a weapon, and I knew it wasn't. I said that is not negotiable. I am not having a couple of writers decide... and so Roger said, 'Well, the boys will probably take the offer from Lew Grade.'

They thought, because they used to act out the Morecambe and Wise show, which they'd written, that they could do the same thing. We were only on the avocado when he threw this bombshell, and I said, 'Well now what do we talk about?' We chatted away, and he said 'Are you sure?', I said I was positive. He said, 'Well what are you going to do?' I said, 'I have no idea, but something will turn up', and it was the following weekend, when Michael Hurll told me, 'Have you heard Eddie Braben's left Ken Dodd?'

So it was that in March 1969, Sid and Dick signed an exclusive contract with ATV as script consultants and associate producers. The move into production was in keeping with some of Green's more arrogant pronouncements about the TV business. 'Producers and directors in comedy are a nuisance, if you've got good writers and performers,' he said in 1965. 'All you need then is a good cameraman. You don't want a lot of clever camera shots spoiling a routine. If anybody starts that with comedy, he's just a frustrated drama producer. I'd sooner have a dyed-in-the-wool theatrical or variety man to work with than a bright boy with ideas. Colin Clews' greatest contribution to the *Morecambe and*

Wise Show was that he sat back on all rehearsals till his two performers and we as the writers had sorted out exactly what we were going to do, and then he concentrated on making sure none of it was missed by the camera.'[15]

Hills and Green had a lot of success. Hills had once declared that he and Green could write a script for Eric and Ernie as they passed on a Tube escalator, and on the last series at ATV, that was almost exactly what they were doing. They had been working on Bruce Forsyth's show for ABC and Morecambe and Wise's show for ATV at the same time, with one of them at Teddington with Forsyth and the other at Elstree with Eric and Ernie one day, before swapping over the next. They'd even been given their own show at ABC, *Those Two Fellers*, the panning of which proved that while they were adequate comic foils, they were never going to be the main event. With no guarantees that Eric would be fit for work any time soon, the ATV contract can be seen as self-preservation, but the manner in which Eric and Ernie found out they'd lost their writers stung.

Ernie was on a plane to Barbados when the steward asked him how he felt about losing his writers. Wise said he knew nothing about it. The steward replied it had been in the papers. Meanwhile, Eric was quoted in reports of the writers' departure as saying, 'This comes as a complete surprise. We are sorry to lose them, but we wish them well. Perhaps now we will start writing our own scripts.'[16] The move had been rumoured a week or so earlier, and Wise had been contacted by the *Express* for comment, but filed it under press kite-flying. Now it was firm. Billy Marsh had been told by Roger Hancock and the pair had agreed that it was down to Sid and Dick to tell Eric and Ernie. 'Unhappily nothing was done about it,' said Ernie five years later, adding magnanimously, 'We blame no one. It's just the way things sometimes happen.'[17] A decade later, the positions would be reversed.

8

All the right notes, in the right order

Although it wasn't obvious at the time, the loss of Hills and Green was a blessing in disguise. It might not have been ideal but for the availability of a particular writer and a flash of executive inspiration. For the previous decade, Eddie Braben had been the main writer for his fellow Liverpudlian Ken Dodd, but the pair had parted over a financial issue. Michael Hurll, who mentioned Braben's availability to his boss, was Dodd's TV producer. The pair were close. Hurll's father, Fred Hurll, chief executive of the Boy Scouts Association, had been a good friend of Billy Cotton Senior, and Hurll had followed 'Young Bill' as producer of the elder Cotton's Band Show.* Young Bill saw an answer to the Sid and Dick problem.

Eric and Ernie knew Braben by reputation, and liked his work, but wondered if he was right for them. Braben's feet were even colder. 'I had watched a lot of their shows and they

---

* There was also a persistent rumour within the BBC that Young Bill and Michael Hurll were half-brothers, as a result of an affair between Old Bill and Hurll's mother.

didn't make me laugh,' he admitted in his memoirs. 'I was not a fan.'[1] However, he needed the work, and so he accepted when summoned to a meeting with Eric and Ernie in Cotton's office at Television Centre. During the course of the meeting, Braben began to see something in these two men that he could use. He saw the way they were with each other. Finishing each other's sentences. Obviously totally at ease with each other. Two almost lifelong friends, closer than many brothers. Braben realised that if he could turn that reality into comedy, the show stood a chance.

It was one of those moments where the planets aligned. When Braben went back to Liverpool, he was able to translate what he'd seen to the page instantly. When they met a week later with a script to go through, Eric and Ernie liked what they read, but were a tiny bit disturbed to have everything typed up ready for them, rather than a single sheet of paper. They wondered if it was too different from what they'd done before. Bill Cotton suggested recording it and seeing how it went. If it went well enough, he'd transmit it on BBC2. It went well enough. That first series of four was Eddie Braben's probationary period as Eric and Ernie's writer, but at the end of it, all concerned agreed it was a perfect fit.

What is obvious is that Braben hadn't merely found something to work with, he knew instantly how to use it. Viewing their first series working together, all of the fundamental elements for the following fourteen years fell into place in that initial three hours. In the opening duologue of the series, both partners acknowledge the events that had kept them off television for nearly a year. Eric addressed it directly, basking in the warmth of the audience's applause and saying 'Keep going, you fool' as he looked into his jacket. Ernie went for a more oblique approach. Eric asked if he'd get to kiss any girls this time. Ernie replied that he'd kissed a girl last time and look what happened then.

It's telling that he asks about kissing rather than anything stronger. For all of their innuendo, Eric and Ernie were, and always would be, trapped, albeit gleefully, in their teenage years where boys 'got off' with girls. Desire was indicated by steamed-up or wonky glasses. Naughtiness was merely hinted at. That said, they weren't always lily-white. On a Royal show in the 1960s, one of their exchanges gets a filthy laugh from the audience, and Eric makes no attempt to give the joke any plausible deniability.

Eric: Incidentally, I want you to work well tonight.

Ernie: Yes?

Eric: Yes, 'cause I've seen him.

Ernie: Seen him? Who?

Eric: He's definitely here. I've seen him. I've had a chat with him back there.

Ernie: Who?

Eric: What do you mean who? Who? The fella. [Mimes polo playing, an obvious reference to the Duke of Edinburgh.]

Ernie: Oh, polo.

Eric: Ohhh, I could have said that couldn't I, you fool?

Ernie: You don't mean…

Eric: Yes, I've seen him back there. Jimmy Edwards. He's here. I've seen him. You remember Jimmy Edwards.

Ernie: Yeah, Jorrocks.

Eric: [Grabs Ernie by the shirt front] Don't be like that. That's not nice. You've got to be careful. [Laughs knowingly] No, we'll plug anything.[2]

At the time, Edwards was in the title role of a sitcom called *Mr John Jorrocks*, and the seemingly innocent Ern pronounces the name exactly like 'Durex'. There is also the possibility that they were mopping up some extra laughs from people who merely heard the similarity to 'Bollocks'. For a seemingly crude gag, it's deceptively multilayered.

The personality changes were in place straight away, in particular Ernie's vanity and self-regard, with Eric puncturing his pomposity at every turn. What is especially noticeable in these first shows is the way that Ernie uses Oliver Hardy as a blueprint for dealing with his idiot friend. The cadences of his voice in the early flat sketches are purest Babe.* Eric flagged up a change of tone at the start. 'There'll be plenty of dollies in the series, but we won't be chasing 'em any more. We won't have sketches in which we have girls like that up to our flat. We think we're too old.'[3]

The main female presence in the new shows was a versatile actress who could do everything from dolly to drudge, Ann Hamilton. She had worked a fair bit with Hills and Green at ABC on *The Bruce Forsyth Show*, and had appeared in one of the final ATV shows, and again once in the first series at the BBC. When Braben started turning in sketches with greater depth, Ammonds, Morecambe and Wise remembered her as being likely to cope with whatever was thrown at her, as indeed she did for the next decade.

The last sketch of the first show is a drama burlesque with Peter Cushing, King Arthur and the Knights of the Round Table. Braben had yet to develop the idea of Ernie as the author of these lavish yet bathetic set pieces, but the concept is similar. During the front cloth sequence, both Wise and Cushing are

* Hardy's nickname.

already in full costume, while Morecambe is in shirt sleeves and apparently unwelcome. Eventually, Morecambe emerges dressed as Sherlock Holmes, persisting with the wrong outfit throughout the sketch.

> Ernie: Mr Cushing, I can't tell you how what a pleasure it is to have you on the show.
>
> Cushing: Why can't you tell me?
>
> Eric: [feigning raucous laughter and slapping his thigh] Another gem in the can. [Cushing starts to laugh for real, causing Eric and Ernie to 'corpse' too] We like stuff like that. Anything subtle. We like anything subtle, don't we?[4]

The first show of the new series was the first time they used 'Bring Me Sunshine' – an obscure American tune of 1966, recorded originally by the Mills Brothers, and found for them by John Ammonds – as a closing song. Over the following years, they closed with other songs, including 'Following You Around', 'We Get Along So Easily Don't You Agree?' and Tony Hatch and Jackie Trent's 'Positive Thinking', but this is the one that became indelibly theirs.*

The 'Tea, Ern?' joke appears in the third show. Normally, if Morecambe particularly liked a line, he'd go out of his way to say to Braben 'Now, that's funny'. But this wasn't praise enough for Morecambe in this case. Before this piece of wordplay had gone anywhere near an audience, he told Braben: 'That is a belter'. Eric's comic instincts were 100 per cent correct: this small gag would become a catchphrase. A joke involving some

---

* This might be heresy, but your author must admit to preferring 'Positive Thinking' to any of the other songs associated with Eric and Ernie.

false legs, and hands holding a top hat and cane appearing from behind a curtain to give the impression that high-kicking crooner Frankie Vaughan was about to come on runs through the first series with Braben, and would become a standby in future years. Meanwhile, it is in show two that one of the defining elements of Braben-era Eric and Ernie falls into place.

When Braben submitted the first bedroom sketch, Eric and Ernie weren't keen on the idea at all. They were worried it had homosexual overtones. Braben pointed out that they must have shared a bed plenty of times in digs for reasons of economy, but still they wouldn't budge. Only when Braben pointed out that it had been good enough for Laurel and Hardy did they cave in and accept the idea. Nonetheless, Eric felt he had to take out some insurance against the set-up being misread.

'You see the point is that Laurel and Hardy did it, in those days, and nobody said it's effeminate or anything,' he told Michael Parkinson in 1972. 'They didn't know what it meant. That's why, I don't know whether you've always noticed on these particular bed routines, I basically always make it as mannish as possible by smoking a pipe. Have you ever met a queer with a pipe?'[5]

The bed sketches were ideal vehicles for the writer and performer. It was a situation that could be filled with anything that two friends might talk about, or it might be the launch pad for a flight of fancy with Braben's Scouse surrealism. It could be whatever the writer and performers wanted it to be. In that first bed sketch, both Eric and Ernie try reading to get to sleep. Eric has a cowboy story – *Waco's Debt* by J. T. Edson – and Ernie is reading *The Wind in the Willows*. Neither book suggests great maturity, and this was a deliberate ploy on Braben's part, underlining their fundamental innocence of outlook. Sometimes he made it blatantly obvious by giving Eric a copy of the *Beano* or *Dandy*.

After the recording of that first sketch, Eric called the writer over and handed him the copy of *The Wind in the Willows* that had been used in the sketch. Inside, he and Ernie had inscribed it 'To Eddie, "Stolen" from BBC props. July 1969'.[6] Braben brought the book to many subsequent recordings and persuaded the guest stars to sign it.

The bed sketch from the 1973 Christmas show is a perfect example of the genre, containing one of the best-known lines from Eric and Ernie's entire career. Eric stands idly by the bedroom window as a police car passes, and observes, 'He's not going to sell much ice cream going at that speed, is he?' Other writers, other acts, might have done this as a stand-alone quickie. Indeed, who remembers the rest of the sketch, with Eric trying to persuade Ernie to let him have the side of the bed furthest from the window, because of the draught? Others might have used it as the punchline to the whole sketch. Here, it's almost thrown away casually, thirty seconds from the end of the six-minute sketch. Ernie is trying to write a 'mammoth spectacular', but Eric keeps interrupting him with asides.

Ernie: Are you going to read your newspaper or annoy me?

Eric: I can do both. Says here 'International film star Sophia Loren has turned down an offer from Sir Lew Grade. She said that the grass was too damp.'

Ernie: You are the lowest person I know.

Eric: That's good coming from you. Me low? Who was it then who won the limbo-dancing competition by just walking under the bar?[7]

The 'ice cream' line is still very funny out of context, and while nobody truly knows what will work until it does, Morecambe knew that this would go down a storm. Before the recording, he told Braben 'I've been waiting all week to say this line'. However, it didn't come from nowhere. The pace of the sketch makes it all the more effective when it comes. The tag to the sketch comes when Eric hoodwinks Ernie into vacating the bed by telling him that the red tint in the sky is a fire at the bank. It's a nice ending, but it's not the biggest laugh in the sketch, and it takes confidence to go on after that. Having started sure-footed in 1969, by 1973 Morecambe, Wise and Braben were unassailable.

Braben was always keen to stress Eric and Ernie's ability to ad-lib and to add to the script. It was never a case of Eric and Ernie merely performing what he wrote. The teetotal writer recalled an occasion in rehearsals when Ernie asked him what he did to relax if he didn't have a drink. Braben replied 'Delius'.

> He looked thoughtful when I said this, and as long as I live, I shall never forget what he said next; it was pure Ernie Wise.
>
> 'Is that powder or liquid?'
>
> There's a warm smile every time I recall that line. I could never have written it.

One line added by Eric became a staple of the opening double routines, but it wasn't his own creation. 'Eric told me he stole the line "Look at me when I'm talking to you". That's what the doll used to say to Arthur Worsley. Arthur never spoke, and he was brilliant. The doll insulting him all the time. Eric said, "I only steal from the best."'[8]

Eric's own ad libs tended to be more acerbic. Taking the stage at the 1970 BAFTA awards, he looks at host David Frost, already jetting between England and America weekly, presenting TV shows on both continents. The withering surrealism of his question 'Are you in New York now?' gets a justifiably big laugh from the industry audience. On this appearance there's also a lovely example of how Eric and Ernie never undermined each other. As they walk up to the stage, Eric veers off and pretends to steal a TV monitor from the wings. Ernie might have been primed by his partner, or it might have just been the instinct that comes from thirty years working together. It could even have been his idea. However, the speed with which Ernie follows his partner gleefully to help him wheel the screen away says a lot about their connection.

Both men were hugely appreciative of Braben. 'Well, he's got the worst job in the world, hasn't he?' said Eric in the 1973 *Omnibus* documentary *Fools Rush In*. 'He got his own little house, with his own little office and he goes in there, let's say, on a Monday morning, with a typewriter and a blank sheet of paper, and then he starts from there. And that's it. That's the hard bit... With Eddie, he thinks of things that we think are very funny, that we wish we could think of, but we can't.'[9] Braben tackled any instances of writer's block by an unconventional method. On the startling tiger-print wallpaper of his study, he drew a television screen. If inspiration flagged, he'd look at the screen and imagine filling it. More often than not, an idea came.

However, that's not to say they regarded everything he provided as perfection. 'We did some pretty heavy editing, Eric, Ernie and myself, but we couldn't have managed without Eddie because he was such a marvellous gag man,' said John Ammonds. The rule was that if one of them didn't like a sketch or a line, it would be cut. There would be no arguing or horse-trading between the pair of them.

The whole first series with Braben is shot through with Eric's willingness to undermine the artifice of the business. Turning and grinning at the camera. The pair of them emerging from behind the curtain separately, only for Eric to blurt out his bafflement at why they did. 'Why didn't we come through together? We were stood there.' These little touches became a vital part of why audiences came to regard Eric and Ernie so highly. They were taking the nation into their confidence. Ernie would appear to protest against Eric's antics, but they were both letting everybody in and saying 'We're on your side. You're with us.'

Braben plays with reality, while keeping everything grounded in truth. Eric is given a fictitious daughter. Obviously, you never see them together, as it's Eric in a wig and flower-power dress. Meanwhile, Ernie is given a daughter called Fanny on a similar principle. However, when Eric says 'We were married at Margate', this is a truthful reference to his own wedding, while raising the question of who he's married to. His wife or Ernie?

One of the best things about these shows, though, is Ernie's obvious exuberance. He smiles and laughs more than he ever did in the ATV days, and launches into dance steps seemingly unbidden, with Eric trying to keep him under control. The harshness has gone. Ernie is positively giddy, like a laboratory beagle being freed to run around for the first time.

As well as giving the shows a first airing in colour, Cotton's decision to premiere the new Morecambe and Wise series on BBC2 meant the programmes could be slotted into the channel's existing *Show of the Week* light entertainment strand. The shows were fortnightly at first, and there was a risk of disappointing viewers in the off-weeks. At the time, BBC2 covered only 80 per cent of the UK, compared to BBC1's 99.5 per cent, and there was also an inbuilt resistance in some households, even those with the required 625-line sets, to the new channel, perceiving it as highbrow and designed for snobs. Putting a broad comedy act who'd made their names on ITV on the second channel could well have helped lower that resistance.

On first transmission, the series didn't make the top 20, but when it was repeated weekly on BBC1[*] in the run-up to Christmas, it was a different matter. The first show was in at number 16, being viewed in 6.3 million homes, the same size of audience that the first series had received on its BBC1 run. The verdict was in. The viewers accepted the new Morecambe and Wise, as had the critics.

Writing in the *Daily Express* the morning after the first show, James Thomas admitted that he had been 'worrying about the switch of writers... Too many TV artists, memorably Tony Hancock, have found a chill switch of popularity when their source of material moved on.'[10] No such calamity had befallen Eric and Ernie; indeed, he detected a 'distinct swing for the better', although he wondered 'with these two if scripts are really necessary. I think they could be funny reading through the London telephone directory.' For a bit possibly, but not for another fourteen years at the top of their profession, and other writers working on the show would come to realise how much Braben brought to the arrangement.

As in the ATV years, the new regime continued with the tradition of ending on a running joke. In the first series with Eddie Braben, the show would end with buxom actress Janet Webb, dolled up to the nines in glittering, glamorous gowns, invading the walk-down at the end, pushing Eric and Ernie aside and basking in everybody else's applause. By the fifth BBC series in 1971, Webb had been promoted to a speaking role.

---

[*] Which had itself gone into colour on 15 November 1969. Nonetheless, the series continued to be premiered on BBC2 for a couple more years.

Thank you everybody, thank you. I'd like to thank all of you for watching me and my little show here tonight. If you've enjoyed it, then it's all been worthwhile. So until we meet again, good night and I love you all.[11]

Webb had first worked with Eric and Ernie in 1964 at ATV, where she played Madame Valenska, a medium in a séance sketch. In the early sketches where Webb worked with Morecambe and Wise, she is presented in an unflattering and unattractive light. Eric refers to her at one point as a 'female Harry Secombe'.

> Eric: What does she do?
> Ernie: Well she sits round the table with us and we hold hands, and then she gets to work.
> Eric: I'm not holding hands with that old bat.[*] What's the matter with you? You can believe in ghosts if you want, but personally I don't believe in them.
> [Valenska returns with an attractive young protégé.]
> Eric: But I'll tell you something else, I'm willing to be convinced.[12]

The way they treated her on screen was very different to her experience behind the scenes. One of her first TV roles had been in a Charlie Drake show, and she'd found the diminutive comedian sullen and difficult. 'He never greeted me once during our work together,' she said. 'Never said "hello", "bye-bye", "good morning" or anything. He completely ignored me.'[13] In contrast, Eric and Ernie 'did all they could to make me feel at home' from the moment she arrived at rehearsals.

***

[*] Webb was only in her mid-thirties at the time.

When she became 'the star' of the early BBC shows, she was presented in a far more positive way. Eric and Ernie revelled in her apparent audacity, carrying a throne for her to sit on, pouring her champagne and lighting her cigars. The *Liverpool Echo* said with pride of Wavertree-born Webb that she was 'the best thing to happen to big girls in a long time... She glories in her abundant inches and you love her for it', encouraging larger women not to cover themselves up. 'I don't see why because you are big you should hide,' Webb observed. 'I defy conventions and I'm never ashamed to show what I've got.'[14]

When Eric and Ernie received the award for best light entertainment programme at the 1971 British Screen Awards, host Richard Attenborough suggested quietly to Webb that he would love it if she invaded the stage as per normal. Shock turning to amusement and delight is evident on Eric and Ernie's faces as they realise what's going on, and Eric hands over the award very willingly.* Eventually, the joke that Webb was the real star of the show became blunted by the fact that she had become a celebrity in her own right, worthy of triple-page tabloid features and commanding £175 for personal appearances. She remained connected to Eric and Ernie at one remove, her husband, Charles Vorzanger, being one of the violinists in Peter Knight's orchestra, but it was time for a change of finale. For the next step, Eric and Ernie called in a very old friend.

Arthur Tolcher was born to be in show business. His father, Charles Tolcher, was a well-established music hall comedian,

---

* The award in question later fell apart. Eric and Ernie would have been permitted a moment of disquiet before they realised the invasion was friendly. Less than five months before, at the Royal Albert Hall, where the awards were held, Bob Hope had been pelted with bags of flour as he tried to entertain the audience at the 1970 Miss World contest.

and he began working with his father in shows in the West Midlands from his early teens. Sibling rivalry led him to take up the harmonica. His father could play, and his brother had one but didn't take to it, so Arthur took it over and persevered to get one over on him. Soon he was good enough to perform professionally, and was billed as 'the Wonder Boy Harmonica Virtuoso'. He did his first broadcast at the age of thirteen on *Sandy Powell's Road Show*, where he was due to do two spots. However, he only got to do one, as the show was cut short to relay the abdicating King Edward VIII's address to the nation from Windsor.

In 1937, he was appearing in *Red Riding Hood* at the Grand in Wolverhampton, and was regarded as enough of a local celebrity to be invited to plant a tree in the new King George V playing field in Bloxwich, where he was born and would live for his whole life. Tolcher was already in *Youth Takes a Bow* when Eric and Ernie joined the show in 1940.

Over the years, as well as becoming a fixture in Birmingham pantomimes for Derek Salberg, proprietor of the Alexandra Theatre, Tolcher would develop a highly skilful act where he played all sizes of harmonica, from a giant bass to a one-inch miniature that nonetheless provided a full octave. However, his greatest fame would come not from his ability, but from it being continually thwarted by time running out. At the end of each show, Tolcher would appear, in tails, from the groundrow trench, playing Pasqual Marquinina Narro's 'Spanish Gypsy Dance' on the harmonica. For a bit of variety, on one occasion there was sufficient time for Tolcher to perform, but he'd left his harmonica in the dressing room.

As well as the finales, Tolcher was used for bit parts here and there. He's the thieving Santa Claus at the start of the 1971 Christmas show, and the goalkeeper in the table football sketch from the 1976 festive special. Eric and Ernie just enjoyed having him around, and the feeling was very much mutual. 'The boys never forgot me,' he said in 1974. 'They always remember their friends.' They had asked him to take part in the shows several years before he was able to join them, being busy all year round as a speciality act. However, whenever schedules coincided, he joined his old associates. 'Just to be there with those two is a tonic,' he explained. 'It's as if the years roll away and we are all kids again.'[15]

Whereas most BBC variety shows at the time had a week's rehearsal before going into the studio, Bill Cotton realised that Eric's health dictated a more leisurely pace. Or rather what should have been more leisurely, as Eric's natural propensity for worry meant that an extended schedule merely prolonged the agony of the tension.

'It was a three-week turnaround,' explains Eddie Stuart, production manager on most of Eric and Ernie's BBC shows. 'If we finished the show on the Sunday, then that next week, we prepared for the show in the office. The start of the second week, the boys came in, and then the third week, the guest star arrived. Sometimes the guest star arrived in the middle of the previous week, but basically that was it. We'd record on Saturday and Sunday, then it was back to the start again. In the first week of those three weeks, John Ammonds would be talking to Eddie Braben and getting the script right, and then we would go into production on that script. John was an excellent script editor. He could take a script to pieces.'[16]

Ammonds knew his strength was with the words, so he decided to ask a friend for help with other aspects of the show. Looking at one of his guest lists and realising that a dance-based item would be ideal, he popped along the circular corridor and asked his friend Ernest Maxin if he had any ideas. Maxin

– already a good friend of Eric and Ernie's, having directed *Running Wild* and on stage in Bernard Delfont summer shows – became responsible for the shows' 'dance direction'.

Meanwhile, when it came to performance, Eric and Ernie themselves had an absolute sense of what worked best. When straight actors came in, they were advised not to ham it up. Francis Matthews was a favourite of theirs, having got to know them on *The Intelligence Men*. In that film, he didn't have much to do, and his stardom came largely from suave roles like the TV detective Paul Temple. However, Matthews loved undermining his image and had superb comic timing, both of which qualities were used by Alan Plater, who remembered a story Matthews told him.

> He turned up at the rehearsal rooms at North Acton, went in, scripts handed out, and Eric said, 'I'm going to say one thing, Francis. One note. We don't think any of it's funny. We play the whole thing assuming none of it is funny. That is the note.' It's such a perceptive note. Look, some of this will get laughs, but if you know it's funny, it won't. You're just people living out your lives within this funny little universe, but you don't think any of it's funny.[17]

Although Eric and Ernie loved working in a theatrical atmosphere, the complexity of the shows, with numerous different sets each week, meant that recording at the BBC Television Theatre on Shepherd's Bush Green would not have been ideal. It was also the scene of the *Running Wild* debacle. So, the larger studios at the Television Centre were used. Everyone's favourite was TC8, because it had been designed specifically as a light entertainment studio, and had been built several years after the others, taking into account the suggestions of those who would use it. TC6 was a popular fallback, and the largest studio, TC1, was pressed into use for the biggest scenes, but performers sometimes felt it harder to reach the audience in the expanded space.

The element of theatre was supplied by the addition of curtains, and an unusual treatment for the studio floor. 'There was a three-foot stage they used to erect and that went across the studio,' Eddie Stuart explains. 'There was one occasion where the scene boys got it wrong and we had to move it, but that was the only time.' When Eric and Ernie walked on to open a show, it didn't sound like a television studio. Also, the slight rise meant that three of the cameras would be pointing up at them, with only the fourth on a Mole-Richardson crane for elevated shots. Thus Eric and Ernie worked over the tops of the cameras to the studio audience, building a closer rapport.

The first two BBC Christmas shows had felt very much like longer versions of the usual format. Kenny Ball and his Jazzmen were present, as was the Danish singer Nina, another semi-regular guest.* Indeed, in 1969, that was exactly what the show had been, as a result of Eric missing the second scheduled recording day, on Sunday 21 December, owing to illness. Ammonds had some of the required material from the first day, including a curtain sketch with a giant Christmas tree, but not enough to make a full show. The planned send-up of *The Barretts of Wimpole Street* with Susan Hampshire, Deryck Guyler and Frank Thornton was one of the most notable casualties. Fortunately, recording for the 1970 series was already underway, and Ammonds was able to knit the

---

* Nina van Pallandt (b. 1932) had been part of the pop duo Nina and Frederik with her then husband, Frederik, Baron van Pallandt, before going solo.

festive material into the show recorded on 1 December for screening early in the new year. Meanwhile, the aborted sketch was remounted for the fourth show of the 1970 series, with Diane Cilento taking the part written for Hampshire. Cilento's then-husband Sean Connery attended the recording at BBC Television Centre, reacting with amusement when Johnny Ammonds cursed her quietly for a mistake, not realising Connery was behind him in the gallery.

In 1970, the planned recording proceeded without a hitch, and included Peter Cushing, William Franklyn, Eric Porter and Edward Woodward. When the Audience Research report on the show came back, Ammonds noted that one of the viewers on the panel commented that they 'particularly like the idea of having well-known actors doing things "out of character" and being treated disrespectfully'.[18] The producer had always prided himself on his ability to get the guests, no matter how elevated, and it was decided to go all out to lure big names to be insulted affectionately. From 1971, the ante was upped. The thing was that if there had been any genuine malice behind the insults, it wouldn't have been funny. Eric had said, 'There's nobody more stagestruck than Ernie and I.'

That show had been recorded over two nights in TC6 at BBC Television Centre. The 1971 show would take four nights to get down on tape, with the first session, in TC8 on 6 December between 8 p.m. and 9.30 p.m., being devoted to a single sketch. However, as the sketch in question would become thirteen minutes of the most celebrated and fondly remembered British television comedy of all time, it was an hour and a half very well spent.

Normally when sketches were pre-recorded to be inserted into a show at a later point, they would be recorded dry and then played to the studio audience at the final session. In this case, however, a smaller-than-usual audience, including around fifty BBC staff members, was present to witness André Previn conducting the Grieg Piano Concerto. Their reaction will have come as some reassurance to Eric Morecambe, who had grave doubts about Previn's suitability and the sketch's potential success.

Talking to Eddie Braben and John Ammonds about future shows, Eric and Ernie had remembered the original version of the sketch from the ATV days. Ammonds thought it would be perfect for the Christmas show, with a slight recasting. In the first version, Ernie had been the conductor, but having been watching *André Previn's Music Night*, a BBC1 series featuring the conductor at work, Ammonds knew who he wanted to step in. The fact that Ammonds was already thinking of Christmas guests in July when the Previn series went out is an indication of the pressure of the job. Eric and Ernie seemed unconvinced. 'I think they knew him as a jazz pianist, not as the principal conductor of the London Symphony Orchestra,' Ammonds recalled. Ammonds canvassed Previn's producer, John Culshaw, who said he'd mention the idea to the conductor, with whom he was due to lunch the next day. Previn's response was immediate and enthusiastic.

I rang him and said I produced Morecambe and Wise. He said, 'Before we go any further, you've got a great show there.' I said, 'Thanks very much. I'm glad you said that because I want you to be on it.' He said he'd do it. I said, 'Can I call your agent and tell them you're interested?' He said, 'Better than that. Ring my agent and tell them I'll definitely do it. My agent is Jasper Parrott.' I rang the agent and said, 'I've just been speaking to your client, André Previn, and he wants to be on the Morecambe and Wise show.' He said, 'How long do you want him for rehearsal?' I said, 'About a week.' There was then a crunch at the other end of the telephone, as he fell on the floor. He said, 'A week? He's travelling round the world.' I said, 'Well, it's not him I'm worried about. Eric and Ernie are used to having the guests for the week. They love rehearsal and I admire them for it.' I compromised at three days. I told Eric the next day and said we'd only got him for three days. Eric said, 'How's he going to learn it?' I said, 'This guy knows every note of Beethoven's Fifth Symphony, he's not going to have any trouble with fourteen pages of dialogue.'

We were in that terrible place, the North Kensington Community Centre at Dalgarno Way, where we used to get the over-sixties singing 'Daisy, Daisy'. Anyway, André wanders in there, and we get round the piano, and the first time we did it, I cried laughing. I thought, 'We've got a good one here because he's a performer as well.' This was just the first read-through. Every time he did it, we did it for about two or three hours, it got funnier and funnier. When he went, I said to the boys, 'This is going to be great.'

The ever nervous Morecambe was mollified by the encouraging start, but only slightly. Then came some news that almost derailed the whole venture.

I got back to my office in the Centre late in the afternoon and I get a call from this agent. He said, 'I'm very sorry, but his mother's very ill in America. He's got to fly to the States and he won't be back until the night before the show.' I thought, 'Christ, how do I explain this to Eric, who's jibbing at three days? Now I've got him hardly at all.' So I told Eric the next morning, and he said, 'Sod him, we don't want him.' I said, 'Whoa, you saw how good he was. We can rehearse, we'll be all right. I'll book a room at the Centre with a piano and we'll rehearse. He lands at five, I'll get a car to get him to the Centre for six, and we'll rehearse until ten.' That's exactly what we did and every time we did it, I cried laughing.

Eventually, André went, Ernie went and I was left with Eric. He said, 'John, this is not going to be as funny as you think it is.' I just shrugged my shoulders because the following night with the audience, it went through the roof. As he came off after the recording, I said, 'You know André, with your comic timing, you could have been a very good comedian.' He said, 'John, I think I'm happier with the baton if you don't mind.' He as you know was marvellous. The tagline was that about three months before Eric died, we were having a drink at Thames or somewhere, and I said, apropos of nothing, 'Do you remember what you said to me the night before that Previn sketch at the Television Centre? You said it wasn't going to be as funny as I thought it was.' I paused, and a smile spread across his face. He said, 'John, I've never been more wrong. It's the funniest thing we've ever done.' I thought that was rather nice. It just shows you that he could be wrong. And some younger producers would have wilted – once he said 'Sod him, we don't want him', that would have been it. I knew it was going to be a gem. He was so marvellous.

Morecambe's uncertainty is visible in the show. Then there is an obvious moment when he realises it's going as well as a sketch possibly could be. Previn says that he'll go and get his baton. Walking away, he does a little half-turn back and announces 'It's in Chicago'. Eric can't stop himself responding to the situation with glee and relief, exclaiming, 'Pow! He's in. I like him.'

The sketch was captured in a single take, with no edits or pick-ups. The audience, who had been warmed up, perhaps incongruously, with some live Flamenco from Los Zafiros, and more appropriately by a few jokes from Barry Cryer, knew nothing of Previn's presence until the tape was rolling and Ernie was introducing him in front of the curtain. After the sketch is over, Eric and Ernie joke with the audience about waiting for a clearance from the videotape department in the basement to say that the recording is satisfactory. Ernie says that the orchestra need to go home because they're tired – the joke being that they've been there for no more than twenty minutes and barely played a note. The after-chatter is also noticeable for Previn's very distinctive laugh.

Although Braben was credited as the only writer, there should perhaps have been a credit for Sid Green and Dick Hills. Braben had refurbished and expanded the Grieg sketch considerably, but some of the most memorable elements were carried over from the original, not least the 'I am playing all the right notes, but not necessarily in the right order' line. The idea of phoning Grieg in Norway was there in 1963, but Braben added 'Fingal's Cave' as the telephone exchange. In the first version, the introduction is too short, but it was Braben who knew that specifying 'by a yard' made it funnier. Morecambe asking the band 'Which one's the fixer?' is presaged in the original ATV version. Noticing that the Stuttgart Symphony Orchestra looks suspiciously like Jack Parnell's band, singling out bassist Lennie Bush and trombonist Nobby Clarke for attention, Eric is assured by Ernie that they are 'Leonardo Buschki' and 'Noberti Fixagig'.*

---

* The 'fixer' was the musician who booked the other musicians. Trombonist Nobby Clarke was the fixer for the Parnell band at ATV, but this was a rare exception to the rule that the job tended to be the province of senior violinists. Throughout Morecambe and Wise's BBC career, the fixer was Jack Mandel.

1. The bill from *Something to Sing About*, Eric and Ernie's first Blackpool summer season, 1953.

CENTRAL PIER BLACKPOOL

ORCHID ROOM

PETER WEBSTER
PRESENTS

'LET'S HAVE FUN'

PRICE 6d.

MORECAMBE & WISE

"LET'S HAVE FUN"
Produced by PETER WEBSTER

1. LET'S HAVE FUN
   MAUREEN ROSE
   ORCHID ROOM LOVELIES

2. MORECAMBE & WISE

3. THREE DEUCES
   CANADA'S AMBASSADORS OF SONG.

4. DENNIS SPICER
   With JAMES GREEN

5. MAUREEN ROSE

6. MORECAMBE & WISE
   With THE ORCHID ROOM LOVELIES

INTERVAL

PLEASE NOTE
SPECIAL
Peter
Webster
SUNDAY
SHOW
at 6.10 and
8.15 p.m.
with
STAR
GUEST
ARTISTS
ONE PRICE
ONLY
2/6
All Seats

7. BLUE SKIES.
   ORCHID ROOM LOVELIES

8. EDDIE GRANT.

9. THREE BELLS.
   ENGLAND'S YOUNGEST HARMONY
   GROUP

10. KENNY BAKER

11. THE ORCHID ROOM LOVELIES

JOAN TURNER
Direct from London Palladium
ALAN CROOKE, at the Piano

12. MORECAMBE & WISE

ALEXANDRA THEATRE
BIRMINGHAM

EVENINGS at 7-0   MATINEES at 2.30
Boxing Day at 2 p.m.

Outstanding Cast already engaged includes

GEORGE LACY

MORECAMBE AND WISE

ANTON and JANETTA   DEREK ROYLE

THE FOUR PLAYBOYS • JOHNNY STEWART • THREE GHEZZIS

LEHMISKI LADIES   ROSELLI SINGERS

LYNNETTE RAE

DRESS CIRCLE 8/6 and 6/-   ORCHESTRA STALLS 8/-
STALLS 5/9.   PIT STALLS 3/6   BALCONY 3/6 and 2/-

REDUCED PRICES FOR CHILDREN AT ALL MATINEES

Special reductions in the Dress Circle and Orchestra Stalls for parties of fifty and over from January,
23rd (Saturdays excepted).
Telephone : MIDland 1231   Box Office 10 a.m. to 7.15 p.m.

Printed at Parkes and Mainwarings Ltd., Dee Street, Birmingham 4.

24 DEC 1960

2. (Above far left) The bill from *Let's Have Fun* at the Central Pier, Blackpool, 1957.
3. (Above left) *Sinbad the Sailor* – the 1960/1 pantomime season at the Alexandra Theatre, Birmingham.
4. (Left) Movie stars: on location in the South of France for *That Riviera Touch*, 1965.
5. (Above) On tour for *Ovaltine*, 1968.

6. (Above) Dick, Ernie, Eric and Sid play cards at the BBC in 1968.
Eric is losing, obviously.

7. (Below) Joan, Eric, Doreen and Ernie at Heathrow, on their way to
represent the BBC at the Montreux Golden Rose Festival, 1970.

8. (Above) Francis Matthews persuades Eric to see his logic in the first show of a new BBC series, 1971.

9. (Below) What's on the box? Two familiar faces.

10. (Above) Comedy is a serious business: assistant floor manager John Adams, production assistant Eddie Stuart, producer John Ammonds, Eric Morecambe and Ernie Wise consider Eddie Braben's script in rehearsal at North Kensington Community Centre, Dalgarno Way, W10, 1973.

11. (Above left) 'The art is to conceal the art' – Eric is having none of that, at Fairfield Halls, Croydon, 1973.

12. (Left) The bill from a typical 'bank raid', 1975.

13. (Above) One good turn: Eric and Ernie pose with John Thaw (Jack Regan) and Dennis Waterman (George Carter), on location for *The Sweeney* in 1978, in return for the TV cops' appearance on their 1976 Christmas Show.

14. (Below) Eric and Ernie report for duty at Thames Television's eddington Lock studios, 1978.

15. (Above) Eric and Ernie with Fulton Mackay at Lensbury Club, Teddington, during rehearsals for *Night Train to Murder*, 1983.

16. (Below) A cross-party gathering at a charity performance of *The Mystery of Edwin Drood*, 1987: David Owen (SDP-Liberal Alliance), Lulu, Ernie, Neil Kinnock (Labour), Jeffrey Archer (Conservative).

Braben also added elements that kept the sketch rooted in variety – Yehudi Menuhin being unable to make it because he's appearing in Old King Cole at the Argyle Theatre, Birkenhead* and Eric's instruction to Mr Preview regarding orchestration. 'The reason I ask is that the second movement is very important to me, you see, in the second movement, not too heavy on the banjos. Keep it down, because wunga-changa, wunga-changa, vulgar, vulgar.' Eric also refers obliquely to violin-playing comic Jimmy Wheeler, who had died the previous year:

Previn: Wait a minute. You got me here under false pretences.
Eric and Ernie: False pretences?
Eric: What's he mean, what's he mean?
Ernie: I told you it wouldn't work. He's expecting Yehudi Menuhin.
Previn: He's a comedian.
Eric : And a very funny one too. I must be honest, he makes me laugh when he puts the violin under his chin, gets the last note, and shouts 'Aye aye, that's your lot' and goes straight to the bar. I like that. I'm very keen on him.[19]

There is also a difference of character at the heart of it. In 1963, Eric seems to realise he's out of his depth. There's still a touch of the old 'gowk' act about him. In 1971, however, Eric is absolutely convinced of his virtuosity. In 1963, Ernie is impatient and critical of Eric. In 1971, Ernie is supportive, mediating between Morecambe and Previn, and equally convinced of his friend's virtuosity. For a change, Morecambe is the pretentious artist. Rather sweetly, although Eric is clearly

* A venue flattened by bombs in 1940.

aware that Ern is a terrible playwright, Ern has no doubts about his partner's musicality.

> Previn: Eric Morecambe is a comic. He can't play the piano.
> Eric: [Putting hand on Previn's shoulder] Just a moment, sir. You seem to doubt my musical prowess.
> Previn: [Putting hand on Eric's shoulder] I certainly do.
> Eric: Let me put your mind at rest, sir, because you are now looking at one of the few men who have actually fished off the end of Sir Henry Wood's promenade. Now follow that with the sealions.
> Ernie: I was there when he did it.[20]

The sketch shows how far they had developed. It had taken eight years to get all the right words in the right order.

Production resumed in TC1 on Friday 17 December, the first of three consecutive days in the studio. It might be expected that guest stars would drop in, do their bit and then go, according to availability. However, it was a measure of the growing importance of the show and the appeal of working with Eric and Ernie that Shirley Bassey was willing to be present for all three of the days, plus two days' rehearsal, on a BBC fee of £500. In contrast, Previn had received only £350 for his services, but he was done and dusted in a day, rehearsal included. The first item to be recorded was Bassey singing her straight number, 'Diamonds Are Forever', the theme song from the James Bond film that was to premier at the Odeon, Leicester Square five days after the show.

The affectionate mockery of the guests that Braben wrote into the scripts was just one of the aspects of Morecambe's personality that he had picked up on and amplified. He could have written the ad lib that Morecambe came out with for the benefit of the crew when Bassey made her entrance, as Ammonds' production manager Eddie Stuart remembers. 'She came onto the set wearing her silver dress, and Eric said, "My God, Shirley, you look like a bloody Brillo pad." She fell about and had to go back to make-up to have her eyes done.'[21]

The rest of the evening's recording was devoted to capturing Glenda Jackson's 1930s-style song and dance routine. The male chorus line in top hat, white tie and tails supporting Jackson was the first time that the show used a line-up of faces from the serious side of the BBC playing against character for laughs. First in the row was Cliff Michelmore, followed by Grandstand's Frank Bough, rugby league commentator and It's a Knockout co-host Eddie Waring, Patrick Moore from The Sky at Night, chat show host Michael Parkinson and newsreader Robert Dougall. Parkinson was the new boy, his BBC show having only started earlier in the year, but it was a seismic moment in television to see a venerable authority figure like Dougall sending himself up by apparently singing soprano.*

The following day's session began with the recording of the now-famous comedy routine involving Bassey. 'John said, "I've got Shirley Bassey. Can you think of anything?",' recalled Ernest Maxin, 'This was with the boots. So I worked out that whole routine. I actually wrote that out on paper so we knew exactly what would happen. It became a talking point. Shirley didn't want to do it. She wasn't that keen. I said, "It'll work. It's not going out live, if it's a disaster, you can cut it out."'[22]

The big number was followed by two short sketches contributed by outside writers, although Braben was the only one to get a credit at the end of the show. In fact, there were

---

* The voices were overdubbed by the Mike Sammes Singers.

two uncredited external contributions. The first was the pre-titles quickie with Eric and Ernie sleeping while Arthur Tolcher burgles them, dressed as Father Christmas. This was written by Ray Whyberd and Jay Dee, Whyberd being the ventriloquist Ray Alan writing under his real name.

The other outsider was a quickie involving the two monks who had been regular characters in Eric and Ernie's BBC shows. It had been sent in by a viewer, Steven Dron of Broughty Ferry near Dundee, who suggested that the monks could pull on candlesticks that were revealed to be beer pumps. Dron's letter was dated 15 November 1970, and the sketch had been in the running for that year's Christmas show before being cut for time.

Finally, on Sunday 19 December 1971 came the main recording session for the show, with an audience present in the cavernous TC1, reacting to the live performance they were witnessing and the pre-packaged items. Barry Cryer was the main warm-up man on this occasion, but the stars always insisted on giving the studio audience a good ten minutes of private performance before the tapes rolled, using the ventriloquist routine from their stage act.*

Logically, although not obviously, given the strange ways of television, the first item to be recorded was the opening double, with Eric brandishing a box containing Christmas presents from the BBC. The pair receive silver tankards, albeit not equal.

Eric: I've only got a little 'un.
Ernie [laughing derisively]: The BBC don't think much of you, do they? The size of it.
[...]

* Of which more later.

Eric: Yours is silver and everything. It's got an inscription on it.

Ernie: Well, maybe there's an inscription on yours?

Eric: Don't be a fool. You couldn't get an inscription on that. You couldn't get a full stop on that thing. That's an insult, that.

Ernie: I'm more than satisfied with mine. [Winks at camera] Thank you, Lord Hill.*

Eric: [to Ernie] Crawler. Look at that.

Ernie: Yes, I know, I told you. The BBC really appreciate talent, don't they?

Eric: That's disgusting, that is.

Ernie: What do you mean, disgusting?

Eric: [addressing camera while doing jacket up as if to leave] I'm ready when you are, Lew. Coming straight over. I'll get the bike.[23]

The exchange plays on the smugness and superiority that Braben had built into Wise's comic persona, and briefly gives Wise the upper hand. It almost harks back to the dynamic of the partnership in the ATV years. The punchline comes when a giant, solid gold tankard is produced and Eric is led briefly to think that it is for him, but he is being set up for another fall. It's for Dick Emery, who makes a brief wordless cameo to collect it.†

* Charles Hill, Baron Hill of Luton, was the chairman of the BBC from 1967 to 1972. During the war, he had become famous for his medical broadcasts as 'the Radio Doctor', before becoming a Conservative MP and, from 1963 to 1967, chairman of the Independent Television Authority.
† Pro rata, Emery is the best paid artist in the show, receiving £75 for a few seconds on screen.

Amusingly, when the show went out, Previn received a similar accolade. 'He was living in a lovely country place, a cottage between Dorking and Reigate, Betchworth. They knew him in the local pub, and they knew he was the conductor of the London Symphony Orchestra, but he said, "When I'd been on Morecambe and Wise, they gave me my own tankard."'[24]

Emery would have been back in the Television Centre bar by the time the recording had moved on to the next item, where Eric and Ernie recorded a chat in front of the curtains with Glenda Jackson as the prelude to the routine recorded two nights before. While the audience were watching the recording, Eric and Ernie were off to get changed into turkey costumes for a sketch on death row. After this, Spanish band Los Zafiros did their spot while the stars changed back into suits – their third and final different suits of the evening – for a routine in front of the curtain with Shirley Bassey, and a separate chat with Francis Matthews, who was to star in the climax of the show, the play what Ernie wrote, Robin Hood. The pre-recorded Bassey items gave the stars time to go back and change for this piece, which appears to have been the climax of the evening.

Although the closing song, 'Following You Around', is listed on the recording schedule as the last item to be taped, with Eric and Ernie in dinner jackets, it seems likely that it was recorded near the start of the evening. Instead of evening dress, they're both wearing the same suits as in the opening double, and their pocket handkerchiefs are folded in exactly the same way as they had been before. Astonishingly, given how much pressure they were under that Sunday, they found time to nip around the famous doughnut of Television Centre to studio TC8 to record a quickie for the Christmas Day *Black and White Minstrel Show*, in which they emerged from dustbins and complained that their dressing rooms were getting smaller. The final editing session for Eric and Ernie's Christmas show began at 11 a.m. on Tuesday 21 December, and was finished by 9.30 p.m. According to BBC figures, the show was appreciated by 19 million viewers, making it the most popular show of the season.

While Braben's scripts routinely required blood, sweat and tears, his instant wit indicated how perfect a fit he was for the boys. Barry Cryer, who served as both warm-up man and scriptwriter for Eric and Ernie, remembers Braben at his sharpest one day in the studio.

> Eddie and I were watching Eric and Ernie doing a run-through one afternoon and there was a break, and a whole crocodile of people came into the audience seats and Eddie said to me, 'Who's that, Baz?' And I said, 'Oh, he's called Brad Ashton. He runs a writing school and he's got permission.' 'Oh right, right.' So Brad came over and I introduced him to Eddie. Eddie says, 'Hello Brad' and Brad said, 'We've met before.'
> 'No, we haven't.'
> 'Yes, yes.'
> 'No, no.'
> Brad said, 'We met in the Gents' at Heathrow', and Eddie said, 'I see you've got a different job now.'[25]

Sometimes the sketch would be based around a prop, Morecambe having told Braben early on in their association that 'they loved to work with props, anything they could hold, pick up or carry'. Morecambe had told the writer, 'if it's a good prop, we'll get the laughs'.[26] Often, the props in question were objects that existed only in Braben's mind, and it fell to the BBC's visual effects department, in particular a designer called Bill King, who worked extensively on Eric and Ernie's shows over the years, to make them into reality. Even bringing to fruition such brainstorms as 'Small suitcase to convert into a banjo... small suitcase to convert into a double bass – as discussed'.

Denis Norden liked to describe writers as 'comedians' labourers', but Braben was more of a bespoke tailor. One of the areas where he made the suit fit perfectly was in evening up the power balance between Eric and Ernie, more in keeping with the supportive real-life relationship he'd observed. In the Sid and Dick years, Eric had always been the fall guy. There were a lot of sketches where he didn't get the girl, or where Ernie, with Sid and Dick's connivance, got the upper hand over his partner. With Eddie Braben, it was much more even-handed. He made Eric cleverer and more worldly. This Eric was playful, flirtatious and obviously attractive to women. Meanwhile, he took the edge off Ernie, making him vain and mean but fundamentally innocent. This Ernie wasn't trying to get one over on Eric. He trusted his friend utterly, and the trust was not misplaced. As much as he mocked his little fat friend in the flat, to the outside world, Ernie had no greater supporter. The dynamic was laid out explicitly in one 1976 show where Australian actress Maggie Fitzgibbon played a journalist visiting Ern at the flat to discuss using his manuscript in a guide for young writers. The manuscript in question had already received a response from a publisher that caused Ern to become unbearably big-headed.

> Ernie: They think that I could become another Somerset
>   Morgan.
> Eric [looking baffled]: Who?

Ernie: Somerset Morgan. He wrote War and Peace by Tolstoy.

Eric [with a mild snigger]: I didn't know that.[27]

The publisher describes the book in their letter as 'verbal compost', which Ern takes as a compliment. When Fitzgibbon arrives, introducing herself as 'Miss Fanagonellan' (which both, obviously, mishear as 'Miss Flanagan and Allen'),[*] and reads out a passage where Ern refers to 'Paris, just outside France', Eric hears alarm bells. While Ern is making coffee (not 'the tea, Ern', for a change – this is serious), Eric challenges Miss Flanagan and Allen:

Eric: This guiding young writers. You want to use Ernie's book as a guide on how *not* to write a book, don't you?

Miss Flanagan and Allen: Oh Mr Morecambe, I'm sure you and I can get around this business, and I can assure you we would have done it in the very best of taste.

Eric: Yes, but he would have been made to look a fool, wouldn't he, really? You know? And, I mean, nobody does that while I'm around, because I've got the concession on that. You know, I mean, you hurt him, you hurt me. You hurt me, you hurt him. One for all, all for one, swords in the ceiling... You know that he can't write. I know that he can't write. He thinks he can, and that's good enough for me.[28]

It's played for laughs, but it's an oddly affecting admission from Morecambe. This sketch contains two other illuminating moments. Ern tries to get rid of Eric by asking him, 'If I give you the money, will you go to the pictures and come back in

* Prompting Eric to say 'Sing Home Town and see what happens'.

about three hours?' This is the sort of thing a parent at the end of their tether would have said to a child, rather than a conversation between two adult friends. And yet, there are so many times when Eric is the patient parent to Ern. Whichever way the energy is flowing, there is an endearing element of arrested development. Everything the pair did is redolent of short trousers, stink bombs and catapults. They were overgrown children who had latched onto the fact that even the supposed adults were making it up as they went along. Even being paid thousands of pounds a show to entertain an audience of millions, they were still those two teenagers trying to make each other laugh on a train.

Having annoyed Ernie, Eric bends over briefly while switching chairs, and Ern mimes a karate chop to the back of his neck that looks very much like it could be genuinely spontaneous. That's part of the trouble with Eric and Ernie. They rehearsed endlessly to make things look effortless and off-the-cuff, but 99 per cent of the time, what seems like an ad lib will have been locked down at the table read. This, however, has the air of something totally in its moment. Eric is unable to see what Ern has done, but feels the draught of air, and looks his friend in the eye, laughing. Ern begins laughing too and has trouble getting out his next line, the one about going to the pictures. It's a moment that illustrates how much they enjoyed each other, and how much they enjoyed being Morecambe and Wise. The flat sketches were an inspired creation. They were nothing like either man's home life, and yet they enshrined basic truths about Eric and Ernie, both as a partnership and individuals.

Meanwhile, with guests, Eric would be insulting, while Ernie would be ingratiating, leading his partner to call him a 'crawler'. Eric would get names wrong. Andrew Preview,

Slasher Distillery. The irreverence was a very Scouse touch by Braben. We can only imagine what The Beatles' guest appearance would have been like with a Braben script. The beauty was that everybody was in on the joke. The viewer who watches the Grieg's Piano Concerto sketch to the very end is rewarded with André Previn's very genuine smile in appreciation of the stars he's just worked with.

The greatest store of disdain was reserved for one person, an East End boy a few years younger than Eric and Ernie who had first met them when he was an up-and-coming comedian on the variety circuit in the 1950s. Gradually, he moved away from the comedy to become a middle-of-the-road singer and television personality, becoming one of ATV's biggest stars in the 1960s alongside Eric and Ernie. When Barry Cryer and John Junkin set the ball rolling with a dig about Des O'Connor in a First World War sketch with Radio 2 DJ Pete Murray in the 1972 Christmas show, it was absolutely fine. Everyone was having a laugh about a mate.

> Ernie: Gentlemen, I've got some wonderful news for you.
> Eric: Des O'Connor's got a sore throat.
> Ern: The Red Baron has been sighted and is about to attack the airfield.
> Murray: Don't panic.
> [Everybody panics.][29]*

The line gets a big laugh. For all of his popularity, critics had made a sport of sneering at O'Connor. 'They've said I'm too

---

* This sketch includes a callback to the Memory Man sketch, when Morecambe shouts 'Arsenal'. It gets no response, as the famous sketch had been recorded but not yet transmitted.

twee and casual,' he said in 1975.[30] There was also a degree of professional enmity in show business: the tall poppy syndrome at work. 'Some performers just can't stand other entertainers having any kind of success.'

O'Connor made it very clear that Morecambe and Wise were the exceptions to this, being smart and magnanimous to know that their jokes at his expense were an accolade. Eric and Ernie only insulted the best. Eric backed this up in his rare serious moments. 'Ernie and I would never knock anybody because we didn't like them,' he explained in 1976. 'Des is among our best friends. We've known him since we were struggling to make a living... We know he won't be upset when we have a go at him.'[31] The genuine friendship gave Eric and Ernie a licence to mock Des, just as Eric mocked Ernie but wouldn't allow anyone else to. 'He came to my daughter's wedding,' said Eric in the 1979 Christmas show, with O'Connor sitting alongside him, instantly undermining the sincerity with 'He wasn't invited, but he came'.

It also served as a lightning rod, blunting the impact of malice from other quarters. 'In a funny way it helped my career as the public saw it was a bit of fun and I wasn't too grand to have a joke on me,' said O'Connor. Indeed, he gave as many jokes as he took. 'I used to send Eric and Ernie jokes to insult me with and people would come up to me and say, "Did you hear what he said?" and I'd say under my breath, "Yes I know, I wrote that one."'[32] In any case, if there had been a genuine problem, Des's agent could easily have straightened it out with Eric and Ernie's agent. All three were represented by London Management, proprietor: William Marsh.

Of course, as with all of Morecambe's jibes, it wouldn't have been funny if it had been based in truth. Just as Ernie had all his own hair and wasn't really mean, Des O'Connor was a good singer, with a string of chart successes to his name. His easy-going manner disguised a considerable talent. His head writer, Tony Hawes,* took great delight in writing special lyrics to songs that tested his technique to the full, the peak being the names of hundreds of Palladium stars set to the tune of the Can Can.

The reputation of the show grew to the point that nearly everybody who was approached to appear said yes. The biggest 'one that got away' was the Hollywood legend James Stewart, who got as far as meeting Eric, Ernie, John Ammonds and production assistant Susan Belbin. 'To be honest, I don't think Jimmy understood the idea of famous people having the piss taken out of them, albeit with the utmost love and affection,' Belbin recalls, 'Also he was in the theatre with *Harvey* at the time and we would have to have fitted the recording in during the run. We were all gutted as you can imagine but wow, the boys, John Ammonds and myself had a wonderful (no pun intended!), afternoon.'[33] As *Harvey* ran at the Prince of Wales† from 9 April to 27 September 1975, it's likely that Stewart's appearance was at least partially a casualty of Ammonds leaving the show as a result of concerns for the overworked Eddie Braben, resulting in there being no series in 1975, only the Christmas show.

Then there was Sarah Miles, who was approached for the 1973 Christmas show. Most guests were happy to trust in Johnny Ammonds and the boys.

The only nearly big mistake we made was with Sarah Miles. She said yes through her agent, but I got suspicious when

---

* Son-in-law of Stan Laurel.
† Coincidentally, where Stewart had seen *Strike a New Note* in 1943, and met Eric and Ernie when he went backstage after.

she asked to see a script. It was always embarrassing because we didn't usually have a script until days before. We'd have an idea of what we were going to do. For example, we'd say, 'Right, we've got Keith Michell and we're going to do the French Foreign Legion.' I'd ad-lib it on the phone. We'd virtually make it up and the agent would say, 'Oh, that sounds good.' But Sarah Miles insisted on a script, so I sent her one and I can just visualise the scene when she's with her husband, Robert Bolt, having just finished *Lawrence of Arabia*, saying 'You'll ruin your career' or words to that effect. It wasn't one of Eddie's best, quite frankly. But anyway, it was in an unedited version. We hadn't had a chance to go through it. I had a call from her agent to say that Miss Miles didn't like the script. I said, 'Well, there it is, you'd better forget it', and we got Hannah Gordon very quickly, who was very good.

The personal manager was the guy who supposedly committed suicide in America.* There was obviously a boyfriend or something. He rang me back and said, 'Have you been putting it about that she walked out of rehearsals?' I replied 'Just a moment, no. Where did you get that from? We've had a hell of a job to get a replacement. I've been working hard and haven't had time to tell lies like that.' She was the only person to turn the show down.

Miles had made quite the impression on Eric, Ernie and John Ammonds when she met them for an initial sounding-out. 'We went for an incredible lunch at Oddies in Shepherd's Bush. Eric had arranged with his driver, Michael, to pick us up at a certain time after the lunch. Right through the lunch, she was using every four-letter word in the book. Poor Ernie

* David Whiting.

was going redder and redder. Eric was all right, but Ernie was a bit old-fashioned with things like that. She wanted a lift back to Television Centre, so in the back there was Ernie, Eric and me with her lying right across the three of us. I think the business end was towards Ernie, which embarrassed him even more. I shall never forget that. She was effing and blinding all the time.'

When recording the shows at the BBC, the audience warm-up was an important part of the studio process. Eric and Ernie would come out and use little bits of their stage act, including the ventriloquist routine, to get the audience laughing. However, to fill in the longueurs between takes, and while sets and cameras were being moved, a comic was enlisted. Barry Cryer, as one of the writers, and aided by a quick wit honed at Danny La Rue's club, had done quite a few in the early BBC days, as had John Junkin, before giving way to Felix Bowness. Later famous for playing disgraced jockey Fred Quilley in the David Croft/Jimmy Perry holiday camp sitcom *Hi-De-Hi*, Bowness's bread-and-butter television work for many years was never seen by the viewers at home, but Johnny Ammonds was worried Eric and Ernie might not take to him.

I was a bit nervous about using him with Eric and Ernie because he goes on a bit and he sits on that front rail of the audience to be near them. But he was magic of course. But they were very pleased the first time we had him and they said 'Book him again'. I went on once. Just to introduce them. I thought I'd take a bit of tape with me just to show them what it was recorded on. The make-up room in studio 8 is at the side, you know and Eric was in there somewhere. I started to say what it was recorded on and of course he came out through the door and all the eyes naturally go to him. He said, 'They don't want to hear about all that rubbish. Get off, you silly sod.'[34]

The whole process of making a Morecambe and Wise show is chronicled in admirable detail by a pair of documentaries made during the recording of the 1973 series. *Scene: Morecambe and Wise* and *Omnibus: Fools Rush In* both follow the production of the seventh show, which includes the now-famous Memory Man/'ARSENAL' sketch. However, the idea that the *Scene* version was a cut-down version of the *Omnibus* is given the lie by the fact that the producer of both, Ronald Smedley, spent almost his entire BBC career in schools and children's programmes. It appears that the schools version was the original proposal, and was scaled up and expanded for mainstream viewing.

There is a suggestion in Michael Aspel's memoirs that he mooted the idea for these documentaries. Morecambe and Wise were regular guests on his children's show *Ask Aspel*, so he had the 'in' already. 'It's not possible to copyright ideas, as I found when I put forward the notion of following a Morecambe and Wise sketch from its inception, through rehearsal and onto the stage. Eric and Ernie were all for it. The BBC said, "Nice idea, afraid we just can't fit it in." They managed to fit it in a couple of years later.' Aspel found that similar situations had been dismissed as coincidence, but this time, it was the case.

The documentaries show how heavily involved Eric and Ernie were in the script editing. They were less involved in the post-production process. Initially they had sat in on editing sessions with Johnny Ammonds, but eventually their producer pulled rank and became the final arbiter. He rather enjoyed the feeling of power, not over his stars, but over the nation.

I remember when I was in hospital, I'd had an asthma attack. My production manager was at the editing session. I said I was thinking about cutting from this to that in the flat sketch. The bloke came back and said, 'Well, I said what you wanted to do, Ernie started to argue. Eric got fed up with arguing and said, "Tell John he can do what he always does, please himself."' I never asked them again. If it works. It was a joy to be able to do it knowing you'd play to such a large audience.

We always overran by about ten minutes or so, and we'd have to cut. One year I couldn't get any editing time. I was editing until midnight on Christmas Eve. I was down in the dungeons at Television Centre and I thought to myself, 'Here am I – it's going to play to 24 million tomorrow night. Here am I, the one man responsible for what goes in and what doesn't.' On the money I was getting it was even more ridiculous. That was the joy of it really. I was absolutely in control.

As much as Eric and Ernie put themselves through to remain at the top – and in time, the constant self-induced stress would prove fatal for Eric – there was also a price to be paid by their leading collaborators. In 1972, Eddie Braben had a nervous breakdown trying to top the achievement of the previous year's Christmas show, and was forced to bow out of writing the festive follow-up, with Barry Cryer and John Junkin taking up the slack. It happened again in 1974, and there was no new Christmas show that year. Instead, Michael Parkinson introduced a compilation of highlights.

Eric and Ernie dancing off set, throwing their hands behind their heads as they go, is so much a part of them that it's tempting to assume it was something they did all along.

However, it wasn't part of their act until 1973. It stemmed from a conversation Ammonds had with them one morning before getting down to serious work. He recalled:

> It was me and Groucho Marx. Me primarily, because I did it one morning in rehearsal at Ealing, the purpose built rehearsal rooms we had there. The first week it was just the three of us. They were there at ten, and I got in slightly after. I said, 'Did you see him last night? Groucho?', because I knew he [Eric] was a fan. There was a Marx Brothers film on. I think it was *Horse Feathers*.* 'He did this crazy dance', and I did it all around this large rehearsal room. They put it in that show, when they danced off after 'Bring Me Sunshine', and it became a trademark.

Eric clarified that it wasn't quite as Groucho did it: 'We fell about laughing because he couldn't do it properly. So we copied him, and not Groucho Marx. We copied Johnny Ammonds and we've done it ever since.'[35]

Their increased television success meant that Eric and Ernie were able to take it easier on the live front. Eric's health and the natural ageing process had changed their attitudes to work. Until his first heart attack, the pace had been relentless. Ernie, in particular, was driven by a need to perform. The hungry years had made them unwilling to pass up on any opportunities. In a sense, they were still those two kids doing their act wherever they could. In the early days, it was to prove they could do it. Once successful, it was to prove they could earn money doing it. 'If we heard there were twenty people wanting to see us, we would go and play to them,' said Ernie, 'and if they gave us

---

* Which had been on BBC1 on 21 April 1972.

the right money, we would perform. Anywhere, just so long as the deal was right.'[36]

After 1968, that changed. Their last summer season had been 1967, and their last appearance in pantomime was 1966. In both cases, 'the work was too hard... we began to spend more time at home, and we liked it'.[37] The variety circuit they'd grown up in had disappeared gradually over a decade from the mid-1950s onwards, but there were the cabaret clubs like Batley, and a growing number of venues, often municipally run, where they were more than welcome. The idea of doing a week in one place had disappeared with the ornate gilt theatres.

Most of the new gigs were one-nighters, or two at the most. 'They seemed so easy and brought us so much cash that "bank raids" were the obvious name for them,' said Eric.[38] 'The boys stupidly thought they couldn't fill it for more than one night,' adds ventriloquist John Bouchier, who toured extensively with Eric and Ernie in the 1970s. 'They had this idea that they were only good for one night.'[39]

There is very likely a degree of false modesty here. They could have done more, but basically they didn't want to. 'To me the beauty of show business in this country is that I can work three months and fish nine months,' said Eric in 1981.[40] They were also conscious of creating a scarcity value in their appearances, so that they became keenly awaited events. The 'bank raids depend entirely on the amount of business that comes in,' Ernie explained. 'The speed of the sell-out has always reflected the size of the popularity. We wouldn't go on to perform to half-empty houses... I don't think we would want to tour if there was no business.'[41]

Morecambe wasn't underselling the attraction of the bank raids when he said that they were 'so easy'. They were using tried and tested material, largely from the ATV days, and restricting themselves to the second half of the show, filling the first half with a mini variety bill. 'The funny thing was, with all of their material, all of their experience, they only had a half an hour spot,' says Bouchier, 'They'd do an hour, but the actual act was only thirty minutes long, and then it was a question and answer thing. They'd get the usual questions. Has he really got a wig and that sort of thing. Thirty minutes in those days was a long time to do on stage.'

Happily, a document of the show exists in the form of a film made privately for Billy Marsh at the Fairfield Halls in Croydon in 1973. One thing that somehow comes through the grainy film nearly five decades later is the sheer love emanating from the audience. The Fairfield Halls had opened in 1962, and had been designed very much along the lines of the Royal Festival Hall, where Tony Hancock staged a comeback show in 1966 to a muted response.* Both were designed as concert halls, not comedy venues. As Ernie remarks, 'I've never worked in an aircraft hangar before.' And yet, in a phrase used by performers, Morecambe and Wise 'got across'.†

Indeed, the goodwill is such that they could almost have just stood there. They could sense when they were losing an audience, and how much they would have to do to get them back. On television, they could joke that the punters were getting in free, but these were people who had paid good

---

* Worse, when Hancock saw the BBC recording of his Royal Festival Hall show, one particularly unforgiving close-up made him respond: 'I look like a fucking frog.'

† As a child, I went with my family to see Cannon and Ball at the Fairfield Halls, at the height of their television fame. Their tremendous warmth meant that they got at least as far as row M of the stalls, where we were. However, I also saw them at the Opera House in Blackpool around the same time, and it was obvious where they worked best.

money. However, the dynamic had changed. When they were variety comics, audiences wanted value for money, and would complain if it was not given. When they were on their 'bank raids', the audiences weren't expecting a full bill. They just wanted to be with Eric and Ernie. They wanted to spend a night with their mates.

Their mates paid them back with local knowledge. Years on the halls had taught them that very little got an audience on side quicker than a local in-joke. Ernie says that he wanted to be 'the talk of Addington estate – Little Siberia', a notorious council estate on the fringes of Croydon.

Other than these modifications, their stage act was basically ATV Morecambe and Wise, but overlaid with the dynamic of their true friendship and/or Eddie Braben's version of it. The climax of the act was the ventriloquist routine that they'd done on television in 1963, but the power balance was less skewed in favour of Ernie. Eric was, obviously, a terrible ventriloquist. He made no attempt to disguise the moving of his lips. In the original television version, Ernie explained where he had gone wrong, and he'd accepted it with relative meekness.

Ernie: I can see your lips moving.

Eric: Yeah, I know, I'm doing it, aren't I? It's me who's doing it. That's why my lips are moving.

Ernie: No, wait a minute, when the dummy talks, you keep your mouth shut.

Eric: Do you?

Ernie: Of course.

Eric: Oh.

Ernie: Didn't you know?

Eric: No. [looks at dummy] Did you know?[42]

This stands in contrast with:

Ernie: Just a moment. I can see your lips moving.
[Eric nods defiantly.]
Eric: Eh?
Ernie: I said I can see your lips moving.
[Eric stifles a laugh and looks away, then taps Ernie on the chest.]
Eric: Well, of course you can, you fool. Because it's *me* who's doing it for *him*. He can't do it on his own. [Raps knuckles on figure's face] He's *wood*. [Pushes figure's head out of body] That's me hand there, you know. [Eric looks at audience.] I'm working with an amateur.[43]

Other elements of the stage act went back to the pre-television days, among them Eric supposedly noticing a fat woman in the front row and commenting on her at length, while Ernie apologises for his partner's rudeness, before Eric realises the non-existent fat woman is a non-existent man. If there was a fat woman in the front row, the gag was out.

Another tried and tested element of the stage show was Eric fooling around with a pair of bongos while Ernie impersonated Sammy Davis Jr badly. What comes across from the film is how much fun they're having. Life had moved on, and from spending every hour together when they were teenagers and young men, they now only saw each other when they were working. In television, they were expected to learn new material, so there was less chance for fooling around. On stage, easy familiarity was the order of the day. It was their chance to just be themselves.

The conscious decision to lead separate lives away from work had been one of the things that preserved the partnership. It was also, in the words of John Bouchier, an acknowledgement of divided loyalties. 'The boys never socialised because the wives didn't get on. Ernie's wife thought that he was the star and that Eric couldn't manage without him, and so consequently, although they were electric on stage, they never mixed. Once they were in the theatre, they were great.'

The 1974 series, the pair's eighth at the BBC, opened with a favourite guest returning. André Previn had found time in his busy schedule to reunite with Eric and Ernie, although for comic purposes he was only present as a result of subterfuge. Wise, smoking a pipe to appear 'mature and dignified', had invited him to the flat, telling him he would be meeting senior executives from the BBC television music and arts department, with regard to an important new work. Eric responds to Ernie's revelation about as well as Previn does when he realises who he's really meeting.

> Not André flaming Previn. He ruined my Grieg's Piano Concerto, that fellow. Do you know that when I go to the British Legion now, they won't let me near the piano.[44]

Previn arrives, and immediately tries to leave, with Morecambe blocking his exit. Captive on the sofa, a horrified Previn works through the trauma of their previous encounter.

> Morecambe: I would like to apologise because, I must be honest, I did damage your career.
>
> Previn: I'm glad you brought that up. I want to talk to you about that, because it took me twenty years to build my reputation as a musician, and in five minutes, you made me into a complete nonentity… Now you two fellas got me here with this ridiculous phoney letter in order to con me into

being on your show… If you two are really the heads of the classical music department of the BBC, I'd be better off on *Opportunity Knocks*.

    Morecambe: I don't know why. You didn't win it last time you were on.

Eric tries to convince Mr Preview that the Grieg was unrepresentative of his piano playing, and demonstrates this by playing 'Honeysuckle Rose' in a version that Les Dawson would have admired.* This aural assault prompts Previn to leave, but as he's half out of the door, Wise instructs Eric to 'phone the Palace and tell them after the show it'll be Benjamin Britten who will be presented to her'. Previn returns and talks them out of Britten.

The big production is a 1920s-style dance band novelty number, with an increasingly irritated Previn as the conductor, while Eric and Ernie sing into a microphone bearing the legend '2LO'. In the background, a band of session musicians, including lead trumpeter Stan Roderick, *Goon Show* guitarist Judd Procter and drummer Ronnie Verrell, who also dubbed the drums for Animal on *The Muppet Show*, struggling not to laugh in the background. The 'Royal' presentation is not quite what Previn was expecting.

    Previn: That's not the Queen. That's Mrs Mills.

    Morecambe and Wise (in unison): She's the queen of the ivories.

---

* The cleverness of Mancunian comedian Les Dawson's (1931–1993) out-of-tune piano playing was in his choice of wrong notes. He played just enough of the tune to make it recognisable, and lull the audience into a false sense of security (even though they knew, indeed anticipated gleefully, what was coming) before throwing in the perfect mistake at the right time.

Previn: How can I…

Morecambe: The Palace this week, the Hippodrome next week.

Previn: How can I get myself into these things? Everybody warned me. Everybody told me don't go. Even the twins. How old are they? Four years old. Little fellas. They said 'Papa, don't go', but me, no, Morecambe and Wise.

[Previn storms out through the curtain.]

Morecambe: Sad he has no sense of humour.

At the end of the show, while singing 'Bring Me Sunshine' over the credits, Previn returns to berate Eric and Ernie, but ends up joining in with the song and doing the Groucho dance off with them.

This sketch, with its callbacks to the Grieg sketch and Previn's sudden snobbery-induced change of manner proving that every man has his price, deserves to be far better known than it is. Once again, Previn's comic timing and facial expressions are a joy to behold, as is the idea that the 1971 Christmas appearance did anything but enhance Previn's global reputation.

By the end of that 1974 series, Johnny Ammonds knew that something had to give. The high standard had been maintained, but at the cost of immense stress all round. With Mike Yarwood's technically exacting shows taking up more and more of his time, he decided it would be him, and told Bill Cotton Jr of his decision.

Poor old Eddie was getting tired. Nervous exhaustion. I'm not surprised. I have no idea how anyone just sits down with a blank piece of paper. I said to Eric that we should get other people in, with Eddie, to reinforce him. We all agreed. Then when the next series came up, Bill said to me, 'Eric wants me to book Eddie Braben.' I said, 'For 100 per cent?' He said, 'Yes.' I said, 'Well, we've been through all this.' Eric stuck to his guns. I said I didn't want to go through it all again. It was a brave thing to do because it was a big show, but I just said I want to come off the show. If that had been my sole source of work on a contract I wouldn't have done it or I would have thought more about it, but I was genuinely concerned about Eddie.[45]

When Ammonds indicated his desire to step aside, the choice of replacement was obvious to all concerned. Ernest Maxin had been choreographing the show from the start as well as producing and directing *International Cabaret*, *The Black and White Minstrel Show* and Charlie Drake's Montreux award-winning comedy series. At first, Maxin was worried he would be treading on Ammonds' toes.

John's office was next to mine, and he was probably my closest friend there. Bill Cotton called me into his office. 'Eric and Ernie want you to take over their show.' I said, 'But look, come on now, you can't change in mid-stream. John's done a great show. They'd be cutting off their nose to spite their face. And I've got to follow a great show.' He said, 'No, John agrees. He feels he needs a change.' I discussed it with John, and I said as long as I've got your OK, and this was in front of Bill Cotton and Billy Marsh.[46]

One way of easing the pressure on Braben was to increase the number of bits of visual 'business', at the expense of the more verbal items; Braben remembered Eric telling him early on that 'they loved to work with props, anything they could hold, pick up or carry'. There was a contrast in approach between Ammonds and Maxin. Ammonds tended to edit on the page, and shoot only what had been written down. Maxin tended to shoot long and edit afterwards.

In Eric's case, giving him something to handle was an outlet for his constant nervous energy, and he was the one who came up with most of the ideas. Sometimes it was simple, just a ukulele. Other times, it was more complex. As a result, the prop lists for the shows are almost as funny as the scripts themselves, and Susan Belbin, then Ernest Maxin's assistant floor manager and later an acclaimed comedy director, played them very much for laughs. Writing a requisition for a 'hand grenade with pin easily pulled out', Belbin specified 'non prac'. While it was as well to specify, the instruction will have been received with amusement by props buyer Bobby Warans.

Ernie's play *The Life of a Bengal Lancer* in show four of the 1976 series is particularly rich in prop requests. Ernie was to be tortured by Khan, played by Anthony Sharp, a favourite straight man, and so the order went in for a 'pair of false legs from the waist down to look like Ernie's, legs to get longer and longer and on a given cue legs to shoot back behind screen from where they came' and with Belbin noting that 'Wardrobe will supply britches and boots for legs'. In the event, the comedy legs don't spring back quite quickly enough, and are still in shot when Ernie emerges from behind the screen.

Belbin also echoed one of Little Ern's own catchphrases when requesting a calendar with the months 'JANUARY FEBRUARY MARCH MAY SORRY APRIL, DECEMBER', calling for 'each leaf to blow off separately to give the effect of the passage of time like what they do in the movies!!'[47]

As amusing as Morecambe's demands were, they had to be built, usually by the show's visual effects expert Bill King, and this cost money. 'Ernest's classic line with Eddie, Eric and Ernie was "Look, you know I love you",' said Gary Morecambe in 2013. 'Instantly, they'd dissolve. The "but" was always coming.' Some involved with the production felt that Maxin didn't say 'but' quite enough, though. When Ammonds had been producing the show, the controls were tighter, with the props ordered as required. With Maxin's more visual approach and his freer attitude to the script, Morecambe would order props on the basis that they might be useful, as Eddie Stuart explains:

There was always the possibility that Eric was going to order too much stuff, but it was only latterly that he was ordering it and it was getting done. There was one occasion where we had six horses. Not real horses, dummy horses. And he didn't use one of them. I tried to put a stop to it. We got this printout [of the show budget] and it said that we were way over the top, so I said, 'Well, I've got to do something about this.' I said to Ernest, 'Look, we've got to stop Eric ordering all this stuff,' and he said, 'Oh, I can't do it. They've got to love me.' So I said, 'OK, I'll do it.' Didn't worry me. I said to Eric, 'Look, this has got to stop because we're spending too much money.' Eric threw a wobbly and walked off. And then after that he wouldn't talk to me. He'd say everything to the AFM, and so in the end I said, 'Oh, this is no use,' and I asked to come off the show. It was a shame, but still, there we are.[48]

Stuart's last show with the pair, the second of the series, had included a request for a cello with legs attached, so that Eric, burlesquing Pablo Casals, could emerge from behind it after an overwrought and emotional solo to reveal he was without trousers. The sketch was cut, but remounted for show three.

Eric's response to Stuart's admonishment was childish, petulant and upsetting, but it wasn't motivated by anything other than perfectionism and the dogged pursuit for a laugh. Stuart, as production assistant, had to balance the books. That wasn't Morecambe's concern. In the case of the cello, it was only a thirty-second quickie, but that was thirty seconds of dialogue that Braben didn't have to sweat over.

It was an argument that Stuart was never likely to win. By 1976, Eric and Ernie knew their power and importance to the BBC, and weren't afraid to use it. Ernie remembered 'Bill Cotton saying at a conference in Montreux, "Gentlemen, you realise, of course, that comedies, like all shows, are getting terribly expensive, you can't do it." I'm sure Ernie Wise would agree with that. I said, "No, I don't. If it gets a big laugh, I don't care what it costs."'[49]

The last show of that 1976 series contained one of the most enduring pieces of Eric and Ernie's BBC career. For some years, Ernie had been nursing the idea of making breakfast to the tune of David Rose's 'The Stripper'. When he mentioned it at rehearsal, Maxin saw the potential instantly, but wondered how to make it work. Inspiration struck when Maxin got home to his wife, actress Leigh Madison.

You know the harder you try to think, the solid concrete sets between the ears. By the time I got home, my wife Leigh said, 'What's the matter with you?' I must have looked drawn and worried. I explained what had happened. She said, 'Don't worry about that. Why don't you go to bed early? Get a good night's sleep and I'll have breakfast all ready for you. What do you want? Do you want grapefruit? Toast?' I said, 'Wait a minute.' I wrote that down and suddenly I could see something, but I didn't know what.

Maxin's son, Paul, recalls the scene at home: 'Dad, he had a lovely old record player with big speakers. He was listening very very loudly to David Rose's "The Stripper". It finished he'd go back to the beginning. I wasn't allowed in. The music was so loud. He was marking it all out on manuscript paper.'

With the melody written down, Maxin went into the kitchen, an event Leigh and Paul viewed with trepidation. 'He was not a man known for his cooking skills. He had one thing, a German pancake called Kaiserschmarrn, and when he made it, it was like a brick with currants in.'[50]

Ernest recalled Leigh laughing at him as he 'went into the kitchen singing this tune and opening/closing the cupboards'. She was less amused by the state her husband left the room in, as Paul remembers. 'He'd made a complete mess of it. Flour and eggs everywhere.'

Maxin argued that the mess was vital to the creativity. 'I did the mixing of the omelettes, now with all those things and the toast popping up, the chopping of the grapefruit, to plant that, the music has got to be written to fit the gag, not just play the song through. So when Ernie was mixing the omelette, I needed the brass to flare. Silence when he took a breather. The chopping of the grapefruit, then separating them, squeezing them.'

This musical consideration is particularly obvious when Eric is opening and closing the cupboards. The melody line is normally swung, but to match the action, here every note is right on the beat – one, two, three, four, two, two, three. Having got everything where he wanted it, Maxin called Peter Knight to put flesh on the bones. 'I'd got all the notes of all the gags for that particular scene. I phoned through to Peter, went through what I wanted note by note. He was terrific. You only had to tell Peter once. I knew I wouldn't have to worry and that it would be there at nine o'clock. And it was. And that seemed to inspire not only Peter, but it inspired Eric and Ernie.'[51]

The importance of the Morecambe and Wise Christmas shows to the BBC can be measured by the fact that Eric and Ernie's fee had risen from £4,500 in 1971 to £10,000 in 1976. However, the extra pressure of expectation had taken a terrible toll on Eddie Braben's health, resulting in bouts of nervous exhaustion, to the point that he had to rule himself out for the 1976 show, as he had in 1972 and 1974. Barry Cryer was contracted to provide half an hour's worth of material, while Mike Craig, Lawrie Kinsley and Ron McDonnell were enlisted to provide the other half.

Rehearsals began on 18 October 1976, in preparation for the unusually large amount of location filming that had been scheduled. The Ernie Wise play was to be a First World War romp, featuring *Sweeney* stars John Thaw and Dennis Waterman, and it would involve motorcycle stunts, shot on location at Caesar's Camp near Aldershot with the Army's White Helmets formation team.

The 1976 Christmas special is notable for the absence of a sketch in the flat. These tended to be where Braben was at his whimsical and innuendo-laden best. Instead, there is a lot of stand-up and front cloth work. The opening routine involves the exchange of Christmas presents, with Eric giving Ernie an enormous feature-packed watch that fails in the basic duty of telling the time. There is a dash of Braben-style self-cleaning filth ('I've never had one that lights up in the dark before.').

However, from the adversity of Braben's absence came two of the memorable visual moments in which Ernest Maxin excelled. Whereas the Hollywood influence on Johnny Ammonds had been more comedic, not least with the Marx

Brothers' dance, Maxin had grown up, like Wise in particular, with an eye for the big dance numbers. When Jack Benny worked at the BBC in the 1950s, the allocated producer was Maxin. The American comedian had developed an idea that all Englishmen wore black jackets and striped trousers. Head of light entertainment Ronnie Waldman had been able to reassure the star that Maxin was not a typical stiff Englander.

> They used to call me Mr MGM – Maxin Goldberg Maxin, Ronnie said, 'He looks like an American.' I used to have a crew cut in those days, and I went to a tailor who cut the suits in an American way. You know, Hollywood-mad. He looks like an American boy. Then Ronnie said, 'He's a Jewish boy.' Jack Benny said, 'I'll take him.' I used to say to them, 'I want lots of silver and glitter, the floor's got to look like black glass, I want festoons with wind machines blowing through the dresses.'[52]

Maxin's visual sense enabled him to translate Hollywood vision into on-screen magic within a television budget. When the idea of recreating Gene Kelly's street scene from *Singing in the Rain* came up during planning, Maxin realised that flooding a television studio was not possible in the way that it had been on the film set, television cameras being electronic, and film cameras then being largely mechanical. However, it soon dawned on producer and performers that the lack of water could be the joke. There would be no rain. The set would be bone dry. Wise would be twirling an umbrella around in the dry, while Morecambe stood by as the hapless bystanding cop, bemused, but becoming the repeated victim of focused drenchings from guttering and the grey water from clothes washing hurled from windows above.

This was the first item to be recorded on the first of the four studio days, Saturday 4 December, along with a quickie featuring Eric as a newspaper vendor selling the 'Morny Stannit'. Maxin's second big number was the first item to go down on tape on the second day, Monday 6 December. The seed of the idea had been sown in Maxin's mind earlier in the year, while working on the Morecambe and Wise series. The studios at BBC Television Centre had observation galleries high up where, unless they were blocked off under exceptional circumstances, staff and authorised visitors could watch activity on the studio floor. Angela Rippon was one such, showing a relative around the studios. Noticing that there was a break in the rehearsals, Rippon chanced her arm.

It was one of the musical numbers, and we'd broken for lunch. Down the iron staircase into the studio came Angela Rippon with an aunt of hers from Devon. The aunt wanted to look around and see the Morecambe and Wise studio. I said, 'Yes, you can show her round the studio.' It was the first time I'd seen Angela from there down. I'd had coffee with her in the canteen, but she was always sat down, and on the *Nine O'Clock News*, she was always from there up. Now I saw these gorgeous legs and said, 'Do you dance at all?' She said, 'Well, I can dance. I went to a dancing school and I love ballet.' I asked if she'd like to come into a Morecambe and Wise show, and she said, 'I'd love to, but I don't think my boss would let me.' I said, 'Would you mind if I went to see him?' I went to see her boss, Alan Protheroe, and I explained. 'We'll say we're going to see Angela's legs for the first time.' So he said, 'Well, I don't mind, providing if it doesn't work, you wouldn't use it.' I said, 'For my sake, I wouldn't.'[53]

Protheroe was easier to convince than Eric:

The next week at rehearsals, first day on the Monday, we were sitting having a cup of coffee in the break and I told them the story. 'I think it would be a great news thing, because the public have only ever seen her from the waist up sitting behind a desk.' Ernie said, 'Yes, great idea.' Eric said, 'No. We've had a lot of stars on this show, Diana Rigg and all these people. No.'

Maxin was about as far from devious as anyone in show business can be, but he wasn't above improving his luck where necessary. Eric was a keen cricket fan. In the flyleaf blurb of his novel, *Mr Lonely*, he listed his only ambition as 'To be at next Centenary Test at Lords'. Sometimes, when the pressure began to feel a bit too much, Eric, Ernie and their producer would chalk a wicket on the wall of the rehearsal room and knock a tennis ball around with a bat. When he asked Maxin if he could miss rehearsals to attend a Lady Taverners' lunch at the MCC, the producer gave him an afternoon pass, but stipulated that he'd have to stay later that evening.

What Morecambe didn't realise was that his producer knew, from the Television Centre rumour mill (the old joke being that the corridors were circular so the rumours could travel faster), that Rippon was also going to be present at the lunch. Maxin had a hunch that once Eric met her, he'd be convinced of her suitability. When Eric returned to rehearsals in the evening, nothing was said, and Maxin assumed that the game was up.

'We just carried on rehearsing and at the end I thought, "It's all over now, we tried." Eric was the last one to go. He closed the door as he went out, a few seconds later, he put his head around the door, and, smoking his pipe, said, "Let's have Angela Rippon in the show."'

Once Rippon's dance debut was down, there was time to record Elton John's song, 'Sorry Seems to Be the Hardest Word', along with a quickie with Elton, Eric and Ernie poking their heads out from behind the curtain. The evening ended with Eric and Ernie in dinner jackets, recording the closing number, 'Positive Thinking'.

The final day of pre-recording, Tuesday 7 December, began with the sketch featuring Eric and Ernie as figures on a table football game, with Arthur Tolcher in goal. Then Eric and Ernie recorded their eccentric dancing routine with Marian Montgomery as she sang 'Goofus'. Surprisingly, the Nolans recorded their song without an audience. The rest of the session was taken up with a couple of pre-tapings for the First World War sketch – the firing squad tag and the split-second cutaway where the candle attaches to the spike of Eric's German helmet.

Finally, on Wednesday 8 December, an audience was ushered into TC8 and warmed up by Felix Bowness for a live recording of Ernie's play with Thaw, Waterman and Kate O'Mara. Meanwhile, Elton John was back, to record the sketch where he attempts to accompany Eric and Ernie as they do a soft-shoe routine, as well as some front cloth gags with the boys for dotting about throughout the show. Oddly, the last thing to be recorded was the opening double.

After the 1976 Christmas show, it was decided that there would be no series following in 1977, only the Christmas show at the end of the year, which would prove to be Eric and Ernie's swansong at the BBC. The year 1976 had been a busy one in television terms. As well as their series and the festive special, they had undertaken some light work for Johnny Downes, founder of *Crackerjack* and the light entertainment department's specialist in children's shows, hosting *It's Child's Play*, a series in which playlets and sketches written by schoolchildren were performed by professional actors including Ralph Bates, Alfie Bass, Sinéad Cusack and Rudolph Walker.

Eric and Ernie acted in the last item in each week, and there is an unrestrained joy about these performances. In the first show, Ernie plays the landlord of an inn, with Eric as a yokel with a puppet dog on his arm explaining to two visiting policemen how the place is haunted. For the information, they require drinks. Eric is on Scotch, Ernie is on sherry and the puppet dog is on tankards of lager. The brio with which the puppet despatches the beer and throws the tankard behind him competes with Eric's piratical interpretation of his own role for some very big laughs.

In the autumn of 1977, Morecambe, Wise, Braben and Maxin geared up to top the previous year's show. After a pre-titles sketch sending up Starsky and Hutch as Starkers and Krutch, Eric and Ernie open with their names in lights behind them. Unfortunately, the rig is too wide for the stage, with the result that only part of it can be seen. Pointing out that it reads 'RECAMBE AND WISE', Eric calls back to his early variety catchphrase by declaring 'I'm not all there', a nice little joke for those in the know, but primarily for the amusement of Ernie.

It wasn't unusual for big stars to call Ernest Maxin at home to ask if there was any chance of appearing on the Morecambe and Wise show. He had a system with his wife, Leigh, and his son, Paul, to make sure he wasn't bothered unduly. 'We used to have this call-screening routine, where either my mother or myself would repeat the name,' Paul Maxin recalls. 'We'd pick up the phone. "530 5377, who's speaking please?", and we were under instruction to repeat the name, so my dad could decide whether he was in or not.'

Surprisingly, there was one very big name offering himself for the 1977 Christmas show who didn't make the producer spring to his feet, even though Paul Maxin admits that it was 'the only time I nearly wet myself'. It was October when Maxin Junior 'picked the phone up, the name came and I repeated the name. Paul McCartney. And my dad was there saying "Call him back". Macca was trying to get on the 1977 Morecambe and Wise Christmas show, promoting "Mull of Kintyre", but they'd already booked Elton John, and they didn't know what to do with him and Wings.'⁵⁴ Maxin had a chat with Johnny Ammonds, who suggested offering McCartney to Mike Yarwood's producer, Jim Moir. Thus it was that the former Beatle got his Christmas Day plug.

The Elton John – or as Eric kept calling him, 'Elephant John' – sequences ran throughout the show, with the star arriving at BBC Television Centre reception and being told to report to room 405. Between sketches, John would be shown continuing his fruitless search for the room, turning up in a sauna with John Laurie, Arthur Lowe and John Le Mesurier from *Dad's Army*, all in full Home Guard uniform, and at a dockside warehouse, where he opened a door and fell straight into the Thames. He finally got to sing his song after the credits had rolled in an empty studio TC8 for the benefit of two studio cleaning ladies, who might well have had the names Erica and Ernestine, so marked was their resemblance to Morecambe and Wise.

Comedic misnaming was a favourite tactic of Braben's, and Elephant wasn't the only one to be rechristened for 1977. When *Poldark* star Angharad Rees appeared, Eric renamed her 'Handgrenade'. The balance was restored in the finale when guest star Penelope Keith kept calling Morecambe 'Derek'. First she appeared in a send-up of Cyrano de Bergerac with

Eric, Ernie and the great Francis Matthews, whose beautiful comic timing and willingness to send himself up made him a perfect and semi-regular guest on Eric and Ernie's shows. Then there was a big MGM-style dance number, with the difference that the set builders hadn't finished the staircase.

The whole show is studded with moments that have been repeated endlessly ever since, but there's one particular item that stands out, where newsreaders and presenters perform 'There Is Nothing Like a Dame' from *South Pacific*. Through the use of stand-ins and some nifty videotape editing, these desk-bound stalwarts of the small screen appeared to be doing rolls and somersaults. Part of the joke is that it is obviously not them, but without the aid of freeze-framing, the effect is convincing. Eric and Ernie loved the idea, but Eric was unconvinced that the execution would go so well, as Ernest Maxin recalled:

After the Angela Rippon show went out, one of the newscasters, I think it was Richard Baker, put his head round my office door and said, 'Do you think you can use me in a show?' I said, 'Yes, I'll have a think about it.' He's a musician. Then later that day, Michael Aspel put his head around my door and I thought, 'Hang on, I'll use them all together.' Of course, Peter Woods had that wonderful face. Anyway, we did this, discussed it. Eric was very much in favour.

When we got to rehearsals, something I hadn't actually realised, I couldn't get them all there at the same time, I got the acrobats. They were all on different duties. I was going through the routine over and over again. Eric was very poorly. This was just before his second heart attack. Once again his lips went blue, he went to the piano in the rehearsal room, leaned on it and said, 'This will never work. I can't see it working.' This was the Wednesday, we were in the studio on Saturday. I said, 'It will all work, because they're all doing the same routine, but they're not all together at one point. Once we get into the studio, they'll all be there.' He said, 'But the time...' I said, 'In fifteen minutes, I promise you. We'll have done the rehearsal and everything. It's an editing job for me that night.' Ernie put in his, 'Look, if it doesn't work, we don't use it.' If it hadn't been for Ernie, that number wouldn't have gone on. I couldn't convince him. Ernie did a great job on that.

So we rehearsed it. Eric said, 'Can I come and watch the edit?' We did the whole thing in fifteen minutes, shot it in fifteen minutes. We finished at about eight o'clock. Eric was so worried. Ernie wasn't worried at all. I said come back at about eleven. He came in. I'd just finished editing it just before he came in. I saw it run through, and it looked great. And he came in. He was ashen white. He said, 'Well?' I said, 'The best thing to do, you come and sit beside me and we'll run the thing.' I watched his face. I could see the reflection in the screen. He was sitting back. As it went on he began to lean forward, and when it came to the dance routine, where it all fitted, I saw the tears were running down his face. It moved me, it really moved me. I have a lump in my throat now talking about it. He said, 'Bloody hellfire, Ernest, it works.' And put his arms around me, gave me a hug.

The show was a success, but writing in the *Observer*, Clive James wondered if it wasn't a little too calculated. It 'stuck to their by-now-classic format... Every component was triple-tested. The sense of adventure was consequently lacking. Eric was twice as funny busking with Dickie Davies on ITV's *World of Sport* on Christmas Eve.'[55] It seems a strange criticism, knowing the pressure on Braben, Maxin and the stars. Christmas specials aren't where the risks are taken. The audience didn't want adventure. They wanted more of the same, only bigger and better than before. Even though all concerned were professionals at the top of their game, Christmas Day in the Maxin household was still tense, as the producer watched the reactions of the family and friends present like a hawk to be certain that it had all worked as planned.

However, on watching the *World of Sport* appearance, it's very easy to see why it appealed so much to James. Being just before Christmas, sporting fixtures were thinner on the ground than usual, and with space to fill between the actual events, Morecambe's appearance seems to be the televisual equivalent of being allowed to bring board games to school on the last day of term.

Morecambe appears while Davies is doing his introduction, clutching a bottle of Haig Scotch whisky and apologising for being late. Davies tells him that in fact he's early for the post-show party. Morecambe sits down next to Davies, complaining that the seat is too low and disappearing behind the desk until only the top of his head is visible. Davies promises some cushions and continues attempting to introduce the programme, while a barely visible Morecambe pretends to start on the whisky under the desk. The framing is perfect. Just the eyebrow and the corner of his glasses and the bottle are enough to provoke raucous laughter from the crew. As does Morecambe's reaction to a clip trailing the wrestling later in the show: 'I'll tell you what. That fella in the red. Big Daddy. He looks like Lew Grade.'

When Morecambe is next visible, the cushions have been provided and he now towers over Davies, telling the presenter he's not as tall as expected, comparing him to Ernie and giving him the double slap he usually reserved for his partner. In a sense, Davies is a substitute for Ernie, and instead of wig jokes, Morecambe homes in on Davies' moustache, tweaking it and declaring 'It's real. The last time I saw anything like that on a top lip, the whole herd had to be destroyed'. Then, as Davies tries to do a link into the skiing, Morecambe tells viewers 'He's reading it' before starting to read Davies' Autocue[*] in unison with the presenter.

Davies attempts to interview Morecambe, and invites the comedian to give demonstrations of his own sporting prowess with a round of darts and an attempt at a frame of snooker, with Morecambe pushing Davies' head down on the table and using the host's neck as a rest. As Davies tries to introduce the next item, Morecambe pretends to have his hand stuck in one of the pockets of the snooker table. Davies delivers another link, sitting on Morecambe's lap, with the comedian pretending to operate him like a ventriloquist's figure. The show ends with the credits rolling over Morecambe shaking hands with the production staff who sat behind Davies and collated the results as they came in.

With the rude intrusions of sporting activity excised, the archive tape runs to just over half an hour, and is a testament to both Davies' professionalism and Morecambe's relentless stream of invention. The presenter keeps going even when he has Morecambe interfering with his hair, rustling a paper bag into his tieclip microphone or resting his feet on his leg.

---

[*] Autocue is the brand name of the leading make of camera-mounted prompting devices, using a screen and an angled mirror to reflect the script into the presenter's line of vision. It has almost become the generic term, though other makes of prompter are available.

Maxin would have entered the new year fully expecting to be asked to do the next Christmas show, but in late January 1978 came the news that Morecambe and Wise were leaving the BBC to join Thames Television. That final Christmas show featured an oddly prescient sketch where Eric and Ernie were shown to be moving out of the flat into a bigger and, Ernie was keen to stress, cheaper property. Negotiations between Billy Marsh and Philip Jones at Thames were underway by the time the show was recorded in mid-December, and Morecambe and Wise both knew they might well be leaving for real. It's possible they suggested the premise for the sketch to Braben. However, neither Braben nor Maxin had an inkling of what was to come. John Ammonds recalls:

> [Eddie] wasn't told, they didn't ask him, if he was going to Thames. This is almost unbelievable unless you know stars. Eric said the same thing about Sid and Dick. When they did that first series, Eric had the heart attack and he went to Portugal to recuperate. On the plane coming back, someone handed him a newspaper and he saw that Sid and Dick had signed up with Lew Grade to produce or something. He said to me 'They didn't even tell us about it', but he did the same thing to Eddie Braben.[56]

This treatment has echoes of the way they had been abandoned by Sid and Dick, but both Eric and Ernie were always clear that the business was as important as the show.

Morecambe mentioned the Thames offer to Bill Cotton Jr at the light entertainment Christmas party, but the executive assured them that the BBC would match whatever Thames offered. Eric and Ernie felt that Cotton couldn't complain. As they pointed out, Thames were only doing what he'd done to

Lew Grade a decade earlier. Nonetheless, Cotton felt slighted by the way it was done. He had gone to America on a business trip early in the new year, assuming that he'd hear more about the Thames proposal from Billy Marsh, and be able to make a counter-offer. It was while in Hollywood, suffering with flu, that Cotton was called by his PA, Queenie Lipyeat, who told him that Eric and Ernie had defected. When Cotton spoke to Marsh, he was told it was a done deal. 'It felt more like a divorce than the end of a working partnership,' he said in his memoirs. 'I was very, very sad about it.'[57]

Lovers of Eric and Ernie could have supplemented their Christmas TV fix with *The Morecambe and Wise Special*, a stocking-filler book in the mode of the Monty Python and Goodies tie-in books that had sold so strongly over the previous few years. Curiously, the credit for the content is given completely to Morecambe and Wise, with no apparent involvement from Eddie Braben.

With or without Braben, the book stands up well. One of the highlights is a double-page spread entitled 'Among His Wigs', with Wise playing up to the age-old gag by modelling various hairpieces, including the 'Madame Pompadour', 'The Very Last of the Mohicans' and 'The Des O'Connor Fright Wig'. There is also a spoof book club advertisement, including 'The Magnificent BBC: A sincere tribute to the clever, generous, kind, good, contracts department from a grateful Eric and Ernie'. It was accompanied by a review, supposedly from BBC director-general Ian Trethowan, calling it 'A welcome piece of grovelling'. There was also a *Keep Fit with Eric* title listed. The next year would make both jokes ring hollow.

9

Crossing the river

Eric and Ernie always said that show business was half the show and half business. For all of their warmth as performers, they were both shrewd when it came to the business part. 'A lot of people said we should never have gone over to commercial television in 1978, but the point is that Thames only did to the BBC what the BBC had done to ATV,' Eric said.[1]

There was to be no series before Christmas 1978, but there was time for a special in October. The first show begins with a sequence shot outside the company's Teddington studios. A green Ford Transit with the BBC TV logo on the side speeds past the gate before reversing back along Broom Road and driving through the gate. Eric and Ernie, in caps and raincoats, are chucked out of the back of the van at the scene dock of studio 1 by unseen hands, their battered suitcases, held together with string, following them, before the van is off. The pair are greeted by an effeminate floor manager, earphones around his neck, who informs them that everyone has been looking forward to working with them and gives Ernie the double-sided face slap. The fourth wall is broken comprehensively. Ernie looks into the camera, wide-eyed, as Eric says: 'They're the same here as what they are at the BBC, only quicker.'[2]

The opening monologue includes a callback to the floor manager's fruity greeting at the studio gate as Ernie informs the audience, 'They've given us every facility. They've bent over backwards', to which Eric replies 'Well, one of them did. Ended up in the river.' After that, it was very much business as laid down by Ammonds.

Since he was freelance, their favourite special effects designer, Bill King, was able to join them at Teddington, but they were without Braben, who had been put under exclusive contract in an echo of their experience with Hills and Green a decade earlier, or Maxin, who was BBC staff. Having filled in for Braben in previous years, Barry Cryer and John Junkin were the obvious choices. Running the show they had Keith Beckett, a producer and director of vast experience. Beckett was a good fit in many ways. Like Maxin, he was a former dancer/choreographer, having worked in both musical comedy and ballet, taking the title role in *Petrouchka* at the Stoll Theatre on Kingsway in 1950. Meanwhile, like Eric and Ernie, he had been a child performer, beginning his career in his teens at the Q Theatre in Brentford. Beckett had moved into television at Tyne Tees in Newcastle in the late 1950s, and had worked extensively at ABC, Thames and London Weekend.

The first Thames Christmas show featured one new sketch that would have held its own in any of the BBC shows. The Syd Lawrence Orchestra had appeared as the musical guests in 1974, and the bandleader was well known to Eric and Ernie from his days in the trumpet section with the BBC Northern Dance Orchestra. The band had become regulars on Les Dawson's Yorkshire Television series *Sez Les*, and when a comedy idea came up requiring a big band to play the Count Basie tune 'Whirlybird', Lawrence was the obvious choice.

The joke was that Lawrence would be lured offstage by a pretty girl, leaving Ernie to conduct the band while Eric attempts to take the fast and furious piano solo, but finds the instrument locked. Eric and Ernie become involved in a silent argument, with their mouth movements fitting the tenor saxophone solo perfectly. Eric goes around the orchestra, lifting each musician off his chair in time with the music, to look for the key. Beaten, he returns to the piano, and Ernie bangs the lid in frustration, which unjams the lock just in time for Morecambe to play the four-note tag at the end of the number. It is a joyous three minutes of fine music and Rolls-Royce comic timing, and the band clearly agree, the saxophone section becoming visibly convulsed during the synchronised argument.

One of the musicians laughing and being manhandled by Eric was lead trombonist Chris Dean, who took over the band when Syd Lawrence retired, and he remembers an 'absolutely hilarious' day at Teddington, taping the sketch. 'It was a very happy day with these two. They were a delight and Eric was a very very funny man. It was just "on" all the time. All the things that went with those two, even though they were being very very professional, they were ad-libbing certain things.'

Elements of the day were less happy for Lawrence, who had little patience with anything that got in the way of music. 'He was a very shy man. He didn't want to be taking part. In the sketch, they were shouting to Syd in the corner, and Syd hated this. Syd's face when he turns round is not the happiest of faces, and it wasn't supposed to be, but that was for real. He didn't have to act. Totally and utterly pissed off.' He was at least saved the responsibility of learning any dialogue. Before the sketch, he appears in front of the curtain with Eric and Ernie, speaking through actor Frank Coda. It's turned into a comedy bit, but Dean explains that it was down to union demarcation. 'Syd wasn't in Equity, he was in the Musicians' Union, so he wasn't allowed to say anything. He wasn't allowed to actually talk.'[3]

Lawrence's recalcitrance amused his musicians. 'We were all just laughing at him because he's got this pot of gold here and he doesn't understand it. He doesn't understand that to have his band working on the Morecambe and Wise show, you've got to put something back. And it's the Christmas show too, it's the big deal, so for God's sake give it something back. That was Syd. He was a fantastic musician, very clever bandleader, but he didn't like anything other than playing.'

Amid the pleasure there was some hard, precise work to be done, with the majority of the burden falling on tenor saxophonist Norman Brown. 'Syd said to Norman, fabulous sax player, "You have to learn the Eddie 'Lockjaw' Davis solo verbatim, exactly, every inflection, you have to learn that." Syd wrote it down, because his transcriptions were better than anybody's. So Norman took it down, but then he also had to learn it off by heart for the miming.'

The music track was pre-recorded for a couple of reasons. One was the physicality of the sketch. 'It was all very funny on the day, having to run along and lift every musician, and trying to get it in time. Of course, musicians being musicians, they're moving up too early, too late or they don't quite get it, so we had to do it a few times.' The other was consistency. 'That was because of the amount of times they had to go through it to make it work. You'd never get the same performance exactly twice. First thing they did was say that they'd been rehearsing to the Count Basie version and ours was exactly the same. Ernie was very much a big band fan, and they both loved the band. They were in raptures listening to it and working with it.'

Eric and Ernie were well ensconced at Thames when the BBC sold some of the old shows to American television, the first time the pair had been seen on the other side of the Atlantic since the late 1960s. BBC Enterprises did a syndication deal with Time Life where the shows were to be repackaged into seventy half-hours, with Eric and Ernie's approval. The move had been prompted by an indiscreet comment Ernie made at a charity function in Billy Butlin's Jersey home to a diarist on the *Daily Express* William Hickey column. 'The BBC are hopeless at this sort of thing,' Ern was quoted as saying. 'What we need is a Lew Grade to sell our show. It's a great shame because we would love to get a break in America.' A BBC spokesman was quoted as saying that 'it seems that Morecambe and Wise have a special sort of humour which does not appeal to Americans. We are trying – really.' There was also the fact that Thames, while not as bullish as Lew Grade's ATV, had a far more aggressive export policy than the BBC.*

In the summer of 1979, Ernie was one of the Thames stars accompanying a sales delegation to Los Angeles led by managing director Bryan Cowgill. The company had arranged to showcase some of its most popular programmes on a local channel where they could be seen by Hollywood buyers. David Hamilton was also on the trip. After the business was done, there was a treat for all concerned. 'Thames were so pleased with the work we did for them in LA that they treated us afterwards to a weekend in Las Vegas,' Hamilton recalls. 'We saw the wonderful Dean Martin in concert. He came out with a drink in his hand, did a little dance routine and said, "Who is

---

* BBC Enterprises was regularly dismissed as a contradiction in terms.

the mother who said it's the legs that go first?" He then looked at the huge orchestra behind him (must have been forty-piece) and said to the audience, "What are all these people doing in my bedroom?" Ernie, sitting next to me, realising we were watching one of the all-time-greats, said, "I don't think he drinks. Nobody who drank could have that perfect timing."'[4]

The BBC/Time-Life deal, when it came, wasn't quite the same as when Grade had sold *Piccadilly Palace* to the ABC network, or when the pair had appeared on the CBS network with Ed Sullivan. The shows were selling to small local stations, which stripped them across five nights a week. It was, as Ernie admitted, 'the bottom rung of the ladder' and it 'didn't represent the biggest slice of money we ever had', but Eric rationalised the situation. 'Even if nobody saw the series, it was on. That's what matters.'[5]

Ernie still harboured dreams of breaking America right to the end of his life, but after Eric's heart attack, it was off the agenda. Realistically, it had been anyway. Eric needed the audience response too much to ever be comfortable in films, and streamlining their act for American audiences lost a lot of what made them Morecambe and Wise. With hindsight, Morecambe had strong views about compromise:

> Eric: As far as I'm concerned, what I'd like to do is, I want to stay here. I'm very happy here. I love it here. We earn money here. We're stars here, and it's great. If the Americans want us to go over there, they've got to do it here. They've got to buy the shows. I won't go over there, and I will not say 'sidewalk', I will not say 'garbage'.
>
> Ernie: That's pavement.
>
> Eric: And rubbish as far as I'm concerned.[6]

As hard as Morecambe and Wise worked, show business was a social thing too. These were the days when every television studio complex had its own bar attached.* These were where stars and staff relaxed and gossiped, often together, with a gleeful disregard for hierarchy. Eric, a ball of tension when working, could often be found in the bar after the show, holding court. Barry Cryer remembers an incident indicative of the dividing line between work and pleasure.

I wrote a two or three minute bit for Eric looking into the camera and I gave it to him in front of a lot of people in the room, the choreographer, the producer and everybody on a bit of paper and he looked at it and said, 'No. You got this wrong, Barry. No, you weren't listening. You got this wrong.' And he handed it back, 'Have another go at it.' I was furious. I thought, what a thing to do in front of everybody. I went off to the bar and was sulking. He came in and he said, 'Hello, long face. What are you dr—' I said, 'You've just bollocked me in front of everybody.' He said, 'Oh, that was there, this is now. What are you drinking?' You know, the friendship and the business were two different things.[7]

Cryer recalls an occasion in the bar at Thames with another big comic name, while Eric and Ernie were getting ready to record a show.

This may surprise you. I was in the bar, I can't remember why. Tommy Cooper came in. He'd been at a meeting or something. He said, 'Ooh, Eric and Ernie are downstairs.

---

* Except Granada, following the opening night in 1956 when host Quentin Lawrence had appeared on air very obviously sloshed.

Come on.' Ooh, I thought, what's on? So Tommy and I went down to the studio and of course the man on the door didn't stop Tommy going in. He couldn't, you know. Tommy walked in and I slid in with him. And Tommy, that big man, went sliding down the side of the audience very quietly, he wasn't spotted. Eric and Ernie were in the middle of their own warm-up and Tommy walked on. Unforgivable. Enormous applause and laughter when he walked on. Eric told me later, he said, 'I could have strangled him.' Ernie loved it. 'Hello Tommy,' says Eric. Tommy could cry. He could turn it on. And he started crying. 'Oh hoo Eric, oh, Eric.' And Eric tried to push him off, and of course Tommy leaned on him and if Tom leaned on you, you couldn't push him off. Ernie was loving it. Eric said 'Tommy, what is it?' At the time, Dick Emery had a very lively love life and divorces and was notorious in the tabloids. Tommy said to Eric, 'Dick Emery's left me.' Enormous laugh, and Tommy walked off. Eric said to me afterwards, 'I could have strangled him,' he said. But looking back, very funny.

Although the financial blandishments offered by Thames, along with the Euston Films connection, had been seductive, Eric and Ernie missed Braben, Maxin and Ammonds.

Eric and Ernie's first Christmas show for commercial television in 1978 – they had never done one during their time at ATV – didn't manage an audience of 21.3 million, as their last BBC show had. However, nothing that Christmas did, and Morecambe and Wise topped the overall festive ratings with 19.15 million, even with screens in the Yorkshire region blacked out by a dispute. They had acquitted themselves well and could look ahead to a busy year at Thames, with their film project finally getting underway, and shooting due to begin in May.

Barely a month after the success of the new show, though, came the news that Eric had been rushed to St Albans City Hospital with exhaustion. Joan reassured the press that it wasn't anything to do with his heart, it was just overwork laying Eric low. 'He does everything in an energetic way and never relaxes,' she said.[8]

Two months later, Morecambe was in hospital again, and this time it definitely was his heart, with the illness being reported, as in 1968, as a 'mild' attack. As had been the case eleven years earlier, it was much more serious than that. However, their 1981 autobiography suggests that the second heart attack happened in January 1979, not March. 'I had three tachycardias in February,' said Eric. 'I didn't feel very well... but after two heart attacks I knew what was going on... Heart attacks are vicious. Tachycardias are nothing in comparison.'[9]

Morecambe was referred by the surgeons at St Albans to pioneering heart specialist Magdi Yacoub, based at Harefield Hospital. One of Eric's valves was faulty and a heart bypass operation would be advisable. It was early days for the procedure, and it came with many risks, but without it the comedian's life expectancy was around eighteen months at best. The seven-hour operation went ahead in June 1979.

Morecambe and Wise had always made themselves very accessible to journalists. Even though they employed a press representative, the main show business correspondents all had Eric and Ernie's home numbers. The hacks knew they could be relied on for a highly quotable answer on any issue. With Eric in hospital, Ernie's phone was ringing off the hook, and he admitted that it was possible that Eric might want to take it easy after this, or even retire. In April, a month after the heart attack was made public, Ern told journalists that a decision would be taken on the future of the partnership in September.

'I'll wait until he is better or until Eric says "enough is enough",' said Ernie loyally,[10] adding that if Eric did decide to leave the business, he would carry on. 'I'm far too energetic to sit around doing nothing.' In the event, the announcement that Eric would be returning to work in time for Christmas came a month early, in August. Their press man, George Bartram, arranged a photocall at Eric's house in Harpenden.* Ernie's appearance was the same as ever, but in his time out of the public eye Eric had grown a moustache.

At the photocall, they suggested they would be back at work in January, with no Christmas show. However, a month later came the announcement that they would be on Christmas Day television. The usual run of rehearsal was beyond Eric. He was edging back in gently. His first public appearance was at a Lord's Taverners event in November. However, Thames knew that there was such an appetite to see them, especially after all that had happened, that a less intensive production would be forgiven just this once.

There was another incentive to do a Christmas show, as Johnny Ammonds had crossed the river to join them at Thames. His exit from the BBC was not blocked by Bill Cotton Jr so much as encouraged, but not because Cotton wanted to see Ammonds go. Ammonds' wife, Wyn, had developed multiple sclerosis, and Cotton knew the way the BBC worked well enough to see that a move to Thames could be hugely beneficial.

---

* Ernie and Doreen Wise began their married life in Doreen's home town of Peterborough. Eventually, they moved to Harrow, then in 1974, to a house by the Thames in Maidenhead.

He came to me one day and he said, 'I just think I ought to tell you that Thames Television have offered me a lot of money to go and produce Morecambe and Wise, but I'm not going to take it.' I said, 'Why not?' He said, 'What do you mean?' I said, 'Why aren't you going?' He said, 'Well, you don't want me to go, do you?' I said, 'Think about it, Johnny. You've got a wife who is very ill. You've been at the BBC long enough to make your pension well worth while. If you've got the opportunity of making a financial killing now by saving the Morecambe and Wise show, take it.' He said, 'I thought you'd try and stop me.' I said, 'Think about it, Johnny. I'm much more interested in you getting your just rewards for all the work you've done than hanging around the BBC. You'll always work, but you might never get another show like this.' So he said, 'Oh.' Then he came back and said, 'I've phoned them up and told them I'll come.' I said, 'You've made the right decision.' I'll never know if it was the right decision, because it diminished him insomuch as his heart and soul was in the BBC. I cared much more about his wife. He had terrible problems, paying for the care, holidays. I was working on the basis that he could cash his pension in, and he probably would get at least half as much again as he got at the BBC, possibly more.[11]

Ammonds oversaw a production where Eric and Ernie would record a couple of new sketches, but the majority of the show would consist of Eric and Ernie chatting with David Frost, and guests including Glenda Jackson and Des O'Connor. The show opened with what appeared to be Eric and Ernie, in top hats and tails, entering down a sweeping staircase. When Morecambe materialised from the back of the set, it became clear that 'Eric' was Garfield Morgan from *The*

Sweeney, wearing a pair of heavy-rimmed glasses. Obviously, the cricket-mad Eric introduces him as 'Mr Garfield Sobers', then, when corrected by Ernie, changes to 'Cliff Morgan'. Morecambe explained that Morgan had done the big entrance because he wasn't allowed to go on the staircase for medical reasons, while running up and down the stairs repeatedly for illustration. Morecambe's original suggested opening, where he was to be carried in on a stretcher, had been vetoed.

The commercial breaks at Thames give the chance for a new take on thwarting Des O'Connor's attempts to sing. He is assured that he will be allowed to do so this time, but every time he gets underway, the adverts cut in. Meanwhile, the finale is a proper reunion, with Arthur Tolcher present, and Janet Webb coming down the grand staircase, barging through to deliver her speech one more time. A placard with chaser lights declares 'NICE TO BE BACK', but most of the lights fuse, leaving only the 'BBC'.

The second heart attack had put Eric off smoking permanently. Before his first coronary, his nervous tension led him to puff his way through up to a hundred cigarettes a day. After it, he stuck with smoking a pipe with greater moderation. Although never a problem drinker like some comedians, Eric still liked to relax with a drink, but in time, weight gain encouraged him to rein that in too. He was also concerned that it could tip over from being a treat to a grim necessity.

While Morecambe was recuperating at home, he turned to writing, but this time not sketches or gags. He wrote a novel. He was far from the first comedian to turn his hand to literature, and like so many who had preceded him, he chose the subject he knew best for his debut: show business. Harry Secombe's *Twice Brightly* had shone an affectionate spotlight on the dying days of variety, while Les Dawson's *A Card for the Clubs* had been gritty and harsh, telling the story of a comic who spent years struggling to get out of the clubs, only to sabotage his success when the big break came.

In *Mr Lonely*, Morecambe followed a similar line to Dawson, writing of Sid Lewis, compère at the Starlight Rooms, who had served his apprenticeship at the fag end of variety and in summer seasons, whose big break eluded him. Eventually, Lewis hits big on TV with a character called 'Mr Lonely', seemingly somewhere between Freddie 'Parrot Face' Davies and Peter Cook's E. L. Wisty* in delivery, hosting a variety show with a topical edge. His success is short-lived, however. He dies outside the Grosvenor House Hotel after an awards ceremony, being hit by a taxi and accidentally stabbing himself through the heart with his trophy.

Although a fairly serious effort, Morecambe said it was 'a very funny book, which surprised me as 90 per cent of it was written when I was desperately ill'.[12] Reviewing it for the *Daily Express*, Spike Milligan made no mention of the book's humorous appeal, preferring to praise its realism. He lauded its 'simplicity with a magnificent eye for the plastic details of the entertainment world' and called it 'the very best example I've read which describes a profession that is looked on, by all except those in it, as glamorous'. Milligan compared *Mr Lonely* very favourably to John Osborne's *The Entertainer*. 'You have to have LIVED it to have WRITTEN it,' he said, calling Osborne's effort 'very good, but lacking that essential ingredient of personal experience'.

It is indeed a fascinating book for its insights into show

---

* Wisty was a boring man who spoke expertly on subjects he did not understand in a monotone, his voice being based on that of Arthur Boylett, one of the non-teaching staff at Cook's school, Radley College.

business, with Morecambe concentrating on the seamier side of it all. Lewis has a loyal wife who can't understand why he bothers with show business and wishes he'd get a normal job.

'Carrie just wanted him to be the type of husband that brought in enough money to live on, to pay the rent, and to go to Yarmouth for a few days every year, the same as her father had done… He wanted to be a star for Carrie but she couldn't understand that. What she wanted for him was to be average. He couldn't understand that.'[13]

Lewis is less loyal, and not averse to the odd extramarital dalliance with singers and showgirls. When Lewis is in Las Vegas, trying, abortively, to break America, he makes arrangements for a tryst with a posh young secretary from Thames Television, who happens, accidentally on purpose, to be honeymooning there at the same time. In Lewis's corner of the business, everyone's at it, it seems. Although Morecambe had protested innocence when he'd stumbled upon the orgy in David Whitfield's dressing room, his debut novel is an indication that he was more worldly than he cared to let on.

It's also interesting in the way that Morecambe inserts a version of himself into the narrative as Lewis's lifelong friend and narrator of the tragic story. Indeed, he was Lewis's best man, and there are faked wedding pictures included as evidence. There are no obvious direct inspirations from real life for the main characters, which is probably wise, as nobody is particularly likeable, and the legal issues would have been legion.

However, there are some cameos. Lewis happens to be in the reception area at BBC Television Centre, waiting for a dressing room key, when a parcel arrives for a Mr John Ammonds. The courier is informed that Mr Ammonds has 'defected… you know, went to the other side'. Also in a scene set at a showbiz party in the Starlight Rooms, there's an encounter with 'Joyce and Lionel', which has to be a reference to Joyce Blair and her brother, Lionel.

'Joyce turned and flung her arms around Sid and hugged him tightly like the old friend he was, while Lionel stepped back and did a dance routine for three seconds that would have taken anyone else a chorus and a half.'[14]

There are a couple of sly digs at Lionel, with him having 'the brownest face in the club' which 'wrinkled into more wrinkles', and him shaking 'his head six times quite hard to prove that his hair was real'.

Another interesting aspect of the book is the contrast between its tone and that of Eric and Ernie's memoirs. In the autobiography, they speak affectionately of their formative years. In *Mr Lonely*, Morecambe makes the variety scene of the 1950s seem like much more of a grim old slog. Lewis begins his career as the feed to a charmless old hack comedian and drunk called Big Ed Low, who 'always finished every sketch he did by dropping his pants, or Sid's pants, or one of the chorus girls' pants, just before the blackout at the end of the sketch'.[15]* Low is on £200 a week, and paying Lewis a mere £17 10 shillings. As for the chorus girls, they were told that they'd 'get a present at the end of the season in September, and Ed usually kept his promise, but the poor kid never saw the present until the middle of the following June'.

Perhaps the fact that Morecambe wrote the majority of the book while recovering from a major heart attack is significant when understanding its dark, bitter tone. A prolonged period of considering his mortality may have made him wonder whether all of the effort he and Ernie had taken to get to the

---

* Low seems to be an unpleasant version of Gus Morris.

top had been worth it. Certainly, around this time, Morecambe started to wonder if he wanted to continue performing.

With Johnny Ammonds back on the team, Eric and Ernie were ready to undertake a regular series in 1980 – half-hour shows, or twenty-five minutes, allowing for adverts. Financially, the move to Thames made sense for Ammonds, but it wasn't the happiest coda to his working relationship with Eric and Ernie. Part of Ammonds' dismay was down to the way things had changed in the six years since he had last worked with Eric and Ernie. At the BBC, the producer had always been impressed by Morecambe's ability to retain the script. He explained:

> At the BBC he was a marvellous study. His memory was terrific, whereas Ernie was the one who had trouble. I can remember rehearsals now at Dalgarno Way with Ernie facing me and Eric behind Ernie. Tackling a paragraph. Anything over one line, and Ernie would seem to be in trouble. He'd be trying to do this speech on the third day's rehearsal and he'd fluff it, and I'd see Eric's eyes go up to heaven. I try to avoid looking at Eric and I say, 'OK Ernie, I think you're getting it, let's have another go.' Eric would say to me, 'John, can't you get him to take the script home?' I'd say, 'He is, but he can't absorb it like you.'

At Thames, Ammonds found that Morecambe was finding it harder to get on top of the material.

> I noticed on several occasions that his memory wasn't as good as it was. Which makes sense with the heart attack. If you've had a stoppage of blood to the brain, however short. It had affected his memory.[16]

While the Thames series are often viewed as more of the same only less so, they continue the tradition of ending with a running joke and contribute perhaps the most fondly remembered of all the finale gags. The idea, established in the opening show of their first Thames series and carried on for much of the Thames era, was beautifully simple. Eric, Ernie and the week's guest star would be in front of the curtain. Ernie would convince Eric that there was no time to sing 'Bring Me Sunshine', and pack him off to the dressing room. Once the coast was clear, the curtains would open, and Ernie would launch into the song with the guest star.

The main set for the Thames shows was simple but effective, marrying a white floor with a white backcloth, or cyclorama, lit in such a way that viewers couldn't see the join. At ATV Elstree, this 'infinity cyc' effect was easy to achieve, because a special trench had been sunk around the perimeter of the studio floor to house rows of lights. Other studios needed to build the floor up, and Eric and Ernie's stage was perfect.

Midway through the song, trudging along the groundrow trench, Eric would appear, leaving the studio clad in a raincoat, an outsized cap, an overlong scarf and carting his personal effects in a carrier bag. Spotting that the show was not in fact over, he would climb back onto the stage, remonstrate with Ernie as the credits rolled and finally all three would leave, doing the traditional dance.

Years later, John Ammonds recalled that this ending was a substitution for a finale that failed to fly. The first three recordings ended with a tenor singer turning up in the final sketch and singing 'The Donkey Serenade', holding a note for a seemingly unfeasible length of time while the sketch concluded and the credits rolled. At the first recording, one of the cameramen approached Ammonds with reservations, which the producer admitted he shared. It had been Eric's idea, and Ammonds mentioned his concerns to Ernie, who agreed but refused to undermine his partner. There was still time to reshoot the endings, but the clock was ticking, so the producer approached Morecambe, who, surprisingly, agreed. 'He was waiting for somebody to say it, because he hadn't the heart to come out and say it himself,' Ammonds said.[17]

Ammonds said the solution 'happened almost by accident', but it hadn't come completely from nowhere. Perhaps unconsciously, the revised pay-off looked back to a show from the first BBC series, twelve years earlier, in which Michael Aspel – then a newsreader and the host of the children's show *Crackerjack* – had been the guest star, and Ernie had been trying to keep Eric out of the finale with Aspel.

The conventional wisdom is that the Thames years were a matter of going out with a whimper. The 1979 Christmas show hadn't even made the top 20, but the 1980 series topped the ratings with audiences of over 16 million. The attractions for the stars were that it was less work for more money. The regular BBC shows had been forty-five minutes, whereas at Thames they were back to making half-hours, which ran closer to twenty-five minutes once the commercials had been taken into consideration. This, theoretically, meant less pressure on Eric, and also on Eddie Braben. However, the writer found it restrictive, being unable to develop meandering sketches as he had at the BBC, and resenting the break-up in pace.

While there is something in this, the Thames shows had their moments. However, they did lose one thing that they had at the BBC, which was guaranteed access to a peak slot on Christmas Day. If 25 December fell on Monday through to Thursday, there was no question that they would be the highlight of the schedules. However, with Thames handing over to London

Weekend Television on a Friday evening, if Christmas Day was on a weekend, ITV scheduling politics meant that there was no chance. Brian Tesler, managing director of LWT at the time, remembers taking Valium to get through the fraught scheduling meetings with the other companies.

This meant that in 1981, the show was bumped to 23 December, then 27 December in 1982, and the final show in 1983 went out on Boxing Day. This last show is a clear sign that Morecambe and Wise were running on empty, creatively, and it's equally clear that both of them knew it. This is not unreasonable for a partnership that had lasted over forty years, but it made comments from a couple of years before ring hollow. 'Although our Christmas shows have always been the flagships of our operation, it doesn't mean to say we will always do one… We have to know whether we can put together a show that is of high enough quality before we start,' said Ernie.[18]

Often, at Thames, the only way to guarantee the quality was to raid the archive and hope that nobody would notice. Their 'Bye Bye Blues' dance routine with Robert Hardy in 1982 was a retread of a sketch that had been done (admittedly twice) at the BBC. Incidentally, the 1982 show contains arguably the most problematic moment of their television career. In a big production number sending up the song 'Chattanooga Choo-Choo', where Eric and Ernie play all the parts, they end the sketch in blackface, as railway stewards, with Eric holding up a cardboard cut-out of Jimmy Savile.* By this time, Eric and Ernie had good reason to be disenchanted with television in general and Thames in particular. The film project that had lured them

---

* At the time, Savile was the front man for British Rail's 'This is the Age of the Train' advertising campaign.

back to commercial television five years earlier had turned into a studio-based production, shot in the conventional multi-camera way on videotape. Their only appearance on celluloid at Thames had been playing themselves in an episode of *The Sweeney*, a reciprocal arrangement after Dennis Waterman and John Thaw's appearance in the 1976 Christmas show.

Co-written with its director Joe McGrath, who had established Peter Cook and Dudley Moore's *Not Only...But Also...* at the BBC before going on to direct films like *The Magic Christian*, *Night Train to Murder* was a 1930s mystery pastiche that took an impressive cast including Fulton Mackay, Pamela Salem and Lysette Anthony to make 90 minutes of television that failed to impress its stars. When shooting finished in March 1983, Eric did his level best to ensure that it wasn't screened. The opening double in the 1983 Christmas show was mostly a word-for-word remake of the watch sketch from the 1976 Christmas show, albeit with a different ending. The 1976 show also provides the 'Old Soft-Shoe' sketch, but with Peter Skellern in place of Elton John. Skellern pushes his own piano on, to an appreciative response from the audience. Eric comments that it's 'the first time I've seen a piano get a round of applause'. This seems a knowing aside. Have the audience been told to applaud, or are they thinking that they're getting Elton John?

It's a pleasant enough reworking, and Skellern was a skilled comic performer in his own right, as well as a talented musician, but it illustrates the law of diminishing returns that was now applying. In the glory days at White City, an artist of the stature of Skellern would have been series material, but not quite big enough for the Christmas show. Similarly with singer Tony Monopoly, featured in a sketch based around the song 'Cabaret'. He's been assured that he will be backed by the finest orchestra available, and the number begins with the full might of Harry Rabinowitz's studio orchestra. However, the curtain pulls back and reveals his real backing band: the Harpenden Hot Shots. Eric is on trombone, Ernie is on drums, and they're joined by a banjo player and a pianist. It's a funny sketch, but it was funnier when they did it with Frankie Vaughan in the 1976 series.

Derek Jacobi and Fulton Mackay were much closer to the Ammonds-era level of guest booking, but their sketch first appeared in one of the ATV shows, in May 1964. In the original, Ernie conspired with Sid and Dick to create a custard pie sketch where only Eric was ever at risk of getting one in the face.

Under Ammonds and Maxin, the guests acted as if they were there under sufferance. The audience at home knew that everyone was having a ball, but that was the joke. Any close-ups were used to underline the horror and shame the guests were pretending to feel. The 1983 Christmas special is a particularly egregious example of missing this exquisite gag. Director Mark Stuart cuts away to close-ups of the guest stars laughing along and looking far too pleased to be there. The same can't be said for Eric and Ernie, who seem, in retrospect, to be very much going through the motions.

The closing number is another lift from the ATV days, featuring Eric and Ernie singing 'Swinging Down the Lane' with a pair of malfunctioning stools. Unique among the revisitations, this one improves on the original. This is unlikely to be hindsight at work. We know now what both Eric and Ernie knew at the time, that this was their last big Christmas show, although neither were quite aware how quickly the decision would be made final. First, Eric gets his hand stuck to the top of his stool, and is rendered immobile. Then the stool top comes away, revealing four prongs, one of which he sits on absent-mindedly. Ernie helps, and the song falls by the wayside as the pair struggle, apart from perfectly timed turns to the camera to sing the title. Then Ernie tries to get the stool top off with his foot. Naturally, it becomes stuck to his shoe. Eventually, freedom is achieved, but when Eric puts his hand on Ernie's shoulder, it becomes stuck again. It's a lovely little routine, deftly executed, and it's a sweetly fitting coda to their forty-odd years in the business. They came in with comedy and a soft-shoe routine, and that's how they went out.

Well, almost. After the Thames Colour Production* caption at the end, continuity announcer Philip Elsmore appears in vision to run down the programmes following later, one of which is *Des O'Connor Tonight*. Eric and Ernie appear behind him, in hats and coats, but still joined at the shoulder, laughing at O'Connor and declaring in unison 'No chance'.

---

* Seemingly still enough of a novelty to be mentioned on the end caption as late as 1988.

10

Half a star

On Sunday 15 April 1984, a beloved comedian dropped dead of a heart attack on live television. Millions were watching *Live from Her Majesty's* when Tommy Cooper collapsed in mid-routine. After the commercial break, the show continued with the tabs closed, just about masking Cooper's slumped form. Les Dennis and Dustin Gee* were the first act afterwards, modifying their act so it worked in front of the cloth, and being carried through what must have been a harrowing moment through sheer professionalism. On the walk-down at the end of the show, with Cooper absent, all those present try to put their best brave showbiz faces on, but Dennis and Gee look like they've been hit by a truck. What viewers suspected was confirmed by the ITN bulletin immediately after the show. Many performers like to claim it's the way they want to go, but this revised that view for most.

---

* Tragically, the fearsomely talented Gee would suffer a heart attack on New Year's Day 1986 in Southport, where he and Dennis were appearing in pantomime. He died two days later.

This devastating event made Eric Morecambe realise that he was doing the right thing by scaling back his professional activities. He had a habit of insisting that he'd take it easy then committing to another series, but this time was different. He had told family and friends that if he had another heart attack it would be fatal, and that if he did another series, he would definitely have another heart attack. It was time for family and fishing, and the odd appearance when he felt up to it. This was a long way from the jokey way he'd told Michael Parkinson that in 1968 he'd have had a heart attack if he'd realised he was having a heart attack.

It had already been reported in February that he intended to take a year off, which came as a surprise to Thames executives, who were expecting him and Ernie to start work on a new series in May. On one occasion, Morecambe went to lunch with Philip Jones, adamant that he would say no, only to agree to another series and a Christmas special. This time, he had no intention of seeing it through. Billy Marsh would smooth it over. In the meantime, there were to be odd guest appearances, including being a panellist on the first edition of a revival of *What's My Line*, hosted live by Eamonn Andrews from the stage of the Royalty Theatre.

Through May 1984, Eric was feeling off-form. A pacemaker had been fitted after the bypass operation, but there had been an accident on set at the recording of the 1983 Christmas show, where he hit his head and suffered a cardiac arrhythmia. Nonetheless, he remained willing to take calls from journalists for a quote when they needed one. When Diana Dors died of cancer on 4 May, Eric was on hand to pay tribute to his 'unique' friend, then again when Sir John Betjeman died on 19 May, calling his work 'a real taste of the twenties and thirties, all steam engines and soot'.[1]

He was all set to go into hospital for tests at the start of June, but there were a couple of commitments to fulfil first. On 17 May, three days after he turned fifty-eight, Eric went back to the Thames studios at Teddington Lock* with Gail to record an edition of the panel game *Whose Baby?*, in which celebrities had to identify the famous parent of the person they were grilling. Then on Sunday 27 May 1984, he was due to appear with his old friend the Welsh comedian Stan Stennett at the Roses Theatre in Tewkesbury. It was to be an informal evening of questions, answers and reminiscence. It was potentially the blueprint for any future public appearances – low stress, no lines to learn, no rehearsal.

The show went well. However, in the audience, Joan became increasingly worried that Eric wouldn't be able to resist too much of a good thing. She wanted to stop the show, but felt powerless to do so from her seat. The audience didn't want to let him go, and he didn't want to go offstage. He took six curtain calls, larking around with the band, playing the xylophone and the drums. Eventually, he went into the wings and collapsed instantly, hitting his head. The traditional, clichéd call went out, asking if there was a doctor in the house.

At home in Berkshire, Ernie Wise's telephone rang. Ever since that late night call in Batley sixteen years earlier, Wise had come to dread such a call. When the phone rings that late, it's never good news. His partner was in Cheltenham General Hospital. He had suffered a third heart attack. A few hours later, another call. John Eric Bartholomew had died.

At 7.22 a.m., a dazed yet composed Ernest Wiseman appeared on ITV's *Good Morning Britain*, being interviewed by John Stapleton. It is a tough watch, but a testament to Ernie's

---

* '...Middlesex, TW11 9NT.'

professionalism that he got through it. Maybe he shouldn't have accepted the call, but the pair had always been open and friendly with journalists, and if Ernie didn't do it, they might not have managed to get anyone appropriate. Throughout, Ernie speaks of Eric in the present tense, having to correct himself instantly. This is understandable as Morecambe had died only a couple of hours before. However, even when Wise appeared on *Desert Island Discs* six years later, the same impulse was there. Talking about the enduring power of the early Abbot and Costello influence, he told Sue Lawley, 'I mean, we copied their material and even to this day, we do a routine with Peter Cushing and bank managers, a money routine that we did all those years ago, pinched from Abbott and Costello, and we still keep it up. Or we did.'[2]

Retrospectively, Ernie felt the same sense of powerlessness that Joan had on the night. The two people who could have told Eric to calm down were in no position to do so. 'There wasn't anything I could do at the time,' he said. 'They said that he did the question and answer and then he was messing about in the show, you know running about all over the place, which I would have stopped him doing if I'd have been with him.'[3]

There would be no more wig jokes. No more 'Get out of that'. Braben had once written a line for Eric for when Ernie disappeared into the wings briefly. 'Don't be too long, I get a cold draught all down one side.' It was a joke, but it was based on the writer's close observation of his friends.

Eric said he was aware there was a space, an uncomfortable emptiness when Ern wasn't there. 'I'm fine. I'm OK for about two minutes. After that it doesn't feel right.'... Offstage they could manage without each other... In the studio, rehearsal room or the variety theatre that was very different. The following has happened when I've gone into Eric's room.

'Have you seen Ernie?'

'He's in the gallery talking to the sound man. Do you want him?'

'No, no, nothing important.'

This has happened in Ern's room.

'Is Eric around?'

'He's at the tea machine. Did you want him?'

'No, I'll talk to him later.'

Each one looking for the other half of himself.[4]

Ern would spend the rest of his life looking for Eric.

He wasn't quite ready to retire, though. He wasn't yet sixty. The trouble was that, in a memorable line of Braben's, Ernie was now 'half a star'. He could only do what he had always done, and for his solo career he began looking back to when he had started, but instead of being 'the Jack Buchanan of tomorrow', he was the Ernie Wise of now, and despite considerable talents, the openings for a song and dance man in 1984, especially one nearing pensionable age, were limited. Ernie decided that a one-man show was the answer.

I said to myself, I've got to do an act of some description. A bookable act. So I put together about an hour and twenty minutes of all I remembered, with 'Knee Deep In Daisies' and all the jokes I remember. Everything. And I went to Australia and did some cabaret in 1985. I went round the cabaret spots. Everybody said, 'Oooh aren't you brave and those tough audiences out there?' They weren't tough at all. They were English people, they were full of reminiscence and they wanted to talk about Flanagan and Allen and all.[5]

In 1987 came what Ernie thought was his big chance to prove himself. American singer-songwriter Rupert Holmes, of piña coladas and getting caught in the rain fame, had written a musical based on Charles Dickens' final, unfinished novel, *Edwin Drood*. Holmes set the story within the framework of a Victorian music hall show – the play within a play what he wrote – and addressed the incompleteness of the text by letting the audience vote on the alternate endings. A success on Broadway, it transferred to the West End and Wise was cast in the dual leading roles of the music hall's chairman William Cartwright and Mayor Thomas Sapsea. Ern was in his element again at last.

> My greatest achievement next to 'Singing in the Rain'. What happened was that I got this… big thick script and a musical score like you've never heard before. A small opera, and I learned the words and I learned the music because I can learn that easier than the words. I can learn music and lyrics much easier than words, and I spent five weeks rehearsing it. We went on at the Savoy Theatre and it came off after ten weeks and I was broken-hearted, because I never got chance to actually get a hold of it.[6]

Offers of pantomime came, but Ernie had various reasons for refusing. When you've had the star dressing room at the Palladium, one further down the pecking order at a provincial theatre is a hard pill to swallow, and having maintained a lifelong friendship with his bank book, as Connie had advised, Ernie didn't need to do it.

> I don't want to be straight man to everybody else. I don't want to be what is it, the mayor or something, you know, or

Baron Hardup. I have to maintain my stature. I think that's very important. I don't want people to say, 'Oh what a shame look at him, fancy him playing that. God, he must need the money' and all that. I really don't want that what do you call it? Pity, I suppose. I don't need the money. I want to go on working, but I want to maintain my position. As you say it is pride, but I'll tell you this much if I was broke I would do it.[7]

While he might not have needed the money, he did eventually need the sound of an audience, and in December 1992 Ernie starred as the King in *Sleeping Beauty* at the Theatre Royal, Windsor, conveniently close to his Maidenhead home. During the production of the show, a documentary crew from the BBC's *40 Minutes* followed his progress for a programme to be called *The Importance of Being Ernie*. When the programme went out, Wise and those close to him found it hurtful and snide.

Eventually, while joking that he was still on his way to Hollywood, Wise realised that he was on a hiding to nothing as a solo act. Show business involves many pigeonholes, and once in one, it's hard to move. The public likes a turn to do what it's always done. The public could accept his horticultural advice, dispensed in his 'Garden Wise' column for the *News of the World*,* but weren't interested in him other than as Little Ern. As with the American experience, Ernie was cursed by timing. If he had found himself going solo ten or fifteen years later, when Bob Monkhouse and Bruce Forsyth were reinventing themselves on *Have I Got News For You*, he might have stood a chance. However, by then, even he, the fitness fanatic, had

---

* Satirised by *Viz* comic as 'Biscuit Wise', in which Little Ern gave his reviews of various baked goods.

begun to experience ill health, being laid low by a series of strokes. Ernie died on 21 March 1999.

If the roles had been reversed, and Ernie had predeceased his partner, Eric would have found it hard to re-establish himself as a solo entertainer. He would have continued to be famous for being who he was, but would most likely have concentrated on writing, popping up at publication time to promote each new release with some prime jifflearsing about.

Had Eric lived ten years longer, there would have been no more big shows, but he and Ernie would have turned up on panel games and chat shows, singly or together. Maybe there would have been the odd guest spot on *Des O'Connor Tonight*. They wouldn't have needed to do anything. They just had to be Eric and Ern, and they'd had a lifetime's rehearsal for that.

'We go back to when I first saw him give his audition,' said Ernie on *Desert Island Discs*. 'When he walked onto that stage as a young boy, with his beret and his lollipop, and sang "I'm not all there, there's something missing", and that is the song when people see me. I'm not all there. They expect to see the two of us.'

11

The short, fat, hairy legacy
of Eric and Ernie

And that is exactly how Eric and Ernie continue to be seen. Eric and Ernie remain the gold standard for double acts, while also being an unattainable ideal. No act could command the audiences they did at their peak. Although they had, while they were still active, become almost synonymous with Christmas, few can have realised that nearly forty years after their last show, they would still be a regular fixture in the festive schedules. The BBC usually repeats one of the Christmas spectaculars. There have been some repeats of the Thames shows, but these seem to have dried up. Each year seems to see a new documentary about them, often finding some new aspect of their career. Within the last three years, we have seen the recovery of several shows that had been thought lost.

While they were always fondly remembered, this ubiquity was not always the case. There was a repeat of the 1973 Christmas show in 1985. After that, in the summer of 1986, BBC1 plundered not its own library but the ATV archives for a run of late 1960s shows with new links by Little Ern, under the title *Vintage Morecambe and Wise*. There was nothing more until 1991, and then it took until 1993 for a Christmas Day repeat of 1977 to begin the apparent new tradition of an Eric and Ernie Christmas show getting an outing in full on 25 December.

Historically, nostalgia seems to begin at the twenty-year point. A decade is too recent and fresh. The bad bits are still in focus. A further decade on, the highlights become enshrined. In the 1970s, there was a massive wave of nostalgia for the 1950s and the rock and roll age. By the early 1990s, it was the 1970s' turn. People who'd grown up watching Morecambe and Wise with their parents were now making and commissioning television. The Christmas specials were largely 'safe'. With no or almost no editing for taste, they could be shown again, something that couldn't be said for some other programmes of the era.

However, Eric and Ernie have been pigeonholed. Unlike a dog, they appear to be just for Christmas. Between 1968 and 1976, they made nine series for the BBC, eight of which survive in full. Bizarrely, BBC2 ran the first surviving ATV series from 1962 in full in late 1999 and early 2000. Meanwhile, there has been only the odd series of compilations from the BBC shows. While available on DVD, they languish while *Dad's Army* is seemingly on constant rotation. Why is this so?

Part of the answer may be quotas. An old show is a repeat, whereas a compilation qualifies as a new programme. They were expensive shows to make, and the repeat fees for guests would make them expensive to repeat as per the original contracts. Reusing the material in compilation form would involve new contracts. Also, the quality of the Christmas shows was such that maybe showing the regular shows could be an anticlimax. With such a massive output, not all of it could be gold, and maybe there is a desire to preserve a myth that it was.

Whatever, the shows still seem to find an appreciative audience, many of whom weren't born when Eric died. To them, some of the guest stars must be baffling, but the beauty of it is that the sketches stand alone. You don't have to understand who Keith Michell was to find what Eric and Ernie do with him funny.

Eric and Ernie finally conquered America posthumously, when *The Play What I Wrote*, by Hamish McColl and Sean Foley, ran for three months at the Lyceum Theatre on Broadway in 2003, having debuted at the Liverpool Playhouse in 2001 before transferring to Wyndham's in London's West End. The genuine celebrities who lined up to be insulted each night in London included Ralph Fiennes and Roger Moore, who, in a chilling echo, suffered a heart attack while on stage. On Broadway, *M*A*S*H* star Alan Alda was one of the guests.

Other stage shows have been inspired by Morecambe and Wise. In 2009, Tim Whitnall's *Morecambe* was one of the big hits of the Edinburgh Fringe, with Bob Golding's portrayal of Eric winning *The Stage* award for best solo performance. Aptly enough, it moved to the Duchess Theatre in London for a short run that Christmas. *Eric and Little Ern*, by Jonty Stephens and Ian Ashpitel, also began at the Edinburgh Fringe before moving to the West End. 'I sat in the audience and I thought I was at a Morecambe and Wise show,' said Gary Morecambe.[1] In 2011, Victoria Wood produced Peter Bowker's affectionate television drama about their early years, *Eric and Ernie*. Gary Morecambe had nothing but praise for the way his grandparents were depicted by Wood and Jim Moir – aka Vic Reeves, one of the double-act performers most frequently compared to Eric.

I think Victoria made her look like she was really driven, which she wasn't. She was quite laid back. She just wanted Eric to get off his arse, really. She really did. She kicked it off. For no reasons of her own. She just saw this lad who was going to end up working in the corner shop, which was fine, but she was very wide-seeing. Victoria actually played that element quite well. And he didn't until he discovered comedy, and he only discovered it by doing piano, dancing and singing. What Jim got brilliantly was the laid-backness. He underplayed it, and George underplayed life. That's how George was. He'd really worked at it. And he was George in the lunch break. He wouldn't talk. We had lunch together the group of us. Not like the guy I remembered. And then I realised he was still George.[2]

Then in 2017, the story of Eddie Braben's involvement with Morecambe and Wise was made into a BBC drama, *Eric, Ernie and Me*, with Stephen Tompkinson as Braben, and Rufus Jones as an uncannily accurate Johnny Ammonds.[*]

There are also the tangible monuments. Eric is commemorated in bronze, in ornithological mode, on the promenade at Morecambe, doing John Ammonds' version of the Groucho dance with a pair of binoculars around his neck.[†] Ernie is

---

[*] As well as interviewing him, I knew and had observed Johnny at close quarters, through our membership of the Coda Club, a monthly gathering for musicians, hoofers and writers. Other members included most of Peter Knight's band. Watching Jones playing him, it was as if he had been reincarnated.

[†] Bafflingly, he is facing the town. Personally, I'd have had this keen ornithologist looking out across the Bay towards Grange-over-Sands, a view I took in many times as a student in Lancaster, and on subsequent return visits.

immortalised in granite. Together, larger than life, they can be found at the entrance to the Winter Gardens in Blackpool.

In the spring of 2021, a show from the BBC series previously thought lost, but found among Eric Morecambe's personal effects by his son Gary, was the centrepiece of a television documentary exploring the enduring appeal of the duo. Thirty-seven years after their last television show, they continue to comfort and delight, bring sunshine, laughter and love. The world needs all of these now more than ever. Long may they provide.

Appendix:

MORECAMBE AND WISE AT WORK

Morecambe and Wise at work

The following is a listing of broadcasts and live work under-taken by Eric Morecambe and Ernie Wise, both together and separately. It is extensive, but not exhaustive, as some appearances will have been uncredited and others unlisted altogether.

Radio appearances

LP = BBC Light Programme
HS = BBC Home Service
HS(N) = BBC North of England Home Service
R1/2 = BBC Radio 1 & 2 combined
R2 = BBC Radio 2
R3 = BBC Radio 3
R4 = BBC Radio 4
R4(N) = BBC Radio 4 (northern transmitters only)

Starring vehicles

You're Only Young Once

Series 1:
HS(N), 9 November 1953–4 January 1954
Mondays, 2000 (shows 1–3, 5, 6, 8, 9), 1900 (show 4), Tuesday 1900 (show 7) – 9x30m
M&W, Mary Naylor, the Hedley Ward Trio, the BBC Northern Variety Orchestra.
Writer: Frank Roscoe.
Producer: Ronnie Taylor.

Series 2:
HS(N), 6 May–24 June 1954
Thursdays, 1900 – 8x30m
M&W, Pearl Carr, Deryck Guyler, the Augmented Northern Variety Orchestra, with the Three Imps and Robert Beatty (show 1), the Horrie Dargie Quintet and Charlie Chester (show 2), Kenneth Connor, The Maple Leaf Four and John Slater (show 5), the Ray Ellington Quartet and McDonald Hobley (show 6), The Radio Revellers and Harry Secombe (show 8).
Writer: Frank Roscoe, with additional material by M&W.
Producer: John Ammonds.
Shows 1, 2, 5, 8 and 6 from this series were given a national airing on the Light Programme, 20 July–17 August 1954, Tuesdays, 2000.

Series 3:
HS(N), 1 October–17 December 1954
Fridays, 1900 – 12x30m

M&W, Hattie Jacques, Deryck Guyler, Herbert Smith, Les Howard, Stan Stennett, Harry Locke.
Writer: Frank Roscoe, with additional material by M&W.
Producer: John Ammonds.

The Show Goes On

LP, 31 March 1955
Thursdays, 1930 – 11x60m
'Variety at high speed introduced by Morecambe and Wise' with The Kordites, the Raymond Woodhead Choir, the Augmented BBC Northern Variety Orchestra conducted by Alyn Ainsworth, and: Max Miller, John Horvelle, Ken Dodd, Violet Carson, Edouin et Rachelle (show 1); Ted Lune, Louise Traill, Freddie Sales, Semprini, the Hedley Ward Trio (show 2); Ken Platt, Petula Clark, Stan Stennett, Frank Cook, The Gaunt Brothers (show 3); Fayne and Evans, Rawicz and Landauer, Ken Dodd, Pearl Carr, Martin Lukins (show 4); Richard Murdoch and Kenneth Horne, Tony Brent, Gladys Morgan, Tollefsen, the Hedley Ward Trio (show 5); Robb Wilton, Rawicz and Landauer, Denis Goodwin, Betty Driver, The Gaunt Brothers (show 6); Ken Platt, Lita Roza, Peter Cavanagh, Harry Baile, Eddie Calvert, The Tanner Sisters (show 7); Jimmy James and Co., Rawicz and Landauer, Stan Stennett, The Beverley Sisters, Martin Lukins (show 8); John Horvelle, Gladys Morgan, Ronald Chesney, Ken Dodd, the Hedley Ward Trio (show

9); Arthur English, Louise Traill, Jack Storey, Edouin et Rachelle (show 10); Ted Lune, Rawicz and Landauer, Jimmy Young, Bill Waddington, Max Geldray (show 11).
Producers: Geoffrey Wheeler and Ronnie Taylor.

Laughter Incorporated

LP, 21 July–22 September 1958
Wednesdays, 2000 – 10x30m
M&W, Sheila Buxton, Rawicz and Landauer (show 1), Semprini (shows 2–5, 7 and 9), Max Geldray (shows 6, 8 and 10), Peter Goodwright (shows 1, 4–8 and 10), Judith Chalmers (shows 1, 4–10), Leonard Williams (shows 2 and 3), Penelope Davis (shows 2 and 3), Alyn Ainsworth and the BBC Northern Dance Orchestra (shows 1–5, 8 and 10), Geraldo (shows 6, 7 and 9).
Writer: Edward Taylor.
Producer: Eric Miller.

The Morecambe and Wise Show

LP, 24 July–28 August 1966
Sundays, 1330 (repeated Wednesdays 2000) – 6x30m
M&W, Anita Harris, Elaine Taylor (shows 1–5), Peter Hawkins (shows 1, 3–5), John Baddeley (shows 2 and 6), Dilys Laye (show 6), the Mike Sammes Singers, Burt Rhodes and his Orchestra.
Writer: Eric Merriman.
Producer: John Browell.

The Eric Morecambe and Ernie Wise Show

Series 1:
R2, 26 January–1 March 1975
Sundays, 1402 (repeated Saturdays 1902) – 6x30m
M&W, Ann Hamilton, Arthur Tolcher with: Michael Segal, Peters and Lee (show 1); Michael Ward, Salena Jones (show 2), Anita Harris (show 3), Wilma Reading (show 4), Laura Lee (show 5), Gay Soper, Lynsey de Paul (show 6), Dennis Wilson and his Orchestra.
Writer: Eddie Braben.
Producer: John Browell.

Series 2:
R2, 5 September–10 October 1976
Sundays, 1402 (repeated Saturdays 1902) – 6x30m
M&W with: Gayle Hunnicutt, Richard Caldicott, April Walker (show 1); Percy Edwards, Salena Jones (show 2), Richard Mathews, Ann Hamilton, Michael Kilgarriff (show 3); Allan Cuthbertson (show 4); Nicola Pagett, Elaine Delmar (show 5), Brian Wilde, April Walker (show 6); Syd Lawrence and his Orchestra (shows 1, 4 and 6), Peter Knight and his Orchestra (shows 2, 3 and 5).
Writer: Eddie Braben.
Producer John Browell.

Series 3:
R2, 4 December–25 December 1977, 25 March 1978, and 1 May 1978
Sundays, 1402–1430 (repeated Saturdays 1902–1930)

Guest appearances and spots

LP, Saturday 6 December 1947,
1740–1815
Beginners Please

LP, Saturday 20 March 1948,
1800–1830
Beginners Please

LP, Thursday 19 August 1948,
1930–2015
Show Time
Dick Bentley (host), David Griffiths,
M&W, Marcia Owen, Peter Sellers,
Saveen, Chick Fowler, The Show
Timers.
Musical director: Frank Cantell.
Producer: Roy Speer.

HS, Tuesday 23 October 1951,
1900–1930
First House: Vaudeville broadcasts
from famous music halls and
theatres.
Tonight: A visit to the Shepherd's
Bush Empire, London to hear Lee
Lawrence, Peter Sellers, M&W.
Introduced by Brian Johnston.

HS, Thursday 10 January 1952,
1230–1300
Workers' Playtime from a stove
foundry in Leeds
Harry Shiels, The Melomaniacs,
Sheila Bennett, M&W, Fred Harries
at the piano.
Producer: Philip Robinson.

HS(N), Thursday 13 March 1952,
2000–2030
Variety Fanfare
Producer: Ronnie Taylor.

LP, Sunday 4 May 1952,
2100–2200
Variety Bandbox
Harry Locke, Patrick O'Hagan,
M&W, Kay Cavendish, Freddie
Sales, the Hedley Ward Trio, Ethel
Revnell, Jimmy Young, the Peter
Knight Singers, Cyril Stapleton and
his Orchestra.
Producer: John Foreman.

LP, Thursday 15 May 1952,
2000–2045
Variety Fanfare
High-speed variety from the North
of England with The Kordites, Eric
Easton, M&W, Patrick O'Hagan,
Michael Howard, Albert Ward,
Les Ward, Al Read, the Augmented
Northern Variety Orchestra
conducted by Vilém Tauský.
Producer: Ronnie Taylor.

LP, Thursday 12 June 1952,
2000–2045
Variety Fanfare
The Kordites, The Norman George
Sextet, M&W, Jimmy Young,
Freddie Sales, Littlewood's Girls'
Choir, Albert Ward, Les Ward,
Michael Howard, the Augmented
Northern Variety Orchestra
conducted by Vilém Tauský.
Producer: Ronnie Taylor.

LP, Tuesday 1 July 1952, 1930–2015
Variety Fanfare
The Kordites, Harold Smart, M&W,
Jimmy Young, Gladys Morgan,
Ken Frith and his Magic Pianos,
Littlewood's Girls' Choir, Ken Platt,
the Augmented Northern Variety
Orchestra conducted by Vilém
Tauský.
Producer: Ronnie Taylor.

LP, Tuesday 22 July 1952, 1930–2015
Variety Fanfare
The Kordites, M&W, Dorothy Squires, Freddie Sales, Larry Macari, Tony Fayne and David Evans, Ken Platt, the Augmented Northern Variety Orchestra conducted by Vilém Tauský.
Producer: Ronnie Taylor.

LP, Sunday 27 July 1952, 2100–2200
Variety Bandbox
Richard Murdoch, M&W, Adelaide Hall, Cliff Gordon, the Harold Smart Quartet, Bill Kerr, Jimmy Young, the Peter Knight Singers, Cyril Stapleton and his Orchestra.
Producer: Bill Worsley.

LP, Tuesday 19 August 1952, 1930–2015
Variety Fanfare
The Kordites, The Gaunt Brothers, Leslie Adams, Les Howard, M&W, Billy Mayerl, Benny Hill, Ted Heath and his Music, Alan Clarke (host), the Augmented Northern Variety Orchestra conducted by Vilém Tauský.
Producer: Ronnie Taylor.

LP, Tuesday 2 September 1952, 1930–2015
Variety Fanfare
The Kordites, Ken Frith and his Magic Pianos, The Stargazers, Harry Bailey, Stanelli, M&W, Anne Ziegler and Webster Booth, Jack Warner, Alan Clarke (host), the Augmented Northern Variety Orchestra conducted by Vilém Tauský.
Producer: Ronnie Taylor.

LP, Tuesday 16 September 1952, 1930–2015
Variety Fanfare
The Kordites, The Malcolm Mitchell Trio, Bob Monkhouse, Littlewood's Girls' Choir, Tommy Reilly, M&W, David Hughes, Ken Platt, the Augmented Northern Variety Orchestra conducted by Vilém Tauský.
Producer: Ronnie Taylor.

LP, Friday 10 October 1952, 2000–2045
Variety Fanfare
The Kordites, Billy 'Uke' Scott, M&W, Ken Frith and his Magic Pianos, Tony Fayne and David Evans, The Radio Revellers, Frankie Howerd, the Augmented Northern Variety Orchestra conducted by Vilém Tauský, Alan Clarke (host).
Producer: Ronnie Taylor.

LP, Friday 31 October 1952, 2000–2045
Variety Fanfare
The Kordites, The Malcolm Mitchell Trio, Bob Monkhouse, Norman George and his Violin, Littlewood's Girls' Choir, M&W, Adelaide Hall, Robb Wilton, the Augmented Northern Variety Orchestra conducted by Vilém Tauský, Alan Clarke (host).
Producer: Ronnie Taylor.

LP, Friday 21 November 1952, 2000–2045
Variety Fanfare
The Kordites, Jimmy Leach and his Organolian Quartet, Roy Lester, John McHugh, M&W, Albert Ward and Les Ward, Elsie Waters and Doris Waters, the Augmented

Northern Variety Orchestra conducted by Vilém Tauský, Alan Clarke (host).
Producer: Ronnie Taylor.

LP, Friday 12 December 1952, 2000–2045
Variety Fanfare
The Kordites, Robin Richmond, Leslie Adams, Sylvia Cecil, M&W, Albert and Les Ward, Vic Oliver, the Augmented Northern Variety Orchestra conducted by Vilém Tauský, Alan Clarke (host).
Producer: Ronnie Taylor.

LP, Friday 9 January 1953, 2000–2045
Variety Fanfare
The Kordites, The Tanner Sisters, Barry Took, Winifred Atwell, M&W, Anne Shelton, Robb Wilton, the Augmented Northern Variety Orchestra conducted by Vilém Tauský, Alan Clarke (host).
Producer: Ronnie Taylor.

LP, Friday 30 January 1953, 2000–2045
Variety Fanfare
The Kordites, The Gaunt Brothers, Eddie Arnold, Ken Mackintosh, M&W, Anne Ziegler and Webster Booth, Ken Platt, the Augmented Northern Variety Orchestra conducted by Vilém Tauský, Alan Clarke (host).
Producer: Ronnie Taylor.

LP, Friday 13 February 1953, 2000–2045
Variety Fanfare
The Kordites, The Tanner Sisters, Leslie Adams, Ken Frith and his Magic Pianos, Peter Cavanagh, Jimmy Young, M&W, the

Augmented Northern Variety Orchestra conducted by Vilém Tauský, Alan Clarke (host).
Producer: Ronnie Taylor.

HS, Thursday 19 February 1953, 1225–1255
Workers' Playtime from a brake-lining factory at Chapel-en-le-Frith
Ken Platt, Lynnette Rae, M&W, Billy 'Uke' Scott, the Jimmy Leach Organolian Quartet, Fred Harries at the piano.
Producer: Philip Robinson.

LP, Friday 27 February 1953, 2000–2045
Variety Fanfare
The Kordites, the Hedley Ward Trio, Eddie Arnold, Tollefsen, M&W, Eve Boswell, Arthur Askey, the Augmented Northern Variety Orchestra conducted by Vilém Tauský, Alan Clarke (host).
Producer: Ronnie Taylor.

LP, Friday 13 March 1953, 2000–2045
Variety Fanfare
The Kordites, the Hedley Ward Trio, Eddie Arnold, Tollefsen, M&W, Eve Boswell, Arthur Askey, the Augmented Northern Variety Orchestra conducted by Vilém Tauský, Alan Clarke (host).
Producer: Ronnie Taylor.

LP, Friday 27 March 1953, 2000–2045
Variety Fanfare
The Kordites, the Hedley Ward Trio, Eddie Arnold, Rawicz and Landauer, M&W, John McHugh, Littlewood's Girls' Choir, Ken Platt, the Augmented Northern Variety Orchestra conducted by Vilém

Tauský, Alan Clarke (host).
Producer: Ronnie Taylor.

LP, Wednesday 29 July 1953,
2100–2200
Blackpool Night
The Three Monarchs, Bill
Waddington, 'An unknown singer
who is on holiday here', M&W,
the Beverley Sisters, Dave Morris,
Allan Jones, Arthur Askey, Reginald
Dixon, the Northern Variety
Orchestra conducted by Alyn
Ainsworth, Jack Watson (host).
Producer: Philip Robinson.

LP, Wednesday 23 September 1953,
2100–2200
Blackpool Night
Ken Frith, Bill Waddington, Bill
Maynard, Les Howard, M&W,
Reginald Dixon, Peter Cavanagh,
The Beverley Sisters, Ken Platt,
the Northern Variety Orchestra
conducted by Alyn Ainsworth, Jack
Watson (host).
Producer: Philip Robinson.

HS, Thursday 22 October 1953,
1225–1255
Workers' Playtime from an electricity
power station near Accrington
M&W, Maureen Rose, Bill
Waddington, The Jimmy Leach
Organolian Quartet, Fred Harries
at the piano, Alan Clarke (host).
Producer: Philip Robinson.

LP, Friday 30 October 1953,
1930–2015
Variety Fanfare
Ken Frith and his Magic Pianos,
John Blythe, The Beverley Sisters,
Jimmy Wheeler, David Hughes,
M&W, Ken Platt, The Kordites,

the Augmented Northern Variety
Orchestra conducted by Vilém
Tauský, Alan Clarke (host).
Producer: Ronnie Taylor.

HS(N), Tuesday 19 January 1954,
1900–1930
Variety Fanfare
Producer: Ronnie Taylor.

HS(N), Tuesday 9 February 1954,
1900–1930
Variety Fanfare
Producer: Ronnie Taylor.

HS, Thursday 18 March 1954,
1225–1255
Workers' Playtime from Finningley,
near Doncaster
M&W, Eddie Calvert, Benny Hill,
Alma Cogan, Jimmy Leach at the
electric organ, Fred Harries at the
piano.
Producer: Alan Clarke.

HS, Friday 26 March 1954.
1900–1945
Henry Hall's Guest Night
Producer: Glyn Jones.

HS, Thursday 29 April 1954,
1225–1255
Workers' Playtime from the
canteen of an engineering firm in
Birmingham
Martin Lukins, M&W, Billie Baker,
Beryl Reid, Harry Engleman at the
piano, Philip Garston-Jones (host).
Producer: Philip Garston-Jones.

HS, Tuesday 3 August 1954,
1225–1255
Workers' Playtime from a factory
canteen in Belfast
M&W, The Ray Ellington Quartet
with Marion Ryan, Frank Murphy,

Jack Cruise, Norman Metcalfe
at the electric organ, Billy White
at the piano.
Producer: Jack McGeagh

HS, Thursday 5 August 1954,
1225–1255
Workers' Playtime from a factory
canteen in Armagh
M&W, Jack Cruise, Robert Wilson,
The Melotones, Norman Metcalfe
at the electric organ, Billy White
at the piano.
Producer: Jack McGeagh

LP, Wednesday 1 September 1954,
2100–2200
Blackpool Night
Vic Oliver, Jimmy Young, M&W,
Johnny Roadhouse, Eddie Arnold,
Sylvia Campbell, Jim Dale,
Reginald Dixon, the Littlewood
Songsters, the Augmented
Northern Variety Orchestra
conducted by Alyn Ainsworth,
Jack Watson (host).
Producer: Eric Miller.

HS, Thursday 9 September 1954,
1900–1930
Having a Wonderful Time
M&W, Frederick Ferrari, Bunny
Doyle, Frank Clarke, Norman
Robinson and his Orchestra.
Producer: Geoffrey Wheeler

HS, Thursday 14 October 1954,
1225–1255
Workers' Playtime from a canteen
in Wallsend-on-Tyne
M&W, The Ray Ellington Quartet
with Marion Ryan, Frankie Burns,
Martin Lukins, Fred Harries at
the piano.
Producer: Geoffrey Wheeler.

HS, Tuesday 18 January 1955,
1900–1930
Spotlight
Ted Lune, M&W, Bruce Trent, Lucille
Graham, the Raymond Woodhead
Choir, the Augmented Northern
Variety Orchestra conducted by
Alyn Ainsworth.
Producer: Eric Miller.

HS, Thursday 24 February 1955,
1225–1255
Workers' Playtime from a canteen
in Cheltenham
Ruby Murray, M&W, Bert Weedon,
Leon Cortez, Harry Engleman
(piano), Vic Mortiboys (bass), Bob
Mansell (drums), Philip Garston-
Jones (host).
Producer: James Pestridge.

LP, Monday 21 March 1955,
1930–2000
Spotlight
Ted Lune, M&W, Brian Reece,
Les Howard, Julie Dawn, the
Raymond Woodhead Choir, the
Augmented BBC Northern Variety
Orchestra conducted by Alyn
Ainsworth, Roger Moffat (host).
Writers: Jack Bradley and Ray
Davies.
Producer: Eric Miller.

LP, Monday 11 April 1955,
1930–2000
Spotlight
Ted Lune, M&W, Andrew Faulds
as 'Jet Morgan', Les Howard,
Carole Carr, the Raymond
Woodhead Choir, Johnny (The
Sax) Roadhouse, the Augmented
BBC Northern Variety Orchestra
conducted by Alyn Ainsworth,
Roger Moffat (host).

Writers: Jack Bradley and Ray Davies.
Producer: Eric Miller.

LP, Tuesday 19 April 1955, 1900–1930
Spotlight
Ted Lune, M&W, Andrew Faulds as 'Jet Morgan', Les Howard, Carole Carr, the Raymond Woodhead Choir, Johnny (The Sax) Roadhouse, the Augmented BBC Northern Variety Orchestra conducted by Alyn Ainsworth, Roger Moffat (host).
Writers: Jack Bradley and Ray Davies.
Producer: Eric Miller.

LP, Tuesday 24 May 1955, 1900–1930
Spotlight
Ted Lune, M&W, Herbert Smith, Les Howard, Lizbeth Webb, the Raymond Woodhead Choir, Johnny (The Sax) Roadhouse, the Augmented BBC Northern Variety Orchestra conducted by Alyn Ainsworth, Roger Moffat (host).
Writers: Jack Bradley and Ray Davies.
Producer: Eric Miller.

LP, Wednesday 29 June 1955, 2100–2200
Blackpool Night
Reginald Dixon, the Horrie Dargie Quintet, Ted Lune, The Kordites, Robert Moreton, Semprini, M&W, Dickie Valentine, Arthur Askey, Littlewood's Girls' Choir, the Augmented BBC Northern Variety Orchestra conducted by Alyn Ainsworth, Jack Watson (host).
Producer: Eric Miller.

LP, Wednesday 10 August 1955, 2100–2200
Blackpool Night
Reginald Dixon, Ken Dodd, Sylvia Campbell, Denis Goodwin, Raymond Woodhead and Harry Heyward ('At two pianos'), M&W, Dickie Valentine, Vic Oliver, Littlewood's Girls' Choir, the Augmented BBC Northern Variety Orchestra conducted by Alyn Ainsworth, host Jack Watson.
Producer: Eric Miller.

HS, Thursday 18 August 1955, 1225–1255
Workers' Playtime from a works canteen at Fleetwood
M&W, Alma Cogan, Joe Crosbie, The King Brothers, Fred Harries at the piano.
Producer: Geoffrey Wheeler.

LP, Wednesday 7 September 1955, 2100–2200
Blackpool Night
Reginald Dixon, The Ray Ellington Quartet, Vic Gordon and Peter Colville, Les Howard, Stan Stennett, Rawicz and Landauer, Jimmy Clitheroe, Lita Roza, M&W, Littlewood's Girls' Choir, the Billy Ternent Concert Orchestra, Jack Watson (host).
Producer: Eric Miller.

HS(N), Wednesday 19 October 1955, 1900–1930
Double Trouble

HS(N), Wednesday 2 November 1955, 1900–1930
Double Trouble

HS, Thursday 21 June 1956,
1225–1255
Workers' Playtime from a factory
canteen in Norwich
Ronald Chesney, Irene Prador,
Margery Manners, M&W, the
Harry Engleman Trio, Philip
Garston-Jones (host).
Producer: James Pestridge.

LP, Wednesday 18 July 1956,
2100–2200
Blackpool Night
M&W, Ethel Revnell, Edna Savage,
Jimmy Clitheroe, Ken Mackintosh,
Reg Thompson, Albert Ward
and Les Ward, Reginald Dixon,
The George Mitchell Singers, the
Augmented BBC Northern Variety
Orchestra conducted by Alyn
Ainsworth, Jack Watson (host).
Producer: Eric Miller.

HS, Tuesday 24 July 1956,
1900–1930
*Northern Variety Parade: Brian Reece
says 'Let's Make a Date'*
The Kordites, M&W, the Augmented
BBC Northern Variety Orchestra
conducted by Alyn Ainsworth.
Writers: Jack Bradley and Ray
Davies.
Producer: John Ammonds.

HS, Tuesday 31 July 1956,
1900–1930
*Northern Variety Parade presents
Variety Fanfare*
The Kordites, Tom Mennard, Tommy
Reilly, Chic Murray and Maidie,
Joan Regan, M&W, the Augmented
BBC Northern Variety Orchestra
conducted by Alyn Ainsworth, Alan
Clarke (host).
Producer: Eric Miller.

HS, Thursday 9 August 1956,
1225–1255
Workers' Playtime from the canteen
of a factory in Rochdale
M&W, David Hughes, Wyn Calvin,
The Four Southlanders, The Harry
Hayward Trio, Randal Herley
(host).
Producer: James Casey.

LP, Friday 24 August 1956,
2030–2115
Morecambe Lights Up
Al Read, Janette Scott, M&W,
Celia Nicholls, Carlo, Franklin
Engelmann, Alan Dixon, the
BBC Northern Variety Orchestra
conducted by Alyn Ainsworth,
Geoffrey Wheeler (host).
Producer: Eric Miller.

HS, Monday 23 October 1956,
1900–1930
The Call Boy
M&W, Petula Clark, Chic Murray,
Joe 'Mr. Piano' Henderson, the
Hindley-Taylor Singers, Tom
Harrison, the BBC Northern Dance
Orchestra conducted by Alyn
Ainsworth, Jimmy Clitheroe (host).
Writer: Frank Roscoe.
Producer: John Ammonds.

HS, Wednesday 26 November 1956,
1225–1255
Midday Music Hall
Leslie Bryant, Lucille Graham,
Billy Burden, Donald Purchase,
M&W, the BBC Revue Orchestra
conducted by Harry Rabinowitz.
Producer: Bill Worsley.

HS, Monday 15 December 1956,
2000–2100
Variety Playhouse

Harry Locke, M&W, Margaret Rawlings, Thomas Round, Peggy Thompson, Tollefsen, the George Mitchell Choir, the British Concert Orchestra conducted by Vic Oliver and Arthur Anton, Vic Oliver (host).
Writer: Carey Edwards.
Producer: Tom Ronald.

HS, Wednesday 18 March 1957, 1220–1255
Midday Music Hall
The BBC Variety Orchestra conducted by Paul Fenoulhet with the Highlights, Bobby Dennis, Patti Lewis, M&W, David Hughes.
Producer: Bill Worsley.

HS, Tuesday 26 March 1957, 1225–1255
Midday Music Hall from an RAF Maintenance Unit in Berkshire
Douglas Maynard, Felix Bowness, Sheila Buxton, M&W, James Moody (piano), Bert Weedon (guitar), Max Abrams (drums).
Producer: Bill Gates.

HS, Wednesday 29 March 1957, 1905–1945
Henry Hall's Guest Night
Henry Hall, M&W.
Producer: John Simmonds.

LP, Thursday 1 May 1957, 2115–2200
The Call Boy
Jimmy Clitheroe, M&W, The Coronets, Leslie Adams, Peter Sinclair, Johnny Roadhouse, the Hindley-Taylor Singers, Tony Melody, Herbert Smith, the BBC Northern Dance Orchestra conducted by Alyn Ainsworth.

Writers: Frank Roscoe and Wally Ashley.
Producer: John Ammonds.

HS, Monday 2 May 1957, 1225–1255
Workers' Playtime from the canteen of a factory in Farnworth
M&W, Patti Lewis, Bud Bennett, Don Harper, The Harry Hayward Trio, Randal Herley (host).
Producer: James Casey.

LP, Sunday 3 July 1957, 2100–2200
Blackpool Night
The Kentones, Leslie Adams, Arthur Haynes, Camilleri, Peter Cavanagh, Jill Day, M&W, Reginald Dixon, The Raymond Woodhead Singers, the BBC Northern Dance Orchestra conducted by Alyn Ainsworth, Jack Watson (host).
Producer: Geoffrey Wheeler.

LP, Sunday 14 August 1957, 2100–2200
Blackpool Night
The Three Deuces, Eddie Molloy, Arthur Haynes, Camilleri, Ted Lune, Anne Shelton, M&W, Reginald Dixon, The Raymond Woodhead Singers, the BBC Northern Dance Orchestra conducted by Alyn Ainsworth, Jack Watson (host).
Producer: Geoffrey Wheeler.

LP, Thursday 31 October 1957, 1230–1300
Workers' Playtime from the canteen of a metal foundry at Nuneaton
Guy Taylor, Irene Prador, Margery Manners, M&W, Harry Engleman (piano), Vic Mortiboys (string bass),

Bob Mansell (drums), Richard Maddock (host).
Producer: James Pestridge.

LP, Thursday 17 February 1958, 2100–2130
The Call Boy
M&W, Bruce Trent, Frank Cooke, Jack Watson, Judith Chalmers, the Hindley-Taylor Singers, Jimmy Leach at the electronic organ and the BBC Northern Dance Orchestra conducted by Alyn Ainsworth.
Writers: Ronnie Taylor and James Casey.
Producer: James Casey.

LP, Tuesday 12 May 1958, 1230–1300
Midday Music Hall
The BBC Northern Dance Orchestra conducted by Alyn Ainsworth, The Fraser Hayes Four, Sonny Jones, Elizabeth Larner, M&W, Roger Moffat (host).
Producer: Eric Miller.

LP, Monday 17 July 1958, 1230–1300
Workers' Playtime from a factory canteen in Rochdale
M&W, Sheila Buxton, Harry Bailey, The Gaunt Brothers, The Harry Hayward Trio, Randal Herley (host).
Producer: James Casey.

LP, Wednesday 23 July 1958, 2030–2130
Blackpool Night
M&W, The Kaye Sisters, Jimmy Clitheroe, Ted Lune, Peter Sinclair, Margo Henderson, The Demijeans, Reginald Dixon, the Littlewood Songsters, the BBC Northern Dance

Orchestra conducted by Alyn Ainsworth, Jack Watson (host).
Producer: John Ammonds.

LP, Wednesday 3 September 1958, 2030–2130
Blackpool Night
M&W, Alma Cogan, George Martin, Russ Conway, Ted Lune, the Maple Leaf Four, Reginald Dixon, the Littlewood Songsters, the BBC Northern Dance Orchestra conducted by Alyn Ainsworth, Jack Watson (host).
Producer: John Ammonds.

LP, Thursday 9 April 1959, 1230–1300
Workers' Playtime from a factory canteen in Stockport
M&W, Sheila Buxton, Denis Goodwin, The Gaunt Brothers, accompanied by The Harry Hayward Trio, Randal Herley (host).
Producer: James Casey.

LP, Monday 23 April 1959, 1230–1300
Workers' Playtime from a VHF Exhibition at Boscombe, Bournemouth
M&W, Marion Keene, Jack Watson, The Terry Sisters, Ron Millington (electric organ), Michael Watson (guitar), Colin Hawke (double bass), Derek Jones (host).
Producer: Brian Patten.

LP, Friday 11 May 1959, 1230–1300
Midday Music Hall
The BBC Northern Dance Orchestra directed by Alyn Ainsworth, M&W, Carlton Crowther, Russ Conway,

Janet Brown, The Four Ramblers, Roger Moffat (host).
Producer: James Casey.

LP, Monday 22 July 1959, 2030–2130
Blackpool Night
Peter Sinclair, Reginald Dixon, Freddie Sales, Marion Ryan, Edmund Hockridge, M&W, The Woodmen directed by Raymond Woodhead, Alyn Ainsworth and the BBC Northern Dance Orchestra, Jack Watson (host).
Producer: Roy Speer.

LP, Monday 10 August 1959, 1230–1300
Midday Music Hall
The BBC Northern Dance Orchestra directed by Alyn Ainsworth, M&W, Russ Conway, Julie Jones, Harry Bailey, The Peter Crawford Trio, Roger Moffat (host).
Producer: Geoff Lawrence.

LP, Monday 12 October 1959, 1230–1300
Midday Music Hall
The BBC Northern Dance Orchestra directed by Alyn Ainsworth, M&W, David Galbraith, Johnny Roadhouse, Sonny Day, Jimmy Leach, Harry Hayward, Roger Moffat (host).
Producer: Geoff Lawrence.

HS, Monday 2 November 1959, 1230–1300
Midday Music Hall
M&W, Sheila Buxton, Reub Silver and Marion Day, The Malcolm Mitchell Trio, Derek Jones (host).
Musical director: Lawrence Adam.
Producer: Brian Patten.

HS, Monday 30 November 1959, 1230–1300
Midday Music Hall
The Coventry Theatre Orchestra conducted by William Pethers, The Four Ramblers, Alan Randall, Bernard Spear, Terry Burton, M&W, Richard Maddock (host).
Producer: James Pestridge.

HS, Saturday 21 December 1959, 1230–1300
Midday Music Hall
BBC Northern Dance Orchestra directed by Alyn Ainsworth, M&W, The Barry Sisters, Jimmy Leach and Harry Hayward, Jimmy Conway, The Gaunt Brothers, Roger Moffat (host).
Producer: Geoff Lawrence.

LP, Thursday 28 January 1960, 1230–1300
Workers' Playtime from a factory canteen in Birkenhead
M&W, Gwen Davies, Jimmy Ryder, The Terry Sisters, The Harry Hayward Trio, Randal Herley (host).
Producer: Geoff Lawrence.

LP, Thursday 7 April 1960, 1230–1300
Workers' Playtime from a heavy chemicals works at Avonmouth
M&W, Janie Marden, Betty Smith, The Avons, Ron Millington (electronic organ), Colin Hawke (double bass), Jack Toogood (guitar), Derek Jones (host).
Producer: Brian Patten.

LP, Monday 21 April 1960, 1230–1300
Workers' Playtime from No. 1

District Police Training Centre, Bruche, Warrington
M&W, Marion Keene, Tom Mennard, The Harry Hayward Trio, Randal Herley (host).
Producer: Geoff Lawrence.

LP, Wednesday 2 May 1960, 1230–1300
Midday Music Hall
Coventry Theatre Orchestra conducted by William Pethers, The Raindrops, Arthur English, Patricia Varley, M&W, Richard Maddock (host).
Producer: James Pestridge.

LP, Wednesday 11 May 1960, 2030–2130
London Lights
John Cameron, Julia Shelley and John Mitchinson, M&W, Stephanie Voss and Jeremy Brett, The Music Masters, Jimmy Thompson, Janet Waters and The Adam Singers, Paul Fenoulhet and the BBC Variety Orchestra.
Writers: Dick Vosburgh, Brad Ashton and Betty Garland.
Producer: Trafford Whitelock.

LP, Thursday 28 July 1960, 1230–1300
Workers' Playtime from the canteen of pharmaceutical and cosmetic laboratories at Eastleigh, Hampshire
M&W, Billie Anthony, Chris Carlsen, The Terry Sisters, Ron Millington (electronic organ), Jack Toogood (guitar), Colin Hawke (bass), Derek Jones (host).
Producer: Brian Patten.

LP, Monday 15 August 1960, 1930–2030
Seaside Night from Weymouth
Cyril Stapleton and his Show Band, Chris Carlsen, The Kingpins, Daisy May with Saveen, Gladys Morgan, Anne Shelton, M&W.
Producer: Eric Miller.

HS, Saturday 10 September 1960, 2000–2100
Holiday Music Hall
John Hauxvell, Vanessa Lee, Léon Goossens, Lance Percival, Joan Turner, M&W, Percy Edwards, Leslie Randall, Joan Reynolds, The Adam Singers directed by Cliff Adams, the BBC Variety Orchestra conducted by Paul Fenoulhet.
Producer: Bill Worsley.

LP, Thursday 6 October 1960, 1230–1300
Workers' Playtime from Nechells Power Station, Birmingham
The Malcolm Mitchell Trio, Yvonne Ash, Rosemary Squires, M&W, Harry Engleman (piano), Sid Gateley (string bass), Bob Mansell (drums).
Producer: James Pestridge.

LP, Thursday 2 March 1961, 1231–1300
Workers' Playtime from Pleck Gas Works, Walsall
M&W, June Marlow, Felix Bowness, The Tracy Sisters, Harry Engleman (piano), Sid Gateley (string bass), Bob Mansell (drums).
Producer: James Pestridge.

LP, Tuesday 21 March 1961, 1231–1300

Workers' Playtime from No.
15 Maintenance Unit RAF at
Wroughton, Wiltshire
M&W, Marion Keene, Douglas
Horner, The Londons, Ron
Millington (electronic organ), Colin
Hawke (double bass), Jack Toogood
(guitar), Derek Jones (host).
Producer: Brian Patten.

LP, Monday 18 September 1961,
2000–2031
Marine Parade
'Stars of show business entertain No.
41 Commando, Royal Marines, at
their Headquarters at Bickleigh,
Devon'
M&W, The Kaye Sisters, Cy Grant,
Betty Smith, Bryan Rodwell (piano),
Jack Toogood (guitar), Ron Bailey
(double bass), Dick Bird (drums),
Derek Jones (host).
Producer: Brian Patten.

LP, Sunday 12 November 1961,
1935–2030
Royal Variety Performance
Shirley Bassey, Jack Benny, George
Burns, Max Bygraves, Maurice
Chevalier, The Crazy Gang,
Sammy Davis Junior, Lionel Blair,
Bruce Forsyth, Arthur Haynes,
The McGuire Sisters, M&W,
Nina and Frederick, The Malcolm
Mitchell Trio, Andy Stewart,
Frankie Vaughan, Kenny Ball and
his Jazzmen, Mr Acker Bilk and
his Paramount Jazz Band, The
Temperance Seven, The Ballet
Trianas, The Baranton Sisters, La
Compagnie des Marottes, Ugo
Garrido, orchestra directed by
Harold Collins, introduced by Brian
Johnston.
Stage direction: Robert Nesbitt
Programme editor: Arthur Phillips.

LP, Sunday 18 August 1963,
1830–1930
Blackpool Night
M&W, Ronnie Hilton, Bill
Waddington, Rawicz and Landauer,
Elizabeth Larner, Tony Melody, The
Four Ramblers, Reginald Dixon,
the BBC Northern Dance Orchestra
conducted by Bernard Herrmann,
Jack Watson (host).
Producer: James Casey.

LP, Sunday 8 September 1963,
1830–1930
Holiday Highlights
Joe Brown and the Bruvvers, the
Peter Crawford Trio, Reginald
Dixon, Ken Dodd, Jimmy Edwards,
Peter Goodwright, Max Jaffa with
Jack Byfield at the piano, M&W,
The Polka Dots, Cliff Richard, The
Shadows, Terry Scott and Hugh
Lloyd, Helen Shapiro with The
Trebletones, The Tornados, Jack
Watson (host).
Producer: John Simmonds.

HS, Wednesday 25 December 1963,
2030–2100
In the Public Ear
Harry Secombe, Eamonn Andrews,
M&W, Tony Hall, the Max Harris
Group, Allan Scott (host).
Producer: John Fawcett Wilson.

LP, Saturday 23 October 1965,
1930–2030
Blackpool Night
M&W, Edmund Hockridge, The
George Mitchell Minstrels featuring
Don Cleaver, Glyn Dawson and
Bob Clayton, Ray Alan with Lord
Charles, Bert Weedon, Reggie
Dennis, The Settlers, Reginald
Dixon, Jack Watson (host), BBC

Northern Dance Orchestra directed by Bernard Herrmann.
Producer: Geoff Lawrence.

HS, Tuesday 29 August 1966, 1220–1255
Desert Island Discs
Roy Plomley (host), M&W.
Records chosen: Count Basie – 'The Kid from Red Bank', Dave Brubeck Quartet – 'Summer Song', Carmen McRae – 'My Future Just Passed', Artie Shaw – 'Begin the Beguine', Beatles – 'Yesterday', Glenn Miller – 'Pennsylvania 6-5000', Jack Jones – 'I Wish You Love', Barbara Ruick – 'Mister Snow'.
Producer: Michael Hall.

LP, Saturday 28 January 1967, 1930–1959
Be Our Guest
'Morecambe and Wise say Be Our Guest for an evening with Ernie at Eric's place.'
Producer: David Allan.

R4, Tuesday 7 May 1968, 1645–1725
Home This Afternoon
'A family magazine introduced by Tim Gudgin, including Eric and Ernie talking to Jeremy Verity.'

R2, Monday 10 March–Friday 14 March 1969, 0900–0955
Family Choice
Ernie Wise introduces your record requests.

R4, Friday 19 September 1969, 2130–2158
What Did You Do in the War, Daddy?
Documentary about the Bevin Boys.
Producer: Richard Kelly.

R4, Sunday 15 November 1970, 1900–1925
Subject for Sunday
M&W talk to John Mountjoy.
Producer: Hubert Hoskins.

R4, Sunday 28 February 1971, 1925–1930
The Week's Good Cause
Eric Morecambe appeals on behalf of the British Heart Foundation.

R2, Wednesday 3 March 1971, 1401–1502
Woman's Hour from the Midlands
Introduced by Maureen Staffer.
Guests of the Week: M&W.

R4, Sunday 20 June 1971, 1925–1930
The Week's Good Cause
Eric Morecambe appeals on behalf of the British Heart Foundation.

R4, Tuesday 31 August 1971, 1930–2015
The Entertainers
Morecambe and Wise: Two of a Kind.
Presented by Frank Dixon.
Producer: Herbert Smith.

R4, Sunday 5 December 1971, 1900–1930
The Best of British Laughs
M&W talk to Barry Took.
Producer: John Browell.

R2, Saturday 25 December 1971, 1402–1440
Morecambe and Wise sing Flanagan and Allen
Eric and Ernie with records.
Producer: Denys Jones.

R2, Saturday 25 December 1971,
1202–1402
Pete's Christmas Stars
'Pete Murray with music and
conversation for your Christmas
lunchtime including Sir Noel
Coward, Petula Clark, Rod Laver,
Robert Morley, André Previn,
Margaret Powell, Kenneth Williams,
Orson Welles, Liberace, Rex
Harrison, Edward G. Robinson,
Debbie Reynolds, M&W.'
Producer: John Billingham.

R4(N), Saturday 18 March 1972,
0820–0845
It's Saturday
Eric interviewed about his days as a
Bevin Boy.
Producer: Barbara McDonald.

R4, Monday 3 April 1972, 1200–
1225
*Eric and Ernie play Morecambe and
Wise*
'A Bank Holiday Roundabout at
33rpm in which they personally
introduce selected grooves from
their BBC record.'
Producer: John Browell.

R2, Friday 21 April 1972, 1130–
1355
The Teddy Johnson Show
Eric and Ernie interviewed.
Producer: Chris Morgan.

R2, Saturday 21 October 1972,
1700–1755
Sports Report
Eric interviewed by Desmond Lynam.
Producer: Bob Burrows.

R4, Thursday 22 February 1973,
0732–0737
Today

Eric interviewed by Alan Parry
about being a director of Luton
Town.
Producer: Bob Burrows.

R2, Friday 4 May 1973,
1902–2000
After Seven
Ray Moore (host), with M&W
interviewed by Duncan Gibbins.
Producer: John Billingham.

R2, Monday 25 June 1973, 0702–
0902
Terry Wogan
Producer: Chris Morgan.

R2, Monday 25 June 1973,
2200-midnight
Late Night Extra
M&W talking about their
autobiography.
Producer: Tony Luke.

R2, Saturday 29 December 1973,
1402–1755
Sport on 2
Luton Town vs Bristol City, with
Eric contributing throughout.
Producer: Bob Burrows.

R2, Saturday 20 April 1974,
1330–1755
Sport on 2
Luton Town vs Millwall, with Eric
contributing throughout.
Producer: Cliff Morgan.

R1, Thursday 18 April 1974,
1730–1745
Newsbeat
M&W interviewed by John Walmsley
about the new *Who's Who*.
Producer: Mike Chaney.

R2, Thursday 2 May 1974,
1405–1435
Sounds Familiar
Ernie Wise, Ray Alan, Ray Fell,
Barry Took (chairman).
Producer: John Cassels.

R4, Wednesday 22 May 1974,
1605–1635
The World of Percy Edwards
Percy Edwards talks to Eric
Morecambe.
Producer: John Fawcett Wilson.

R2, Thursday 4 July 1974,
1405–1435
Sounds Familiar
Janet Brown, John Le Mesurier,
Ernie Wise, Barry Took (chairman).
Producer: John Cassels.

R2, Thursday 4 July 1974,
1405–1435
Sounds Familiar
Diana Dors, Ben Warriss, Ernie Wise,
Barry Took (chairman).
Producer: John Cassels.

R4, Sunday 15 September 1974,
1110–1115
The Week's Good Cause

M&W appeal on behalf of the
Royal Air Forces Association.

R4, Thursday 26 December 1974,
1345–1500
Eric and Ernie's Hall of Fame
Producer: Edward Taylor.

R4, Wednesday 5 February 1975,
1105–1130
Sounds Natural
Eric Morecambe discusses with
Derek Jones his combined

enthusiasm for birdwatching
and fishing.
Producer: John Burton.

R2, Tuesday 1 April 1975,
2102–2202
The Impresarios
Jack Hylton part 1: Michael Craig
with Chappie D'Amato, Arthur
Askey, Ernie Wise.
Writer: Frank Salter.
Producer: David Rayvern Allen.

R2, Tuesday 8 April 1975,
2102–2202
The Impresarios
Jack Hylton part 2: Michael Craig
with Bud Flanagan, Beverly Hylton,
Ernie Wise, Frank Duncan, Fraser
Kerr.
Writer: Frank Salter.
Producer: David Rayvern Allen.

R2, Tuesday 13 May 1975,
2102–2202
The Impresarios
George Black and Sons: Michael
Craig with Arthur Askey, Alfred
Black, Pauline Black, Dan Collins,
Bud Flanagan, Pat Kirkwood, Leslie
Macdonnell, Eric Morecambe,
Ernie Wise, Elsie and Doris Waters.
Written: Frank Salter.
Producer: David Rayvern Allen.

R4, Tuesday 27 May 1975,
1045–1100
Morning Story: Comedian's Choice
Ernie Wise reads 'The First Lesson
and How to be a Neighbour' from
How I Became a Yorkshireman by
Patrick Ryan.
Producer: Herbert Smith.

R2, Thursday 2 October 1975,
1902–1930

Games People Play
Sports quiz: Peter West (chairman),
   Eric Morecambe, Bernard Cribbins,
   Chris Brasher, Barry John.
Producer: Richard Willcox.

R2, Thursday 9 October 1975,
   1902–1930
Games People Play
Sports quiz: Peter West (chairman),
   Eric Morecambe, Bernard Cribbins,
   Chris Brasher, Barry John.
Producer: Richard Willcox.

R4, Sunday 2 November 1975,
   1110–1115
The Week's Good Cause
Ernie Wise appeals on behalf
   of the Parish Church of St
   Mary Magdalene, Ecton,
   Northamptonshire.

R4, Monday 3 November 1975,
   0905–1000
Start the Week
Richard Baker interviews M&W.
Producer: Leslie Robinson.

R4, Friday 26 December 1975,
   1330–1445
Eric and Ernie's Second Hall of Fame
'In which Eric Morecambe and
   Ernie Wise introduce some more
   favourite entertainers of a few years
   ago, including: Sid Field, Flanagan
   And Allen, George Formby, Ronald
   Frankau, Will Fyffe, Tommy
   Handley, Will Hay, Max Miller,
   Gillie Potter, Suzette Tarri, Wheeler
   and Wilson and Robb Wilton and
   reminisce with David Wilmott.'
Producer: Edward Taylor.

R2, Sunday 4 January 1976,
   1530–1602
Be My Guest

'Ernie Wise says Be My Guest
   and invites you to join him as
   he takes time out from writing his
   latest "play" to recall particular
   milestones in his career.'
Producer: John Knight.

R2, Sunday 11 January 1976,
   1530–1602
Be My Guest
'Eric Morecambe says Be My
   Guest and invites you to join him
   as he looks back over 30 years in
   show business.'
Producer: John Knight.

R2, Friday 23 April 1976,
   1902–1930
Funny You Should Ask
Ernie Wise, Diana Dors, Jack
   Douglas, Peter Jones (host).
Questions compiled by Michael
   Pointon.
Producer: Bob Oliver Rogers.

R2, Friday 28 May 1976,
   1902–1930
Funny You Should Ask
Ernie Wise, Diana Dors, Jack
   Douglas, Peter Jones (host).
Questions compiled by Michael
   Pointon.
Producer: Bob Oliver Rogers.

R2, Monday 26 July 1976,
   1902–1930
It's a Funny Business
Mike Craig interviews Eric
   Morecambe.
Producer: Mike Craig.

R2, Saturday 25 December 1976,
   1202–1205
Eric Morecambe and Ernie Wise
   appeal on behalf of the Wireless
   for the Blind Fund.

R2, Monday 14 February–Friday 18
February, 1647–1845
The John Dunn Show
An interview with Eric, extracted
through the week.
Producer: John Meloy.

R2, Tuesday 23 August 1977,
2205–2302
Hubert Gregg
Guests: Leslie Heritage, Pat Keene,
Nigel Lambert, Eric Morecambe.
Producer: David Rayvern Allen.

R2, Tuesday 27 September 1977,
0902–1130
Pete Murray's Open House
Pete Murray (host), M&W.
Producer: Angela Bond

R1, Sunday 4 December and
Saturday 11 December 1977,
0802–0830
Playground
David Rider interviews M&W.
Producer: Don George.

R4, Sunday 1 January 1978,
1100–1130
Local Time
Francis Matthews (host), Eric
Morecambe.
Producer: Jenny De Yong.

R2, Monday 29 May 1978, 1402–
1430
Good Luck, Scotland
'An all-star entertainment as a
prelude to the World Cup. Ernie
Wise and friends introduce Co-
Co, Janet Brown, Michael Hext
(Young Musician of the Year),
Peter Morrison, Tom Conti, Helen
McArthur, Wilfrid Brambell and
Harry H. Corbett as Steptoe and
Son in "Scotch on the Rocks"

written by Ray Galton and Alan
Simpson, The Pipes and Drums of
the Royal Scots Dragoon Guards
and The Max Harris Orchestra.'
Producers: Bobby Jaye/Ian Fenner.

R2, Saturday 21 July–4 August 1979,
1202–1302
Star Choice
Ernie Wise presents his favourite
records.
Producer: Jack Dabbs.

R4, Wednesday 28 November 1979,
1402–1500
Woman's Hour with Sue MacGregor
Guest of the Week: Eric Morecambe.

R4, Wednesday 9 January 1980,
1945–2030
On the Town: in Leeds
Geoffrey Boycott, Lord Boyle,
John Brown, Barney Colehan,
Terry Cryer, Willis Hall, Lord
Harewood, John Harrison, David
Lloyd Jones, Monica Lowden, Jane
Macgill, Francis Matthews, Patrick
Nuttgens, Christine Warner, Fanny
Waterman, Ernie Wise, Judith
Barker, Lolly Cockerell, George
A. Cooper, Petra Davies, Eileen
Derbyshire, Liza Flanagan, Lorraine
Peters, Jake Thackray, Liz Ambler,
Ray Brown, Harry Gration, Peter
Hawkins, Brian Thompson (host).
Producer: David Rayvern Allen.

R4, Monday 31 August 1981,
1402–1500
Woman's Hour with Sue MacGregor
Producer: Wyn Knowles

R2, Tuesday 10 November 1981,
2000–2100
The Crazy Gang Story

Tommy Trinder, M&W, Peter Glaze, Charlie Chester, Richard Murdoch, Hubert Gregg, Leslie Crowther (host).
Producer: Steve Madden.

R2, Saturday 3 April 1982, 2000–2200
Saturday Night is Gala Night
From the Royal Festival Hall: The Festival Dance Orchestra conducted by Bernard Ebbinghouse, Rose Brennan, Leslie Douglas, Billy Munn, Ernie Wise, the Syd Lawrence Orchestra, Eleanor Keenan, Jeff Hooper and The Serenaders, Alan Dell (host).
Producer: Jack Dabbs.

R2, Sunday 23 May 1982, 1402–1730
Sunday Sport on Two Special
Eric talking to George Hamilton about the World Cup.
Producer: Bryan Tremble.

R4, Sunday 13 June 1982, 0850–0855
The Week's Good Cause
Eric Morecambe talks about the work of the Coronary Prevention Group.

R2, 16 September 1982, 2302–0100
Round Midnight
Peter Clayton talks to Eric.
Producer: John Bussell.

R2, Friday 5 November 1982, 1200–1400
Gloria Hunniford
Eric talking about *The Reluctant Vampire*.
Producers: Lawrie Monk, Colin Martin and Phil Hughes.

R2, Sunday 15 January 1984, 1900–1930
Sport and... Humour
Brian Johnston, Eric Morecambe, Michael Bentine, Max Boyce.
Producer: Dave Gordon.

R2, Wednesday 22 January 1984, 2200–2230
Give Us a Conch
'Paddy Feeny chairs a riotous evening of natural history where Eric Morecambe, Pam Ayres, David Bellamy and Sheila Anderson battle for the glittering conch shell.'
Producer: Melinda Barker.

R2, Wednesday 28 March 1984, 2200–2230
Give Us a Conch
Eric Morecambe, Pam Ayres, David Bellamy and Sheila Anderson, Paddy Feeny (host).
Producer: Melinda Barker.

R2, Thursday 31 May 1984, 2200–2230
Castle's Corner
Roy Castle, Eric Morecambe, Charles Collingwood.
Writers: Charlie Adams and Jon Lea.
Producer: Ron McDonnell.

R2, Thursday 26 July 1984, 2200–2230
One of a Kind
'An appreciation of Eric Morecambe OBE, presented by Roy Castle with: Mrs Joan Morecambe, John Ammonds, Eddie Braben, Dickie Davies, Sid Green and Dick Hills, Dickie Henderson, Robert Morley, Harry Secombe, Stan Stennett, Frankie Vaughan and Ernie Wise.'
Producer: Mike Craig.

Television

Starring vehicles

Running Wild

BBC TV, 21 April–30 June 1954
Wednesdays, mostly 2140 – 6x30m.
M&W, Alma Cogan (shows 1–4), Jill
   Day (show 6), Ray Buckingham,
   Hermione Harvey, Four in a Chord.
Producer: Bryan Sears.
Director: Ernest Maxin.

Double Six

BBC TV, 11 August–9 September
   1957
Sundays, mostly 2130 – 5x30m
'A high speed television revue with
   Morecambe and Wise, John Gower,
   Ted Lune, Patricia Bredin, Eileen
   Dyson, The Jack Billings Dancers,
   BBC Northern Dance Orchestra
   conducted by Alyn Ainsworth.'
Producer: Ronnie Taylor.

Two of a Kind (series 1–3) / The Morecambe and Wise Show (series 4–6)

Series 1:

ATV, 18 September–7 December 1961
Thursdays, 2000, 9x30m
Guests: Chris Barber, Janie Marden
   (show 1); The Confederates
   (show 2); Mr Acker Bilk and his
   Paramount Jazz Band (show 3);
   the McGuire Sisters (show 4); the
   Peters Sisters (show 5); Cleo Laine
   (show 6); Gary Miller, Monty
   Sunshine's Jazz Band (show 7);
Micky Ashman's Ragtime Jazz
   Band, Valerie Masters (show 8); the
   Kaye Sisters, Alex Welsh and his
   Band (show 9).
Musical director: Jack Parnell.
Writers: S. C. Green and R. M. Hills.
Producer: Colin Clews.

Series 2:

ATV, 30 June–22 September 1962
Saturdays, mostly 2130, 13x30m
Guests: Terry Lightfoot's Jazzmen,
   The Kaye Sisters (show 1); Kenny
   Ball and his Jazzmen, The Beverley
   Sisters (show 2); Alex Welsh and his
   Band, The Beverley Sisters (show 3);
   The Beverley Sisters, Mr Acker Bilk
   and his Paramount Jazz Band (show
   4); The Mike Cotton Jazzmen,
   Susan Maughan (show 5); Chris
   Barber's Band, Ottilie Patterson,
   The Beverley Sisters (show 6); The
   Clyde Valley Stompers, The Beverley
   Sisters (show 7); Eric Delaney and
   his Band, Teddy Johnson and Pearl
   Carr (show 8); George Chisholm
   and his Jazzers, Teddy Johnson and
   Pearl Carr (show 9); Humphrey
   Lyttelton and his Band, Lita Roza
   (show 10); Alex Welsh and his
   Band, Janie Marden (show 11);
   The Mike Cotton Jazzmen, Teddy
   Johnson and Pearl Carr (show 12);
   Jack Parnell and his Debonaires,
   Teddy Johnson, Pearl Carr (show
   13).
Musical director: Jack Parnell.
Writers: S. C. Green and R. M. Hills.
Producer: Colin Clews.

Series 3:

ATV, 15 June–7 September 1963

Saturdays, 2030 (shows 1 and 2), 2130 (shows 3–13)

Guests: Joe Brown and his Bruvvers, the Mike Sammes Singers (show 1); the Mike Sammes Singers, Mr Acker Bilk and his Paramount Jazz Band (show 2); The King Brothers, Barbara Law, Murray Kash (show 3); Sheila Buxton, the Mike Sammes Singers (show 4); The King Brothers, Janie Marden (show 5); The King Brothers, Susan Maughan (show 6); The King Brothers, Sheila Southern (show 7); Roy Castle (show 8); Shani Wallis, the Mike Sammes Singers (show 9); The King Brothers, Maureen Evans (show 10); The King Brothers, Kathy Kirby (show 11); Eric Delaney and his Band, Lucille Gaye (show 12); The King Brothers, Rosemary Squires (show 13).

Musical director: Jack Parnell.

Writers: S. C. Green and R. M. Hills.

Producer: Colin Clews.

Series 4:

ATV, 4 April–27 June 1964

Saturdays, 2025, 13x35m

Guests: Eddie Calvert and the 'C' Men, The Raindrops (show 1); Janie Marden, Yvonne Antrobus, Kenny Ball (show 2); The Beatles (show 3); Chris Rayburn, The Viscounts, Pearl Lane, Janet Webb (show 4); Jackie Trent, Penny Morrell, Yvonne Antrobus, Freddie Powell, Acker Bilk (show 5); Patsy Ann Noble, The Fraser Hayes Four, Sally Williams, Janet Webb (show 6); Sheila Buxton, Alan Curtis, Yvonne Antrobus, Edmund Hockridge (show 7); The King

Brothers, Freddie Powell, Kathy Kirby, Marilyn Gothard, Janet Webb (show 8); Joe Brown and his Bruvvers, Joy Marshall, Pearl Lane, Jeannette Bradbury (show 9); The Four Macs, Jo Williamson, Dickie Valentine (show 10); Valerie Masters, Gladys Whitehead, Alan Curtis, Jo Williamson, The Bachelors (show 11); Ray Ellington, Barbara Law, Penny Morrell (show 12); Thelma Taylor, The Migil 5, Sandra Boize, Jo Williamson, Sally Douglas, Valerie Van Ost, Christina Wass, Julie Devonshire, Susan Maughan (show 13).

Musical director: Jack Parnell.

Writers: S. C. Green and R. M. Hills.

Producer: Colin Clews.

Series 5:

ATV, 22 January–19 March 1966

Saturdays, 2120, 9x35m

Guests: Lulu, Paul and Barry Ryan (show 1); The Morgan James Duo (show 2); Jackie Trent, The New Faces (show 3); Millicent Martin (show 4); Georgie Fame and the Blue Flames, Julie Rogers (show 5); The Settlers, Barbara Law (show 6); The King Brothers (show 7); Janie Marden, The Shadows (show 8); Herman's Hermits, Teddy Johnson, Pearl Carr, Jackie Poole (show 9).

Musical director: Jack Parnell.

Writers: S. C. Green and R. M. Hills.

Producer: Colin Clews.

Series 6:

ATV, 1 October 1967–31 March 1968

Sundays, various dates and times

Regulars: M&W, Millicent Martin.

Show 1: 1 October 1967, 2025–2125 – Freddie and The Dreamers,

Jimmie Rogers, Kirby's Flying Ballet, The Paddy Stone Dancers, the Mike Sammes Singers [as the Michael Sammes Singers], Jack Parnell and his Orchestra.

Show 2: 22 October 1967, 2025–2125 – The Small Faces, Bobby Rydell, Jill Curzon, Valerie Van Ost, Jenny Lee-Wright, The Paddy Stone Dancers, Jack Parnell and his Orchestra.

Show 3: 12 November 1967, 2025–2125 – The Hollies, Tom Jones, Diana Williams, Eddie Molloy, The Paddy Stone Dancers, the Mike Sammes Singers, Jack Parnell and his Orchestra.

Show 4: 10 December 1967, 2025–2125 – Manfred Mann, George Maharis, Jill Curzon, Margaret Nolan, Freddy Powell, Mike Briton, Diana Williams, Roger Jacombs, The Paddy Stone Dancers, the Mike Sammes Singers, Jack Parnell and his Orchestra.

Show 5: 31 December 1967, 2025–2125 – The New Vaudeville Band, Frankie Avalon, Janet Webb, Diana Williams, Jenny Lee-Wright, Valerie Stanton, Sally Douglas, The Paddy Stone Dancers, the Mike Sammes Singers, Jack Parnell and his Orchestra.

Show 6: 14 January 1968, 2020–2120 – The Moody Blues, Tommy Leonetti, Jenny Lee-Wright, Daphne Odin-Pearse, Jackie Poole, Roger Jacombs, Mike Briton, The Paddy Stone Dancers, the Mike Sammes Singers, Jack Parnell and his Orchestra.

Show 7: 4 February 1968, 2025–2125 – The Tremeloes, Peter Nero, Wanda Ventham, Sheila Bernette, Joe Cusatis, Gene Cherico, Jenny Lee-Wright, The Paddy Stone Dancers, Jack Parnell and his Orchestra.

Show 8: 25 February 1968, 2025–2125 – Eric Burdon and The Animals, Gene Pitney, Gladys Whitred, Dinny Powell, Jenny Lee-Wright, Sally Douglas, Jackie Poole, Jonathan Barrett, The Paddy Stone Dancers, the Mike Sammes Singers, Jack Parnell and his Orchestra.

Show 9: 17 March 1968, 2025–2125 – Georgie Fame and The Fame Group, Bobby Vinton, Diana Williams, Jimmy Lee, Mike Briton, Roger Jacombs, The Paddy Stone Dancers, the Mike Sammes Singers, Jack Parnell and his Orchestra.

Show 10: 31 March 1968, 2025–2125 – The Dave Clark Five, Cliff Richard.

Writers: S. C. Green and R. M. Hills.
Directors: Colin Clews/Philip Casson.
Producer: Colin Clews.
Transmitted in colour in the US as *Piccadilly Palace*.

The Morecambe and Wise Show

Series 1:

BBC2, 2 September–21 October 1968 Mondays, 2050–2120, 8x30m.
Regulars: M&W, Sid Green, Dick Hills.
Guests: Georgia Brown, Los Zafiros, Jenny Lee-Wright, Bettine Le Beau (show 1); Acker Bilk and his Paramount Jazz Band, Roy Budd, Jenny Lee-Wright, Sheila Bernette, Caron Gardner, Bettine Le Beau, Judy Robinson, Tina Martin, Jenny Russell (show 2); Trio Athénée, The Paper Dolls, Jenny Lee-Wright, Ann Hamilton, Jimmy Lee (show 3); Bruce Forsyth, Jenny Lee-Wright,

Kenny Ball and his Jazzmen (show 4); Ronnie Carroll, Kenny Ball and his Jazzmen, Jenny Lee-Wright, Michele Barrie, Jane Bartlett, Wendy Hillhouse, Bebe Robson (show 5); Edmund Hockridge, Jenny Lee-Wright, Kenny Ball and his Jazzmen (show 6); Michael Aspel, Chris Langford, Jenny Lee-Wright, Jimmy Berryman, Lesley Roach, Kenny Ball and his Jazzmen (show 7); Matt Monro, Kenny Ball and his Jazzmen, Jenny Lee-Wright, Sandra Fehr, George Fisher, Jane Bartlett, Thelma Bignall, Linda Hotchkin, Johnny Harris and his Orchestra (show 8).

Musical director: Alyn Ainsworth.
Writers: S. C. Green and R. M. Hills.
Producer: John Ammonds.

Series 2:

BBC2, 27 July–7 September 1969
Sundays, fortnightly, mostly 2215, 4x45m
M&W, Ann Hamilton, Janet Webb with: Peter Cushing, Bobbie Gentry, Kenny Ball and his Jazzmen, Vince Hill, Constance Carling, Diana Powell (show 1); Trio Athénée, Malcolm Roberts, Kenny Ball and his Jazzmen, Janet Webb, Constance Carling, Gilly Fraser (show 2); Juliet Mills, Moira Anderson, The Pattersons, Kenny Ball and his Jazzmen, Lynda Thomas (show 3); Edward Woodward, Kenneth McKellar, The Pattersons, Kenny Ball and his Jazzmen, Peter Cushing, Karen Burch, Rex Rashley, Richard Scott (show 4).

Musical director: Peter Knight.
Writer: Eddie Braben, with additional material by Mike Craig and Lawrie Kinsley on shows 1, 2 and 4.

Producer: John Ammonds.
Christmas special: BBC1, 25 December 1969, 2015–2115
M&W, Fenella Fielding, Frankie Vaughan, Nina, Sacha Distel, The Pattersons, Kenny Ball and his Jazzmen, Alan Curtis, Diane Keen, Rex Rashley.

This show was a combination of specially recorded material and sequences recorded for the show to be transmitted on 11 February 1970, due to Eric missing the second day's recording through 'flu.

Musical director: Peter Knight.
Writer: Eddie Braben.
Producer: John Ammonds.

Series 3:

BBC2, 14 January–22 April 1970
Wednesdays, fortnightly, mostly 2110 – 7x45m
M&W, Ann Hamilton, Janet Webb with: Herman's Hermits, The Pattersons, Kenny Ball and his Jazzmen, Robert Webber, Jenny Lee-Wright (show 1); Ian Carmichael, Kenny Ball and his Jazzmen, Nina, The Pattersons (show 2); Fenella Fielding, Sacha Distel, The Pattersons, Kenny Ball and his Jazzmen, Diane Keen, Alan Curtis (show 3); Diane Cilento, Frank Thornton, Vince Hill, Deryck Guyler, The Pattersons, Kenny Ball and his Jazzmen (show 4); Edward Chapman, Clodagh Rogers, The Pattersons, Kenny Ball and his Jazzmen, Jennifer Flint (show 5); Nina (show 6 – Montreux special); Richard Greene, Nana Mouskouri, The Athenians, The Pattersons, Kenny Ball and his Jazzmen, Rex Rashley (show 7).

Musical director: Peter Knight.

Writer: Eddie Braben, with Sid Green, Dick Hills and Lawrie Kinsley on show 6.
Producer: John Ammonds.

Series 4:
BBC2, 1 July–26 August 1970
Wednesdays, fortnightly, mostly 2110 – 5x45m
M&W, Ann Hamilton, Janet Webb with: Eric Porter, Jan Daley, Trio Athénée, Michael Ward (show 1); Kenneth McKellar, George A. Cooper, Margery Mason, Samantha Jones, Jenny Lee-Wright (show 2); Nina, Craig Douglas, Jenny Lee-Wright, Thelma Bignall, Lillian Padmore, Melita Clarke, Penny Beeching (show 3); Fenella Fielding, Ray Stevens, Sylvia McNeill, Frank Tregear, Leslie Noyes (show 4); Barbara Murray, Dusty Springfield, Michael Redgrave, Robin Day, Flora Robson, Felix Aylmer, Bruce Davis, Peter Davis, Alan Curtis, Penelope Beeching (show 5).
Musical director: Peter Knight.
Writer: Eddie Braben.
Producer: John Ammonds.

Special:
BBC1, Thursday 8 October 1970, 2015–2100
M&W, Ann Hamilton, Janet Webb, Paul Anka, Patricia Lambert, Kenny Ball and his Jazzmen, Gordon Clyde, Brychan Powell.
Musical director: Peter Knight.
Writer: Eddie Braben.
Producer: John Ammonds.
This programme was an all-new one-off to start a repeat run on BBC1.

Christmas special:
BBC1, Friday 25 December 1970, 2015–2115
M&W, Ann Hamilton, Janet Webb, Peter Cushing, William Franklyn, Nina, Eric Porter, Edward Woodward, Kenny Ball and his Jazzmen, Alan Curtis, Rex Rashley, George Day, John Higgins, Clinton Morris.
Musical director: Peter Knight.
Writer: Eddie Braben.
Producer: John Ammonds.

Series 5:
BBC2, 8 April–15 July 1971
Thursdays, fortnightly, 2120 – 7x45m
M&W, Ann Hamilton, Janet Webb with: Flora Robson, Esther Ofarim, Peter & Alex, David March (show 1); Arthur Lowe, Robert Young, Susan Maughan, Rex Rashley, Frank Tregear, Janet Webb, John Le Mesurier, John Laurie, James Beck, Arnold Ridley, Ian Lavender (show 2); Frank Ifield, The Settlers, Richard Caldicot, Michael Ward, Gordon Clyde, Grazina Frame, Brychan Powell (show 3); Jack Jones, Michael Mulcaster, Sheila Southern, Gordon Clyde, Rex Rashley, Grazina Frame, Frank Tregear, Lillian Padmore, Stanley Mason, Arthur Tolcher (show 4); Glenda Jackson, Mary Hopkin, Ronnie Hilton (show 5); Ian Carmichael, Matt Monro, Kiki Dee, Peter & Alex, Charles Rayford, Melanie Fraser (show 6); Trio Athénée, Design, Rex Rashley, Gerald Case (show 7).
Musical director: Peter Knight.
Writer: Eddie Braben.
Producer: John Ammonds.

Series 6:

BBC1, 19 September–31 October 1971

Sundays, 1925, 6x45m

M&W, Ann Hamilton, Janet Webb with: Francis Matthews, Anita Harris, Ann Way, Robert Young, Kenny Ball and his Jazzmen, A. J. Brown, Bert Palmer (show 1); Keith Michell, Design, Kenny Ball and his Jazzmen, Angie Grant (show 2); Cilla Black, Percy Thrower, Ronnie Carroll, Kenny Ball and his Jazzmen (show 3); John Mills, Mrs Mills, Trio Athénée, Kenny Ball and his Jazzmen, Arnold Diamond, Tony Melody (show 4); Nina, The Pattersons, Kenny Ball and his Jazzmen, Frank Tregear, John Scott Martin, Christine Shaw, Jennifer Watts (show 5); Tom Jones, Design, Kenny Ball and his Jazzmen, Gordon Clyde, Rex Rashley (show 6).

Musical director: Peter Knight.

Writer: Eddie Braben.

Producer: John Ammonds.

Christmas special:

BBC1, Saturday 25 December 1971, 2000–2105

M&W, Shirley Bassey, Glenda Jackson, Francis Matthews, André Previn, Los Zafiros, Dick Emery, Frank Bough, Robert Dougall, Cliff Michelmore, Patrick Moore, Michael Parkinson, Eddie Waring, Ann Hamilton, Kenneth Hendel, Rex Rashley, Arthur Tolcher, Ken Alexis, the Mike Sammes Singers.

Musical director: Peter Knight.

Writer: Eddie Braben.

Producer: John Ammonds.

Christmas special:

BBC1, 25 December 1972, 2015–2115

M&W, Glenda Jackson, Jack Jones, Vera Lynn, Pete Murray, Kenny Ball and his Jazzmen, Ann Hamilton, Janet Webb, Ian Carmichael, Fenella Fielding, Bruce Forsyth, Eric Porter, André Previn, Flora Robson, the Mike Sammes Singers.

Musical director: Peter Knight.

Writers: Barry Cryer, John Junkin, Mike Craig, Lawrie Kinsley.

Producer: John Ammonds.

Series 7:

BBC1, 5 January–23 March 1973

Fridays, 2015, 12x45m

M&W with: Cliff Richard, Vikki Carr (show 1); Robert Morley, Vicky Leandros, Reg Lye, New World, Ann Hamilton, Janet Webb (show 2); Lulu, Rostal and Schaefer, Henry Cooper, Percy Edwards, Allan Cuthbertson, Damaris Hayman, Les Rawlings, Johnny Shannon (show 3); Susan Hampshire, Georgie Fame, Alan Price, The Settlers, Ann Hamilton, Janet Webb, Jenny Lee-Wright, Percy Edwards (show 4); Frank Finlay, Wilma Reading, Design, Ann Hamilton, Janet Webb, Maryetta Midgley, Vernon Midgley (show 5); Helen Reddy, Alex Welsh and his Band, Raymond Mason, Allan Cuthbertson, Frank Williams, Michael Brennan, Mike Yarwood, Grazina Frame, Christine Shaw (show 6); Anita Harris, Reg Lye, Anthony Sharp, Ann Hamilton (show 7); Wilma Reading, Springfield Revival, Allan Cuthbertson, Ann Hamilton, Jan Rossini (show 8); Hannah Gordon, Mary Travers, Christopher Neil,

Anthony Sharp, Raymond Mason, Christine Shaw, Hatti Riemer (show 9); Roy Castle, Pete Murray, Anne Murray, The Pattersons, Raymond Mason, Les Rawlings, Johnny Vyvyan, John East, Hugh Elton, Charles Finch, Eric French (show 10); Nana Mouskouri, The Black and White Minstrels, Sooty, George Hamilton IV, Harry Corbett, Grazina Frame, Constance Carling, Johnny Vyvyan (show 11); Peter Cushing, Wilma Reading, Alan Price, Georgie Fame, Ann Hamilton, Bernie Winters (show 12).
Musical director: Peter Knight.
Writers: Eddie Braben, except show 10 – Barry Cryer, Mike Craig and Lawrie Kinsley.
Producer: John Ammonds.

Christmas special:
BBC1, Tuesday 25 December 1973
M&W, Vanessa Redgrave, Hannah Gordon, John Hanson, The New Seekers, Arthur Tolcher, Yehudi Menuhin, Rudolf Nureyev, Laurence Olivier, André Previn.
Musical director: Peter Knight.
Writer: Eddie Braben.
Producer: John Ammonds.

Series 8:
BBC1, 27 September–1 November 1974
Fridays, 2015, 6x45m
M&W, Arthur Tolcher with: André Previn, Magnus Magnusson, Gladys Mills, Wilma Reading (show 1); Ludovic Kennedy, Wilma Reading, Allan Cuthbertson, Gordon Gostelow, Anita Tibbles (show 2); The Syd Lawrence Orchestra, Wilma Reading, Jo Rowbottom, Aimée Delamain, Grazina Frame,

Roy Sampson (show 3); Richard Baker, Wilma Reading, A. J. Brown, Raymond Mason (show 4); Hughie Green, David Dimbleby, Wilma Reading (show 5); June Whitfield, Wilma Reading, John Quayle, Jenny Lee-Wright (show 6).
Musical director: Peter Knight.
Writer: Eddie Braben.
Producer: John Ammonds.

Christmas special:
BBC1, Friday 25 December 1975, 1940–2045
M&W, Diana Rigg, Des O'Connor, Gordon Jackson, Robin Day, Diane Solomon, Brenda Arnau,
Musical director: Peter Knight.
Writer: Eddie Braben.
Producer: Ernest Maxin.

Series 9:
BBC1, 7 January–19 April 1976
Wednesdays, 2015, 6x45m
M&W with: Gilbert O'Sullivan, Dilys Watling, The Vernons, Peter O'Sullevan, Arthur Tolcher, Eve Blanchard (show 1); Michele Dotrice, Frankie Vaughan, Patrick Moore, Tammy Jones (show 2); Lena Zavaroni, The Spinners, Allan Cuthbertson, Ann Hamilton (show 3); Jackie Darnell, Allan Cuthbertson, Anthony Sharp, Kenny Ball and his Jazzmen, Ann Hamilton (show 4); The Karlins, Vincent Zara, Ann Hamilton (show 5); Diane Solomon, Champagne, Maggie Fitzgibbon, Jenny Lee-Wright (show 6).
Musical director: Peter Knight.
Writer: Eddie Braben.
Producer: Ernest Maxin.

Christmas special:

BBC1, Saturday 25 December 1976, 1945–2045

M&W, Elton John, Des O'Connor, John Thaw, Dennis Waterman, Angela Rippon, Kate O'Mara, Marian Montgomery, The Nolans, Gertan Klauber, Arthur Tolcher.

Musical director: Peter Knight.

Writers: Barry Cryer, Mike Craig, Lawrie Kinsley and Ron McDonnell.

Producer: Ernest Maxin.

Christmas special:

BBC1, Sunday 25 December 1977, 2055–2200

M&W, Penelope Keith, Elton John, Angharad Rees, Francis Matthews, Arthur Lowe, John Le Mesurier, John Laurie, Richard Briers, Paul Eddington, James Hunt, Stella Starr, Michael Parkinson, Angela Rippon, Michael Aspel, Richard Baker, Frank Bough, Philip Jenkinson, Kenneth Kendall, Barry Norman, Eddie Waring, Richard Whitmore, Peter Woods, Sandra Dainty, Jenny Lee-Wright, Valerie Leon, the Mike Sammes Singers.

Musical director: Peter Knight.

Writer: Eddie Braben.

Producer: Ernest Maxin.

It's Childsplay

BBC1, 30 July–3 September 1976

Fridays, mostly 1850, 6x30m

M&W with: Jean Anderson, Alfie Bass, Ralph Bates, Joan Benham, Rudolph Walker, Edward Hardwicke, Jon Laurimore, Gillian Phelps (show 1); Arthur Lowe, Suzanne Neve, Hilary Tindall, Michael Bevis, Roger Bizley,

Tony Cundell, Bill Pearson (show 2); Sinéad Cusack, Ian Ogilvy, Jill Townsend, Simon Williams, Darien Angadi, Roger Bizley, Ray Callaghan, Susan Field, Patrick Jordan, George Little, Keith Marsh, Norman Mitchell, Conrad Phillips, Joe Ritchie, Jo Rowbottom, Richard Shaw (show 3); Michael Aldridge, Blake Butler, Peter Jones, Penelope Keith, Bert Palmer, Peter Sallis, Zena Walker, Edward Burnham, Jane Cussons, Alison Glennie, Roy Holder, Donald Morle (show 4); Christopher Cazenove, Beryl Cooke, Glynn Edwards, Clifford Evans, Carmel McSharry, Richard Morant, Angharad Rees, Helen Shingler, Joshua Le-Touzel (show 5); Keith Barron, Dora Bryan, Michael Gough, Norma West, David King, Colette O'Neil (show 6).

Directors: Brian Penders (shows 1, 2 and 4)/Colin Strong (shows 3, 5 and 6).

Producer: Johnny Downes.

The Morecambe and Wise Show

Special:

Thames, Wednesday 18 October 1978, 2000–2130

M&W, Donald Sinden, Judi Dench, Frank Coda, Leonard Sachs, Peter Cushing, Ann Hamilton, Kenneth Watson, Jeffrey Gardiner, Yvonne Costello, Cherida Langford, Rodney Myers, Mike Potter, Davey Tons, John Lilleywhite, John Little, Daniel Rolnick, Kim Butler, Amanda Mealing, Jenny Westbrook, Derek Griffiths.

Musical director: Peter Knight.

Writers: Barry Cryer and John Junkin.
Producer: Keith Beckett.

Christmas special:

The Morecambe and Wise Christmas Show
Thames, Monday 25 December 1978, 2100–2215
M&W, Leonard Rossiter, Nicholas Parsons, Frank Finlay, Harold Wilson [as Sir Harold Wilson], Anna Dawson, Jenny Hanley, Jan Hunt, Frank Coda, Syd Lawrence and his Orchestra, Jillianne Foot, Denise Gyngell, Yvonne Dearman, Italia Conti Stage School, the Mike Sammes Singers, Eamonn Andrews.
Musical director: Peter Knight.
Writers: Barry Cryer and John Junkin.
Producer: Keith Beckett.

Christmas special:

Christmas with Eric and Ernie
Thames, Tuesday 25 December 1979, 2045–2145
M&W, David Frost, Glenda Jackson, Des O'Connor, Arthur Tolcher, Janet Webb.
Musical director: Peter Knight.
Script associate: Neil Shand.
Directors: John Ammonds/Keith Beckett.
Producer: John Ammonds.

Series 1:

Thames, 3 September–8 October 1980
Wednesdays, 2000, 6x30m
M&W with: Terry Wogan, Ann Hamilton (show 1); Hannah Gordon, Hugh Paddick, Frank Coda (show 2); Dave Prowse, Anthony Chinn, Raymond Mason, Fiesta Mei Ling (show 3); Deryck Guyler,

Gerald Case (show 4); Suzanne Danielle, Tessa Wyatt, Valerie Minifie (show 5); Gemma Craven (show 6).
Musical director: Peter Knight.
Writer: Eddie Braben.
Producer: John Ammonds.

Christmas special:

The Morecambe and Wise Christmas Show
Thames, Wednesday 25 December 1980, 2030–2130
M&W, Peter Barkworth, Peter Cushing, Jill Gascoine, Sir Alec Guinness, Peter Vaughan, Gemma Craven, Hannah Gordon, Glenda Jackson, Mick McManus.
Musical director: Peter Knight.
Writer: Eddie Braben.
Producer: John Ammonds.

Series 2:

Thames, 1 September–13 October 1981
Tuesdays, 2000, 7x30m
M&W with: Gemma Craven, Kate Lock, Kay Korda (show 1); Richard Vernon, Max Bygraves (show 2); Diane Keen (show 3); George Chisholm, Hannah Gordon, Richard Vernon, Frank Coda (show 4); Peter Bowles, Suzanne Danielle, Faith Brown, April Walker (show 5); Robert Hardy, Ian Ogilvy, Kay Korda (show 6); Joanna Lumley, Richard Vernon, Frank Coda (show 7).
Musical director: Peter Knight.
Writer: Eddie Braben.
Producer: John Ammonds.

Christmas special:

The Morecambe and Wise Christmas Show

Thames, Wednesday 23 December 1981, 2000–2100

M&W, Ralph Richardson, Robert Hardy, Suzannah York, Ian Ogilvy, Alvin Stardust, Suzanne Danielle, Steve Davis, Valerie Minifie.

Musical director: Peter Knight.

Writer: Eddie Braben.

Producer: John Ammonds.

Series 3:

Thames, 27 October–8 December 1982

Wednesdays, 2030, 7x30m

M&W with: Richard Briers, Diana Dors, Bonnie Langford, Peter Salmon (show 1); Trevor Eve, Wayne Sleep, Jimmy Young, Penny Meredith (show 2); Roy Castle, Peter Salmon (show 3); Colin Welland, Isla St. Clair, Penny Meredith (show 4); Patricia Brake, Royce Mills (show 5); Alan Dobie, Marian Montgomery, Una Stubbs, Kay Korda, Penny Meredith (show 6); Nigel Hawthorne, Patricia Brake (show 7).

Musical directors: Peter Knight and Don Hunt.

Writer: Eddie Braben.

Producer: John Ammonds.

Christmas special:

The Morecambe and Wise Christmas Show

Thames, Monday 27 December 1982, 2100–2200

M&W, Robert Hardy, Rula Lenska, Richard Vernon, Diana Dors, Denis Healey, Glenda Jackson, Jimmy Young, Wall Street Crash, André Previn.

Musical director: Peter Knight.

Writer: Eddie Braben.

Producer: John Ammonds.

Series 4:

Thames, 7 September–19 October 1983

Wednesdays, 2000, 7x30m

M&W with: Margaret Courtenay, Anna Dawson, Maggie Moone, Jenny Lee-Wright, Patricia Samuels (show 1); David Kernan, Jenny Lee-Wright, Valerie Minifie (show 2); Cherry Gillespie, Anita Graham, Penny Meredith, Jean Reeve, Valerie Minifie (show 3); Stutz Bear Cats, Denise Kelly, David Hamilton, Jenny Lee-Wright, Marie-Elise, Jean Reeve, Peter Finn (show 4); Cherry Gillespie, Anita Graham, Jenny Meredith (show 5); Margaret Courtenay, Stutz Bear Cats, Peter & Jackie Firmani (show 6); Harry Fowler, Peter Finn, Valerie Minifie (show 7).

Musical directors: Harry Rabinowitz and Don Hunt.

Writer: Eddie Braben.

Producer: Mark Stuart.

Christmas special:

The Morecambe and Wise Christmas Show

Thames, Tuesday 26 December 1983, 2045–2145

M&W, Gemma Craven, Nigel Hawthorne, Derek Jacobi, Felicity Kendal, Burt Kwouk, Patrick Mower, Nanette Newman, Peter Skellern, Tony Monopoly, Fulton Mackay, Jennie Linden.

Musical director: Harry Rabinowitz.

Writers: Eddie Braben, with Sid Green and Dick Hills.

Producer: Mark Stuart.

Special: Eric and Ernie's Variety Days

Thames, Wednesday 2 March 1983, 2000–2100
Michael Aspel, M&W.
Producer: David Clark.

Thames, Thursday 3 January 1985, 2030–2200
Night Train to Murder
M&W, Fulton Mackay, Lysette Anthony, Kenneth Haigh, Pamela Salem, Margaret Courtenay, Richard Vernon, Edward Judd, Roger Brierley, Penny Meredith.
Writers: Eric Morecambe, Ernie Wise and Joe McGrath.
Director/Producer: Joe McGrath.

Guest appearances and spots

BBC TV, Tuesday 27 June 1939, 2100–2130
Jack Hylton and his Band
Jack Hylton, Bruce Trent, June Malo, Peggy Dell, Ernie Wise, Maureen Potter, Maureen Flanagan, Freddie Schweitzer, Primrose, Doreen Stephens.

BBC TV, Friday 28 September 1951, 2015–2045
George Elrick's Parade of Youth
M&W, Maurice French and Joy, Christine Taylor, The Four in Accord, Rita Martell, Ron Parry, June Birch, Rita Frith and the Youth Paraders.
Musical director: George Clouston.
Producer: Bryan Sears.

BBC TV, Friday 28 August 1953, 2110–2210
Stars at Blackpool

Reginald Dixon, The Three Monarchs, M&W, Winifred Atwell, Nat Jackley, Eve Boswell, Albert Modley, introduced by Marianne Lincoln, the Northern Variety Orchestra conducted by Alyn Ainsworth.
Director: Derek Burrell-Davis.
Producer: Barney Colehan.

BBC TV, Saturday 24 October 1953, 2120–2220
Variety Parade
Max Bygraves, Eve Boswell, Gladys Morgan with Frank Laurie and Joan Laurie and Bert Hollman, Ivor Moreton and Dave Kaye, M&W, Brian Andro, Ernest Maxin, The Tiller Girls, The George Mitchell Glee Club.
Musical director: Eric Robinson.
Producer: Bill Lyon-Shaw.

BBC TV, Saturday 12 December 1953, 2130–2240
Face the Music
Henry Hall, Elsie and Doris Waters, Turner Layton, Belita, Sally Barnes, Carole Carr, Stanelli, M&W, Marcel Cornelis, Sid Phillips, Peter Glover, Bobby Beaumont, Raymond Holder, The Peter Knight Quintet.
Musical director: Eric Robinson.
Producer: Graeme Muir.

BBC TV, Wednesday 23 December 1953, 2140–2240
Pantomime Party from the Mecca Locarno ballroom, Leeds
Stan Stennett, M&W, Freddie Sales, June Bishop, Mary Millar, Ken Roberts, Phyllis Holden, the Zio Angels, Josef Locke, and 'international ballroom dancers' Syd Perkin and Edna Duffield, George Begley and Madge Larney,

Frank Gibson and Joan Finnigan,
Marianne Lincoln (host), Northern
Variety Orchestra conducted by
Alyn Ainsworth.
Producers: Derek Burrell-Davis and
Barney Colehan.

BBC TV, Thursday 23 May 1955,
2215–2245
Let's Have Fun
Jimmy Clitheroe, Joy Harris,
The Kordites, Ken Dodd, Kenny
Baker, M&W, Peter Webster.
Producer: Barney Colehan.

ATV, Sunday 27 November 1955,
2000–2100
*Sunday Night at the London
Palladium*
Arthur Worsley, Elizabeth Seal,
M&W, David Whitfield, The
London Palladium Girls, The
London Palladium Orchestra,
Tommy Trinder (host).
Producer: Bill Lyon-Shaw.

ATV, Sunday 5 February 1956,
2000–2100
*Sunday Night at the London
Palladium*
Joan Regan, Derek Roy, M&W,
The Ganjou Brothers and Juanita,
The Maruthins, The London
Palladium Girls, The London
Palladium Orchestra, Tommy
Trinder (host).
Producer: Bill Lyon-Shaw.

ATV, 21 April–23 June 1956
The Winifred Atwell Show
Saturdays, 2015 – 10x45m
M&W, Teddy Johnson and Pearl
Carr, Jennifer Jayne, The George
Carden Dancers, Winifred Atwell
(host).

Writers: Johnny Speight, John Law
and Bill Craig.
Producers: Dicky Leeman, except Bill
Lyon-Shaw on show 1.

BBC TV, Sunday 1 July 1956,
1945–2115
Variety Cavalcade
Eddie Arnold, Max Bacon, Harold
Berens, Peter Brough, Harry
Brunning, George Buck, Billy
Burden, Peter Cavanagh, Jack Daley,
Billy Danvers, George Doonan,
Jimmy Edwards, G. H. Elliott,
George Elrick, Arthur English,
Cyril Fletcher, Terry Hall, Herschel
Henlere, Bobby Howes, Jewel and
Warriss, Hetty King, Lee Lawrence,
M&W, Joy Nichols, Dave and Joe
O'Gormon, Bob and Alf Pearson,
Wilfred Pickles, Brian Reece, Eddie
Reindeer, Ethel Revnell, Clarkson
Rose, Anne Shelton, Randolph
Sutton, Elsie and Doris Waters,
Albert Whelan, Robb Wilton.
Musical director: Arthur Wilkinson.
Producer: Graeme Muir.

BBC TV, Sunday 21 October 1956,
1400–1430
Let's Make a Date
Brian Reece (host), Janie Marden,
M&W (appearing in the 'Better
Half' segment, in which comedians'
wives talked about their husbands).
Producer: Barney Colehan

BBC TV, Wednesday 28 November
1956, 2045–2130
Vic Oliver Presents
Vic Oliver (host), Robert Beatty,
M&W, Pearl Carr and Teddy
Johnson, Hall, Norman and Ladd,
Kazuko Yamaguchi.
Producer: Graeme Muir.

BBC TV, Monday 3 June 1957,
2030–2100
*Blackpool Show Parade presents Let's
Have Fun*
M&W, Joan Turner, Kenny Baker,
Denis Spicer, Maureen Rose, The
Three Belles and The Orchid Room
Lovelies.
Producer: Barney Colehan.

BBC TV, Monday 23 September
1957, 2115–2200
Stars at Blackpool from the Spanish
Hall at the Winter Gardens
Brian Reece (host), The Three Deuces,
Kenny Baker, The Boliana Ivanko
Quartet, Karen Greer, M&W, The
Tanner Sisters, Anne Shelton, Ken
Dodd, the BBC Northern Dance
Orchestra conducted by Alyn
Ainsworth.
Producer: Barney Colehan.

ATV, Saturday 2 November 1957,
2030–2130
*Bernard Delfont presents the David
Whitfield Show*
David Whitfield, Charlie Cairoli and
Paul, M&W, Margo Henderson,
Jack Parnell and his Orchestra.
Producer: Albert Locke.

BBC TV, Thursday 1 May 1958,
2220–2300
The Good Old Days
Norman and Niki Grant, Professor
Alex Matison, Roger Carne
with Willie Heckle, Sally Barnes,
Raymond Bennett, M&W, Leonard
Sachs (chairman).
Musical director: Alyn Ainsworth.
Producer: Barney Colehan.

BBC TV, Tuesday 15 July 1958,
1930–2000
Wish You Were Here

'At Morecambe and Heysham to
meet Morecambe and Wise, to
look into the Central Pier Pavilion
to see an extract from "Starlights"
and to join Geoffrey Wheeler
and holidaymakers at the Super
Swimming Stadium to see part of
the "Aqua Cascades". With Jimmy
Leach and his Organolian Quartet.
Introduced by Peter West in the
Central Pier Ballroom.'
Producer: Ray Lakeland.

BBC TV, Tuesday 22 July 1958,
1930–2000
Northern Lights
'Jack Watson introduces you to some
of the stars visiting the Northern
holiday resorts.' M&W, Lonnie
Donegan, Chic Murray and Maidie,
The Diamond Twins, The Three
Quarters, the BBC Northern Dance
Orchestra conducted by Alyn
Ainsworth.
Producer: Barney Colehan.

ATV, Sunday 15 March 1959,
2000–2100
*Sunday Night at the London
Palladium*
M&W, Johnnie Ray, Arlene Fontana,
The London Palladium Boys and
Girls.
Producer: Albert Locke.

ATV, Saturday 4 April 1959,
1955–2055
The Bob Monkhouse Hour
Bob Monkhouse, Denis Goodwin,
M&W, The Pamela Devis Dancers,
Jack Parnell and his Orchestra.
Producer: Alan Tarrant.

BBC TV, Friday 3 July 1959,
2000–2035
Blackpool Show Parade

M&W, Jimmy James and Company, Vendryes, the Trio Vedette, David Galbraith, the Zio Angels.
Producer: Barney Colehan.

ATV, Saturday 26 December 1959, 1930–2025
This Particular Show
Tommy Steele, The Malcolm Clare Dancers, M&W, Jack Parnell and his Orchestra.
Producer: Alan Tarrant.

BBC TV, Saturday 26 December 1959, 2245–2345
The Good Old Days
M&W, Betty Jumel, Cardew Robinson, Noberti, Smoothey and Layton, The Manton Brothers, Patricia Bredin, Leonard Sachs (chairman).
Musical director: Alyn Ainsworth.
Producer: Barney Colehan.

BBC TV, Thursday 3 March 1960, 1820–1845
Little Miss Music
'Sheila Buxton in an informal programme of melody, with Alyn Ainsworth and the BBC Northern Dance Orchestra, and guest artists, Morecambe and Wise.'
Producer: Barney Colehan.

ATV, Thursday 24 March 1960, 2135–2230
Val Parnell's Star Time
Dickie Valentine, The Dallas Boys, M&W, Jack Parnell and his Orchestra, Alma Cogan (host).
Producer: Stephen Wade.

ATV, Sunday 3 April 1960, 2000–2100
Bernard Delfont's Sunday Show

Yma Sumac, John Hanson, The King Brothers, M&W, Des O'Connor, Dennis Spicer, Molly Picon, The Tiller Girls, Harold Collins and his Orchestra, Robert Morley (host).
Producer: Albert Locke.

ATV, Saturday 14 May 1960, 2000–2055
Val Parnell's Saturday Spectacular
Dickie Valentine, Arthur Haynes, Dolores Hawkins, M&W, Jack Parnell and his Orchestra, The George Carden Dancers.
Writers: Dick Hills/Sid Green.
Producer: Josephine Douglas.

ATV, Sunday 29 May 1960, 2000–2100
Bernard Delfont's Sunday Show
Leo de Lyon, M&W, Anne Shelton, Daniel Massey, Dilys Laye, Diana Coupland, Meier Tzelniker, Wally Patch, Victor Spinetti, Sheila Hancock, Martin Lawrence, The Tiller Girls, Harold Collins and his Orchestra.
Producer: Alan Tarrant.

ATV, Saturday 9 July 1960, 1955–2055
The Rise Stevens Show
Rise Stevens, Russ Conway, Roy Castle, Ivor Emmanuel, M&W, The George Carden Dancers, The Michael John Singers, Jack Parnell and his Orchestra.
Producer: Josephine Douglas.

ATV, Saturday 6 August 1960, 1955–2055
Val Parnell's Saturday Spectacular
Alma Cogan, The Everly Brothers, Gary Miller, M&W, Margo Henderson, Graham Stark, Peter Noble, The Tommy Linden Dancers,

The Barney Gilbraith Singers,
The Jack Parnell Orchestra.
Producer: Dicky Leeman.

ATV, Saturday 1 October 1960,
1930–2030
Val Parnell's Saturday Spectacular
Paul Robeson, Patrice Munsel, Emile
Ford, M&W, Jack Parnell and his
Orchestra
Producer: Francis Essex.

ATV, Sunday 23 October 1960,
2000–2100
*Sunday Night at the London
Palladium*
Connie Francis, Beryl Grey, M&W,
Ugo Garrido, The London
Palladium Girls and Boys, Don
Arrol (host).
Producer: Albert Locke.

ATV, Sunday 13 November 1960,
2000–2100
*Sunday Night at the London
Palladium*
M&W, Ravic and Babs, The Tiller
Girls, Don Arrol (host).
Producer: Albert Locke.

ATV, Sunday 1 January 1961,
2000–2100
*Sunday Night at the London
Palladium*
The Andrews Sisters, M&W, The
London Palladium Girls and Boys,
Don Arrol (host).
Producer: Albert Locke.

ATV (Midlands only), Friday 17
February 1961, 2315–0000
ATV's Fifth Anniversary Show
Jerry Allen, Pat Astley, Alfie Bass, Bill
Fraser, Patricia Cox, Susan Denny,
Leslie Dunn, Roy Edwards, Alan
Grahame, Ken Ingarfield, Jimmy

Jewel and Ben Warriss, M&W,
Jean Morton, Eula Parker, The
Ponytones, Evadne Price, Peter
Regan, Beryl Reid, Lionel Rubin,
The George Carden Dancers, Jerry
Allen's Anniversary Orchestra.
Producer: Reg Watson.

ATV, Saturday 18 February 1961,
1940–2030
Val Parnell's Saturday Spectacular
Lonnie Donegan, Ruby Murray,
M&W, Miki and Griff, The
Malcolm Goddard Dancers, Jack
Parnell and his Orchestra.
Producer: Dicky Leeman.

ATV, Saturday 1 April 1961,
1940–2030
The Russ Conway Show
Dave King, M&W, Janie Marden, The
Patton Brothers, Danny Williams,
Joe Mudele, Bobbie Kevin, Ernie
Shears, Jack Parnell and his
Orchestra, Russ Conway (host).
Producer: Francis Essex.

ATV, Sunday 12 November 1961,
1930–2225
Royal Variety Performance
Shirley Bassey, Jack Benny, George
Burns, Max Bygraves, Maurice
Chevalier, The Crazy Gang,
Sammy Davis Junior, Lionel Blair,
Bruce Forsyth, Arthur Haynes,
The McGuire Sisters, M&W,
Nina and Frederick, The Malcolm
Mitchell Trio, Andy Stewart,
Frankie Vaughan, Kenny Ball and
his Jazzmen, Mr Acker Bilk and
his Paramount Jazz Band, The
Temperance Seven, The Ballet
Trianas, The Baranton Sisters, La
Compagnie des Marottes, Ugo
Garrido, orchestra directed by
Harold Collins.

Stage direction: Robert Nesbitt
Television director: Bill Ward.

ATV, Sunday 18 August 1963,
2025–2125
Summer Spectacular
Jo Stafford, Robert Morley, Stanley
Holloway, M&W, The Dior
Dancers, The Polka Dots, Larry
Taylor Jr., Terry Brewer, The Road
Stars, The John Tiller Girls, The
Lionel Blair Dancers, Jack Parnell
and his Orchestra.
Writers: Dick Hills/Sid Green.
Producer: Bill Ward.

ATV, Sunday 24 November 1963,
2025–2125
*Sunday Night at the London
Palladium*
M&W, Nina and Frederick, The
Square Pegs, Jack Parnell and
his Orchestra, Bruce Forsyth
(host).
Producer: Jon Scoffield.

ATV, Sunday 4 October 1964,
2025–2125
*Sunday Night at the London
Palladium*
M&W, Millicent Martin, The King
Brothers, The Wychwoods, The
London Palladium Girls and Boys,
Norman Vaughan (host).
Producer: Colin Clews.

BBC1, Saturday 8 November 1964,
1950–2230
Royal Variety Performance
The Bachelors, Cilla Black, Tommy
Cooper, Gil Dova, Gracie Fields,
Lena Horne, David Jacobs, Kathy
Kirby, Brenda Lee, Millicent Martin,
The Moiseyev Dance Company,
M&W, Bob Newhart, Ralph Reader
and the Gang Show, Cliff Richard,

The Shadows, Dennis Spicer, Jimmy
Tarbuck, The Tiller Girls, orchestra
conducted by Eric Tann.
Producer: Duncan Wood.

BBC1, Tuesday 28 November 1964,
1715–1740
Juke Box Jury
Lulu, Jean Metcalfe, M&W, David
Jacobs (host).
Producer: Neville Wortman.

BBC1, Tuesday 9 March 1965,
2300–2325
Variety Club Awards
Kenneth Rive (Chief Barker), M&W,
Richard Attenborough, Rita
Tushingham, Millicent Martin,
Laurence Olivier, Peggy Ashcroft,
Jimmy Tarbuck, Jack De Manio,
Eric Sykes, Bernard Braden, Bernard
Delfont (presenter).
Producer: Ray Colley.

ATV, Sunday 21 March 1965,
2100–2155
*Sunday Night at the London
Palladium*
M&W, The Supremes, Potassy, The
Tiller Girls, Norman Vaughan
(host).
Producer: Colin Clews.

BBC1 Midlands, Monday 30 May
1966, 1805–1826
Midlands Today

ATV, Sunday 2 October 1966,
2025–2125
The London Palladium Show
Kate Smith, M&W, Tom Jones, Bob
Monkhouse, Millicent Martin, The
Clark Brothers, Jimmy Tarbuck
(host).
This programme was recorded in
monochrome and colour.

Directors: Albert Locke (colour)/
Colin Clews (monochrome).
Producer: Bill Ward.

BBC1, Sunday 20 November 1966,
1925–2250
Royal Variety Performance
Des O'Connor (host), The Bachelors,
Bal Caron Trio, the England football
team, Sammy Davis Junior, Jack
Douglas, Hugh Forgie, Christopher
Gable, Nadia Nerina, Juliette Greco,
Frankie Howerd, Kenneth McKellar,
Henry Mancini, Marvo and Dolores
(bearing a remarkable resemblance
to M&W), Matt Monro, the Pietro
Brothers, Gene Pitney, the Seekers,
Tommy Steele.
Producer: Bill Cotton Jr.

BBC2, Sunday 20 November 1966,
2300–2345
Late Night Line Up
Eric and Ernie interviewed by
Michael Dean.

ATV, Sunday 27 November 1966,
2025–2125
The New London Palladium Show
Roger Moore, M&W, The Bachelors,
Joe Brown, Millicent Martin,
Arno and Rita Van Boden, Jimmy
Tarbuck (host).
This programme was recorded in
monochrome and colour.
Directors: Albert Locke
(monochrome)/Colin Clews
(colour).
Producer: Bill Ward.

ABC/ATV co-production, Sunday 4
December 1966, 2035–2310
A Royal Gala
Peter Adamson, Dave Allen, Michael
Bentine, The Beverley Sisters,
Margot Bryant, John Carlisle, Violet

Carson, The Dave Clark Five, Peter
Cook and Dudley Moore, Kenneth
Cope, Ian Cullen, Robert Dorning,
Pamela Duncan, Maurice Durant,
Sonia Fox, Anita Harris, Hughie
Green, Frank Ifield, Rosemary
Leach, Anne Lloyd, Jimmy Logan,
Arthur Lowe, Philip Lowrie,
William Mervyn, Una McLean,
Cathy McGowan, Michael Miles,
Bob Monkhouse, M&W, Barbara
Murray, Pete Murray, David Nixon,
Alfred Ravel, Patricia Phoenix, Cliff
Richard, Edith Savile, Monica Rose,
Sandie Shaw, The Shadows, Jackie
Trent, Frankie Vaughan and The V
Group, The Walker Brothers, Jack
Watling, William Wilde, Patrick
Wymark, The Tiller Girls, The
London Palladium Boys and Girls,
Bel Canto Singers, Pipes & Drums of
1st Battalion of Kings Own Scottish
Borderers, The London Palladium
Orchestra, Eric Tann, Jack Parnell,
Bob Sharples, Eamonn Andrews
(host), David Frost (host), Bernard
Braden (host), Ted Rogers (host).
Musical director: Eric Tann.
Writers: Harry Driver, Vince Powell,
Sid Green, Dick Hills, Maurice
Wiltshire and Eric Merriman.
Director: Colin Clews.
Producer: Albert Locke.

TWW, Sunday 3 March 1968,
2235–2335
All Good Things
The final programme from the ITV
company Television West and Wales,
featuring an encounter between
Eric, Ernie, Bryan Michie – TWW's
programme controller – and host
Bernard Braden.
Bernard Braden, M&W, Ivor
Emmanuel, Clifford Evans, Anita
Harris, Manfred Mann, Stan

Stennett, Lord Derby, Tommy Trinder, Clifford Morgan, Bryan Michie, Osian Ellis, Pendyrus Male Voice Choir, Tessie O'Shea, Stanley Unwin, Billy Burdon, Howard Winston, Danny Blanchflower, the Mike Sammes Singers, Dick Vosburgh, Bob Miller and The Millermen.
Director: John Scriminger.
Producer: Peter Dulay.

BBC1, Wednesday 20 November 1968, 1800–1840
The Wednesday Show with David Jacobs
David Jacobs (host), M&W, Des O'Connor, Lynda Baron, Deena Webster, orchestra conducted by Ken Jones.
Director: James Moir
Producer: Stewart Morris.

BBC Midlands, Tuesday 17 December 1968, 1800–1824
Midlands Today
Interview with Ernie about what he's doing while Eric is ill.

BBC1, Wednesday 25 December 1968, 1840–2045
Christmas Night with the Stars
Louis Armstrong, Nana Mouskouri, Petula Clark, Rolf Harris, Jimmy Logan, Lulu, Kenneth McKellar, Cliff Richard, The Seekers, The Young Generation, M&W (hosts).
Musical director: Alyn Ainsworth.
Writers: Dick Hills/Sid Green.
Producer: Stewart Morris.

BBC2, Tuesday 31 December 1968, 2300–2400
Pick of the Year – Line Up
Ernie introduces an extract from a programme of his choice.

BBC2, Saturday 7 June 1969, 2015–2100
One Pair of Eyes: No, But Seriously
Marty Feldman talks to Peter Sellers, Sandy Powell, Eric Morecambe, Peter Brough and Archie Andrews, Dudley Moore, Annie Ross and Jon Hendricks, Johnny Speight, Denis Norden and Barry Took.
Producer: Francis Megahy.

LWT, Sunday 8 March 1970, 2225–2330
British Academy Film Awards: Frost at the Palladium
Petula Clark, Josephine Tewson, Rod McKuen, Eric Morecambe, Frank Owens, Ernie Wise, Christopher Morahan, Verity Lambert, Paul Watson, Nigel Ryan, Ian Macnaughton, John Howard Davies, Yvonne Littlewood, Mark Stuart, John Alderton, Wendy Craig, Marty Feldman, Edward Woodward, Roy Dotrice, Vanessa Redgrave, Jean Simmons, Rod Steiger, Shirley MacLaine, Rock Hudson, Jack Benny, Ronnie Barker, Ronnie Corbett, David Frost (presenter).
Musical director: Harry Rabinowitz.
Writers: Barry Cryer/John Esmonde/ Bob Larbey/Denis Goodwin/David McKellar/David Nobbs/Neil Shand/ Peter Vincent/Dick Vosburgh/Ian Davidson.
Producer: Philip Casson.

BBC1, Sunday 24 May 1970, 2015–2215
A Royal Television Gala Performance
Dave Allen, Arrival, Tony Bennett, Cilla Black, Basil Brush, Derek Fowlds, Vera Lynn, Rod McKuen, M&W, The Young Generation, Alyn Ainsworth and his Orchestra.

Writers: George Martin/Eddie Braben.
Producer: Stewart Morris.

BBC1, Thursday 1 October 1970,
    2150–2235
Morecambe & Wise's Cinema
'Eric Morecambe and Ernie Wise,
    Britain's most successful comedy
    team, talk to Michael Aspel about
    their career in the music-hall, the
    cinema, and television. They also
    choose and discuss scenes from
    some of their favourite films.'
Director: Peggy Walker.
Producer: John Buttery.

BBC1, Friday 16 October 1970,
    1725–1744
Ask Aspel
Michael Aspel, M&W
Director: Frances Whitaker.
Producer: Iain Johnstone.

BBC1, Thursday 4 March 1971,
    2120–2150
British Screen Awards
Dustin Hoffman, Peter Sellers, John
    Mills, M&W, Mia Farrow, Judy
    Geeson, Margaret Tyzack, Barbara
    Murray, Sacha Distel, The Young
    Generation, Richard Attenborough
    (host).
Producer: Philip Lewis.

BBC1, Thursday 18 November 1971
Holiday 72 with Cliff Michelmore
Ernie interviewed on film about
    Malta.
Producer: Tom Savage.

BBC1, Sunday 26 September 1971,
    2305–2335
She and She
Esther Rantzen and Harriet Crawley
    interview M&W.
Director: Simon Wadleigh

Producer: Desmond Wilcox
Editor: Bill Morton.

BBC1, Saturday 25 December 1971,
    1615–1700
The Black and White Minstrel Show
The George Mitchell Minstrels
    featuring Ted Darling, Dai Francis,
    Margaret Savage, Andy Cole and
    Les Rawlings with The Television
    Toppers, M&W, orchestra directed
    by Alan Bristow.
Producer: Ernest Maxin.

BBC1, Sunday 26 December 1971,
    1700–1805
Wildlife Spectacular
HRH The Duke of Edinburgh, KG,
    Kenneth Allsop, Jeffery Boswall,
    Robert Dougall, Adam Faith,
    Joyce Grenfell, Rolf Harris, Spike
    Milligan, Eric Morecambe, Johnny
    Morris, Eva Rueber-Staier, Peter
    Scott, Harry Secombe, Tony Soper.
    Introduced by Peter Cushing and Dr
    David Bellamy.
Producer: Richard Brock.

BBC1, Tuesday 28 December 1971,
    2225–2315
Presenting Keith Michell
Keith Michell, Marian Montgomery,
    M&W, Nina, Richard Wattis,
    Helena and Paul Michell, the
    Norman Maen Dancers, The Mike
    Sammes Singers, orchestra directed
    by Peter Knight.
Producer: Yvonne Littlewood.

BBC1, Sunday 27 February 1972,
    1455–1515
Ask Aspel
Michael Aspel, M&W.
Producer: Granville Jenkins.
BBC North, Tuesday 11 April 1972
Wise Without Morecambe

BBC1, Saturday 11 November 1972,
2330–0030
Parkinson
Michael Parkinson, Raquel Welch,
Stephane Grappelli, M&W.
Director: Roger Ordish.
Producer: Richard Drewett.

BBC1, Thursday 18 January 1973,
1300–1330
Pebble Mill at One
Tom Coyne interviews Eddie Braben
with M&W joining in.
Producer: Roger Ecclestone.

BBC1, Thursday 18 January 1973,
1406–1429
Scene: Morecambe & Wise
Schools programme based on same
footage as *Omnibus: Fools Rush In*.
Programme: Ronald Smedley.

BBC1, Sunday 18 February 1973,
2235–2325
Omnibus: Fools Rush In
'This film for Omnibus follows the
two weeks of rehearsal that led up
to the recording of last Friday's
Morecambe & Wise Show. "Fools
Rush In" was Eric and Ernie's
original billing nearly 30 years ago
– right at the bottom, in very small
letters. Now they are Britain's best-
known comedians, with a regular
and growing audience of nearly
20 million people. Producer John
Ammonds, writer Eddie Braben, as
well as Eric and Ernie talk about
the skill and sheer hard work of
comedy.'
Producer: Ronald Smedley.

BBC1, Wednesday 21 February 1973,
1715–1740
Val Meets the VIPs

'Valerie Singleton talks to people who
have earned the title Very Important
Persons. An audience of children
will join in and put their questions
to the VIPs who this week are
Morecambe and Wise.'
Producer: Jill Roach.
Thames (plus Westward, Channel
and Grampian only), 13 September
1973, 1430–1450
Good Afternoon
M&W, Mavis Nicholson
(interviewer).
Producer: Diana Potter.

BBC1, Monday 17 September 1973,
1800–1840
Nationwide
Eric and Ernie talk about their
autobiography.
Producer: Michael Bunce.

BBC1, Saturday 24 November 1973,
2315–0015
Parkinson
Michael Parkinson, Glenda Jackson,
Marjorie Wallace, M&W.
Director: Brian Whitehouse.
Producer: Richard Drewett.

BBC1, Monday 18 February 1974,
1800–1845
Nationwide
Ernie demonstrates a 'dog dance
routine'.
Producer: Michael Bunce.

BBC2, Monday 18 March 1974,
1935–2000
*Look Stranger: Wildlife in the Back
Bedroom*
Eric introduces a film about wildlife
artist Gordon Beningfield.
Producer: Jennifer Jeremy.

BBC1, Friday 19 April 1974,
1800–1850
Nationwide
Eric and Ernie talk about inclusion in
Who's Who.
Producer: Michael Bunce.

BBC1, Tuesday 14 May 1974,
1845–1915
*This Is Your Lunch: Morecambe and
Wise*
M&W, André Previn, Glenda Jackson,
Robert Morley, Robin Day, Graham
Hill, Francis Matthews.
Producer: Mary Evans.

BBC1, Saturday 6 July 1974
World Cup Grandstand
Eric talking about football.
Producers: Sam Leitch/Alan Chivers.

BBC2, Monday 8 July 1974,
2215–2245
Read All About It
Ernie talking about his book of the
week and taking part in discussion.
Producers: Melvyn Bragg/Julia
Matheson.

BBC1, Sunday 14 July 1974,
2215–2245
André Previn Meets
'First of a series of informal
conversations between the musical
maestro and his friends and
acquaintances in various walks of
life.'
Director: Roy Tipping.
Producer: Walter Todds.

Thames, Thursday 17 October 1974,
2315–2345
Fifty Bighearted Years
Arthur Askey, Max Bygraves, Jimmy
Edwards, Stanley Holloway, Arthur

Lowe, Eric Morecambe, Ernie Wise,
Bill Shankly, Pete Murray (host).
Director: Steve Minchin.
Producer: Grahame Turner.

BBC1, Sunday 22 December 1974,
2220–2325
*Omnibus: Cuckoo – Mr Laurel and
Mr Hardy*
Eric and Ernie (narrators).
Producer: Robert Vas.

BBC1, Wednesday 25 December
1974, 2325–0020
*Michael Parkinson takes a Look at
Morecambe & Wise*
Producer: John Ammonds.

BBC1, Friday 28 March 1975,
1635–1715
Festival of Entertainment
Cleo Laine and John Dankworth, the
Daughters of Heaven, Sheila Steafel,
Roger Whittaker, Shimada, Eric
Morecambe, the Flying Germains.
Producer: Douglas Hespe.

BBC1, Thursday 24 April 1975,
1800–1855
Nationwide
Ernie interviewed about seaside
entertainment.
Producer: Stuart Wilkinson.

BBC1, Saturday 19 July 1975,
1745–1820
Jim'll Fix It
M&W fixing it for Nicola Perry to
slap Eric around the face and for
Juliet Smith to impersonate Janet
Webb.
Director: Phil Bishop.
Producer: Roger Ordish.

BBC1, Friday 31 October 1975,
1800–1905

Sportswide – part of *Nationwide*
Taking part in draw for *Daily Express* national five-a-side tournament with Jimmy Hill.

Thames, Wednesday 5 November 1975, 1525–1555
Looks Familiar
Eric Morecambe, Diana Coupland, Jack Parnell, Percy Edwards, Denis Norden (host).
Director: Daphne Shadwell.
Producer: David Clark.

Thames, Wednesday 17 December 1975, 1525–1555
Looks Familiar
Eric Morecambe, Joyce Blair, William Franklyn, Mick McManus, Denis Norden (host).
Director: Daphne Shadwell.
Producer: David Clark.

BBC1, Wednesday 16 June 1976, 1800–1850
Nationwide
Eric on commuterland.
Producer: John Gau.

BBC1, Friday 27 August 1976, 1800–1850
Nationwide
Ernie presenting a prize at the *Nationwide* greyhound race.
Producer: John Gau.

Thames, Tuesday 14 September 1976, 1520–1550
Looks Familiar
Vera Lynn, Eric Morecambe, Ernie Wise, Denis Norden (host).
Director: Robert Reed.
Producer: David Clark.

Thames, Tuesday 16 November 1976, 1520–1550

Looks Familiar
Vera Lynn, Eric Morecambe, Ernie Wise, Denis Norden (host).
Director: Robert Reed.
Producer: David Clark.

BBC1, Thursday 9 December 1976, 2125–2215
The Big Time
'Tony Peers, a comedian at Butlin's Holiday Camp, is given the chance to appear in BBCtv's Seaside Special – if he can make his act good enough. He meets some of the top names in comedy – Arthur Askey, Bill Cotton, Ken Dodd, Roy Hudd, Spike Milligan, Bob Monkhouse, Morecambe & Wise and three scriptwriters, who advise him how to tackle The Big Time.'
Producer: Esther Rantzen.

BBC1, Sunday 1 May 1977, 2215–2255
Everyman: What's So Funny About Religion Anyway?
John Pitman talks to Ken Dodd, Frank Carson, Kenneth Williams, Eric Morecambe and Spike Milligan.
Producer: Jim Murray.

BBC1, Wednesday 17 August 1977, 1645–1710
Ask Aspel
Michael Aspel, M&W.
Producer: Frances Whitaker.

LWT, Saturday 24 December 1977, 1230–1500
World of Sport
Eric guesting as co-host with Dickie Davies.
Director: John Scriminger
Editor: Stuart McConachie.

BBC2, Friday 6 January 1978,
2100–2130
Pot Black
Eric makes the draw for the series.
Director: Jim Dumighan.
Producer: Reg Perrin.

LWT, Friday 3 February 1978,
2230–2330
The Sun Television Awards
Buddy Greco, Bruce Forsyth, Larry
Grayson, Jenny Hanley, Mick
Robertson, Nerys Hughes, Miriam
Karlin, Cliff Michelmore, Bill
Oddie, Barry Norman, Judith
Chalmers, Nicholas Parsons, Ernie
Wise, Arthur Mullard, John Noakes,
Leonard Rossiter, Gordon Jackson,
Gemma Jones, Joanna Lumley,
James Bolam, Michael Aspel, Noel
Edmonds, Robert Dougall, Brian
Lapping, Diana Dors, Ronnie
Barker, Ronnie Corbett, Russell
Harty, Abba, Eric Morecambe,
Honor Blackman, John Thaw,
Dennis Waterman, Anthea Redfern,
David Soul, Paul Michael Glazer,
Melvyn Bragg, The Page Three
Dancers, Alyn Ainsworth and his
Orchestra, Dickie Davies (host).
Director: Paul Smith.
Producer: Richard Drewett.

Thames, Wednesday 22 February
1978, 2000–2030
Looks Familiar – 100th edition
Eric Morecambe, Ernie Wise, Patricia
Hayes, Denis Norden (host).
Director: Ronald Fouracre.
Producer: David Clark.

Thames, Wednesday 19 April 1978,
2000–2030
Looks Familiar
Eric Morecambe, Ernie Wise, Betty
Driver, Denis Norden (host).

Director: Ronald Fouracre.
Producer: David Clark.

BBC1, Monday 21 August 1978,
1910–2010
It's a Celebrity Knockout
Stuart Hall, Eddie Waring, Arthur
Ellis (referee), Barry John, Raymond
Baxter, Meriel Tufnell, David
Hamilton, Linda Lusardi, Robin
Askwith, John Blythe, Tommy
Boyd, Patricia Brake, Tim Brooke-
Taylor, Paul Burnett, Eddie Capelli,
Judith Chalmers, Jacqueline Clarke,
Julie Dawn Cole, John Craven,
Pat Crerand, Barry Cryer, Linda
Cunningham, Roger de Courcey,
Neil Durden-Smith, Jessie Evans,
Tony Gale, Graeme Garden, Bob
Grant, Jenny Hanley, Anita Harris,
Rachel Heyhoe Flint, Frazer Hines,
Derek Hobson, David 'Kid' Jensen,
John Junkin, Diane Langton,
George Layton, Legs & Co.,
Liverpool Express, Victor Maddern,
Tony Mahoney, Mick McManus,
Ann Moore, Patrick Moore,
Eric Morecambe, Don Moss,
Bill Oddie, Richard O'Sullivan,
Nicholas Parsons, Lance Percival,
Nora Perry, Doctor Magnus Pyke,
Chris Ralston, Tim Rice, Cardew
Robinson, William Rushton, Sheila
Steafel, Ray Stevens, Mike Swann,
Shaw Taylor, Bob Wilson, Norman
Wisdom.
Director: Keith Phillips.
Producer: Cecil Korer.

Thames, Thursday 23 November
1978, 2100–2200
The Sweeney
Hearts and Minds: John Thaw,
Dennis Waterman, Garfield Morgan,
M&W, Caroline Blakiston, Edward
De Souza, Edward Hardwicke,

George Mikell, Jenny Quayle, Miles Anderson, Jack Klaff, John Moreno, Joseph Charles, Paul Freeman, James Winston, Alan Bodenham, George Irving, Jean Boht, Ronald Forfar, Garry McDermott, Martyn Whitby, Anthony Smee, Simon Browne, Barbara Grant, John Fielding.
Writers: Donald Churchill and Ted Childs.
Director: Mike Vardy.
Producer: Ted Childs.

ATV, Tuesday 12 December 1978, 2030–2100
Variety Club Tribute Dinner to Morecambe and Wise
M&W, Leslie Crowther, Maudie Edwards, Dickie Henderson, Aimi MacDonald, Derek Nimmo, George Elrick, Noele Gordon, Dora Bryan, Glenda Jackson, Larry Grayson, Terry Hall and Lenny The Lion, Terry Wogan (host).
Producer: John Pullen.

Anglia, Monday 19 February 1979, 2230–2300
Morecambe and Stone
Eric Morecambe, Chris Kelly (commentator), Richard Stone (artist).
Producer: David C Kenten.

BBC1, Friday 16 March 1979, 1755–1900
Nationwide
Ernie talking about Eric's second heart attack.
Producer: Hugh Williams.

BBC1, Wednesday 18 April 1979, 2100–2110
A Chance to Meet
Bob Evans interviews Eric and Ernie.

Producer: Garry Knight.

BBC1, Wednesday 24 October 1979, 1755–1900
Nationwide
Ernie presenting award to Richard Baker and singing with him.
Producer: Hugh Williams.

BBC1, Sunday 23 December 1979, 1810–1815
Ernie Wise appeals on behalf of the Peterborough Cathedral Trust.

Thames, Wednesday 3 February 1982, 2000–2100
Two of a Kind
Eric and Ernie discuss double acts with Alan Whicker.
Script associate: Sid Colin.
Producer: David Clark.

BBC1, Wednesday 24 February 1982, 2010–2100
Batley
Neil Sedaka, Charlie Williams, Gene Pitney, Shirley Bassey, Cilla Black, Cannon and Ball, Bernie Clifton, Con Cluskey, Paul Daniels, Ken Dodd, Gracie Fields, The Grumbleweeds, Vince Hill, Engelbert Humperdinck, Eartha Kitt, Danny La Rue, Lulu, Vera Lynn, Johnny Mathis, Eric Morecambe, Cliff Richard, Derek Smith, Alvin Stardust, Freddie Starr, Frankie Vaughan, Mike Yarwood, Michael Parkinson (narrator).
Producer: Rod Taylor.

Thames, Tuesday 16 March 1982, 1645–1715
CBTV Channel 14
Steve Steen, Jim Sweeney, M&W.
Director: Stuart Hall.
Producer: Dale Le Vack.

Thames, Thursday 18 March 1982,
2130–2330
British Academy Awards
Bob Monkhouse, Princess Anne,
Ian Ogilvy, Jan Leeming, John
Mortimer, Lulu, Lionel Jeffries,
Barry Norman, M&W, Nanette
Newman, Roy Plomley, Mike
Yarwood, Selina Scott, Anthony
Andrews, Dilys Powell, Arthur
Lowe, David Croft, John Boulting,
Roy Boulting, David Puttnam, John
Hurt, Denholm Elliott, Hannah
Gordon, Geoff Love, Trevor Eve,
Angela Lansbury, Burt Lancaster,
Topol, Bill Forsyth, Lindsay
Anderson, Denis Norden (host).
Producer: Anthony Cartledge.

BBC2, Thursday 12 August 1982
1855–1920
Six Fifty-Five Special
Eric promoting *The Reluctant
Vampire.*
Director: John G. Smith
Producer: Stephanie Silk
Editor: Peter Hercombe.

BBC2, Thursday 4 November 1982,
2030–2100

Russell Harty
Harty interviews Eric and Gary.
Director: John Rooney.
Producer: Ken Stephinson.

LWT (regional), Sunday 19 December
1982, 1400–1500
Sunday Sunday
James Galway, Elaine Paige, Jeremy
Beadle, Rex Harrison, Henry Kelly,
Matthew Kelly, Eric Morecambe.
Director: Nick Vaughan-Barratt.
Producer: Charles Brand.

Thames, Monday 2 April 1984,
1900–1930
What's My Line?
Eric Morecambe, Barbara Kelly, Jilly
Cooper, Patrick Mower, George
Gale, Eamonn Andrews (host).
Producer: Malcolm Morris.

Central, Saturday 7 April 1984,
1030–1214
The Saturday Show
Jimmy Greaves, Tommy Boyd, Isla
St Clair, David Rappaport, Eric
Morecambe.
Director: Richard Bradley.
Producer: Glyn Edwards.

Stage work

All variety engagements ran for the week commencing on the date in question unless otherwise indicated.

25 April 1938 – Empire, Leeds
Audition for Bryan Michie (EW)

16 January 1939 – Astoria, Streatham
Band Waggon (EW)

23 January 1939 – Empire, Nottingham
Bands May Come: Jack Hylton, Peggy Dell, Freddy Schweitzer, June Malo, Gerda and Ulrick Newman, Maureen Potter, Doreen Stevens, Jack Woodroffe, Ernie Wise, the Two Dancettes, Ralphone and Page, Raymond Smith, Ben Jade and Coy, Jean Rema, Paul Roach and Vicki Burns.

30 January 1939 – Empire, Finsbury Park
Bands May Come: Jack Hylton, Peggy Dell, June Malo, Gerda and Ulrick Newman, Maureen Potter, Doreen Stevens, Jack Woodroffe, Ernie Wise, Vic Oliver, the Two Dancettes, Ralphono and Page, Dennis Lawes, Rex Roper and Maisie.

20 March 1939 – Royal, Dublin
Bands May Come

10 April 1939 – Hippodrome, Portsmouth
Bands May Come: Jack Hylton, Ernie Wise, Freddie Schweitzer, Peggy Dell, June Malo, Primrose.

17 April 1939 – Hippodrome, Bristol
Bands May Come: Jack Hylton, Ernie Wise, June Malo, Primrose, Bruce Trent, Maureen Potter, Doreen Stephens, Maureen Flanagan, Freddy Schweitzer, Deveen and the New York Blondes, Stoll and Gould, Billy Scott-Coomber and his Grenadiers, Iris Sadler, Dan Young, Six Hoffmans.

1 May 1939 – Empire, Sheffield
Bands May Come: Jack Hylton, Coleman Hawkins, Ernie Wise, Dennis Lawes, Hatten and Manners, George and Jack d'Ormonde, Danny Lipton and the four Liptonettes.

9 July 1939 (one night only) – Pier Pavilion, Southsea
Jack Hylton, Freddy Schweitzer, Peggy Dell, 'Primrose', Ernie Wise.

27 November 1939 – Empire, Finsbury Park
Band Waggon: Arthur Askey, Richard Murdoch, Fred Kitchen, Dolly Elsie, Doreen Stephens, Freddy the funny man (Schweitzer, having dropped his surname because of the War), Johnnie Lockwood, Ernie Wise, Borstal Boys, Pointer, Gray and Dawn Trio.

4 December 1939 – Empire, Glasgow

Band Waggon: Max Wall (standing in for Askey), Richard Murdoch, Charlie Smart, Jack Hart, Dolly Elsie, Doreen Stephens, Ernie Wise.

11 December 1939 – Empire, Newcastle
Band Waggon: Max Wall (standing in for Askey), Richard Murdoch, Ernie Wise.

26 December 1939 – Hippodrome, Portsmouth
Band Waggon: Richard Murdoch, Max Wall, Charles Smart, Two Dancettes, Jack Hylton's Bandwaggoners, Ernie Wise.

1 January 1940 – Empire, Nottingham
Band Waggon: Richard Murdoch, Max Wall, Charles Smart, Jack Hylton's Bandwaggoners, Ernie Wise.

7 January 1940 (one night only) – Pavilion, Bath
Band Waggon: Arthur Askey, Bruce Trent, June Malo, Dolly Elsie, Doreen Stephens, Ernie Wise, Johnny Lockwood, Bert Waller, Freddy, Jack Hylton.

15 January 1940 – Hippodrome, Dudley
Band Waggon: Max Wall (standing in for Askey), Richard Murdoch, June Malo, Doreen Stephens, Ernie Wise, Bert Waller.

29 January 1940 – Palace, Blackpool
Band Waggon: Max Wall (standing in for Askey), Richard Murdoch, Charlie Smart, Bert Waller, Doreen Stephens, Ernie Wise, Marion Pola, Trixie and Jean, Dolly Elsie, Freddy,

Bruce Trent, Johnny Lockwood, Sunny Farrar, Jack Hylton's Bandwaggoners. Opened a day late due to 'transport difficulties'.

19 February 1940 – Empire, Swansea
Band Waggon: Max Wall (standing in for Askey), Richard Murdoch, Charlie Smart, Fred Kitchen, Doreen Stephens, Ernie Wise, Marion Pola, Trixie and Jean, Freddy, Bruce Trent, June Malo, Sonny Farrar, Jack Hylton's Bandwaggoners.

26 February 1940 – New Theatre, Cardiff
Band Waggon: Max Wall (standing in for Askey), Richard Murdoch, Charlie Smart, Fred Kitchen, Doreen Stephens, Ernie Wise, Marion Pola, Trixie and Jean, Freddy, Bruce Trent, June Malo, Sonny Farrar, Jack Hylton's Bandwaggoners.

11 March 1940 – Alhambra, Bradford
Secrets of the BBC/Youth Takes a Bow (EW).

18 March 1940 – Empire, New Cross
Band Waggon: Max Wall (standing in for Askey), Richard Murdoch, Charlie Smart, Fred Kitchen, Doreen Stephens, Ernie Wise, Marion Pola, Trixie and Jean, Freddy, Bruce Trent, Julie Dawn, Sonny Farrar, Jack Hylton's Bandwaggoners directed by Fred Bretherton.

Youth Takes a Bow tour: Bryan Michie, Adelaide Hall, Tessie O'Shea, Gerry Moore, Ted Ray, George Moon, Dick Bentley, Patillo and Pesco, the Ilzuka Brothers, Angers and Waller, Marie Louise, the Dennis Family, Eric Morecambe,

Ernie Wise (not all performers were present for the whole tour).

25 March 1940 – Empire, Nottingham

1 April 1940 – Empire, Sheffield

8 April 1940 – Birkenhead

15 April 1940 – Empire, Swansea

22 April 1940 – Hippodrome, Portsmouth

29 April 1940 – Hippodrome, Brighton

6 May 1940 – Empire, Finsbury Park

20 May 1940 – Hippodrome, Birmingham

27 May 1940 – Empire, Stratford

3 June 1940 – Palace, Plymouth

3 June 1940 – Palace, Manchester

10 June 1940 – Palace, Manchester

17 June 1940 – Palace, Blackpool

24 June 1940 – Empire, Glasgow

1 July 1940 – Empire, Leeds

8 July 1940 – Empire, Liverpool

29 July 1940 – Hippodrome, Ilford

12 August 1940 – Empire, Kingston

19 August 1940 – Empire, Chiswick

26 August 1940 – Hippodrome, Lewisham

2 September 1940 – Empire, Swansea

9 September 1940 – New, Northampton

14 October 1940 – Opera House, Leicester

6 January 1941 – Empire, Swansea

13 January 1941 – Empire, Newport

20 January 1941 – Hippodrome, Brighton

27 January 1941 – Empire, Sheffield

10 February 1941 – Hippodrome, Wolverhampton

17 February 1941 – Hippodrome, Bristol

24 February 1941 – New, Cardiff

3 March 1941 – Hippodrome, Manchester

10 March 1941 – Empire, Wood Green

17 March 1941 – Theatre Royal, Bath

24 March 1941 – Palace, Plymouth

7 April 1941 – Palace, Blackpool

5 May 1941 – Hippodrome, Preston

19 May 1941 – Empire, West Hartlepool

26 May 1941 – Theatre Royal, Hanley

2 June 1941 – Metropolitan, Edgware Road

9 June 1941 – Empire, Nottingham

16 June 1941 – Hippodrome, Norwich

23 June 1941 – Hippodrome, Golders Green

14 July 1941 – Hippodrome, Birmingham

28 July 1941 – Empire, Glasgow

4 August 1941 – His Majesty's, Aberdeen

18 August 1941 – Empire, Newcastle

25 August 1941 – Empire, Liverpool

1 September 1941 – Empire, Edinburgh

8 September 1941 – Empire, Leeds

20 October 1940 (one night only) – Winter Gardens, Morecambe,

9 December 1940 – New, Oxford

15 December 1940 – (one night only) – Odeon, Manchester

21 April 1941 – Royal County, Bedford

21 July 1941 – Hippodrome, Coventry

15 September 1941 – Empire, Sheffield

17 November 1941 – Palace, Burnley, Eric billed just as 'Morecambe'

1 December 1941 – Royalty, Chester

8 December 1941 – New, Northampton

5 January 1942 – Metropolitan, Edgware Road

12 January 1942 – Royal Hippodrome, Chatham

Billy Cotton and his Band, Scottie, Chown Ding, The Two Billys, Joan Bamford, The Zamofells, Ernie Wise and Morecambe.

18 March 1943 – Prince of Wales, London
Strike a New Note

Lord John Sanger's Circus and Variety tour: Speedy, Ernie Wise (with Eric Morecambe), Molly Seddon, the Pearl Moss Girls
31 March 1947 – Crowborough
1 April 1947 – Mayfield
2 April 1947 – Ticehurst
3 April 1947 – Lamberhurst
4 April 1947 – Goudhurst
5 April 1947 – Cranbrook
7 April 1947 – Rye
8 April 1947 – Tenterden
9 April 1947 – Hawkhurst
12 April 1947 – Brook Field, Uckfield
14 and 15 April 1947 – Hoopers Wharf, Lewes
16 and 17 April 1947 – Tanfield Ground, Horsham
18 April 1947 – Colonel's Ground, Godalming
10 May 1947 – West End Field, Melksham
12 May 1947 – Recreation Ground, Corsham
13 May 1947 – Recreation Ground, Bradford on Avon
14 May 1947 – Circus Field, Trowbridge
15 May 1947 – Fair Field, Westbury
17 May 1947 – Cook's Paddock, Shepton Mallet
19 May 1947 – Frogpool Meadow, Cullompton
19 May 1947 – Recreation Ground, Wells
20 May 1947 – Recreation Ground, Crediton

30 June 1947 – Chudleigh
1 July 1947 – Topsham
2 July 1947 – Budleigh Salterton
3 July 1947 – Sidford
4 July 1947 – Honiton
5 July 1947 – Axminster
7 July 1947 – Chard
8 July 1947 – Crewkerne
9 July 1947 – Sherborne
10 July 1947 – Gillingham
11 July 1947 – Blandford
12 July 1947 – Wimborne
19 July 1947 – Titchfield
21 July 1947 – Havant
22 July 1947 – Emsworth
23 July 1947 – Selsey
24 July 1947 – Arundel
2–4 October 1947 – Goose Fair, Nottingham

22 December 1947–24 January 1948 – Grand, Brighton
Jack and the Beanstalk: Wallace Lupino, Barry Lupino, Lauri Lupino Lane, Heather Furnell, Eve Eacott, M&W, Mickey McConnell, Ernest Dubois, Dudley and his Midgets.

4 May 1948 (one night only) – Comedy Restaurant, London
Lyric Lodge of Instruction: Bryn Gwyn, Jack Rowlands, Carlo, Lawrie Day and Mabel Dyer, M&W, Joyce Stoker and Audrey Cleaver, Fred Wildon, Ernest Bertram, Stanley Mole.

24 December 1948–26 February 1949 – Empire, Swansea
Goody Two Shoes: Sonny Jenks, Joy Hayden, Vic Marlowe, Bobbie Medlock, Hugh Rene, M&W, Stuart Pearce, Sheila Bennett, Eileen Rogan Girls.

Front Page Personalities tour: The
Amazing Fogel, Lionel King, The
Two Pirates, Gloria Mayne, Reggie
Dennis, The Sensational Denvers,
M&W, Sylvia, the Late Extra
Lovelies.
28 February 1949 – Savoy,
Scunthorpe
7 March 1949 – Empire, York
14 March 1949 – Palace, Grimsby
28 March 1949 – Theatre Royal,
Hanley
4 April 1949 – Hippodrome,
Boscombe
11 April 1949 – Plaza, West
Bromwich
18 April 1949 – Hippodrome,
Norwich
25 April 1949 – Feldman's, Blackpool
2 May 1949 – Theatre Royal, Lincoln
9 May 1949 – Shakespeare, Liverpool
16 May 1949 – Hippodrome, Aston
6 June 1949 – Queen's, Poplar
13 June 1949 – Tivoli, Hull
20 June 1949 – Queen's, Rhyl
27 June 1949 – Hippodrome,
Wolverhampton
4 July 1949 – Capitol, Didsbury
18 July 1949 – Metropolitan,
Edgware Road
25 July 1949 – Palace, Chelsea
1 August 1949 – Empress, Brixton
8 August 1949 – Hippodrome,
Ipswich
15 August 1949 – Opera House,
Cheltenham
22 August 1949 – Regal, Southend
5 September 1949 – Empire, Bristol
19 September 1949 – Princesses,
Crayford
3 October 1949 – Palace, East Ham
10 October 1949 – Grand, Clapham
17 October 1949 – City Varieties,
Leeds
24 October 1949 – Shakespeare,
Liverpool

7 November 1949 – Palace,
Huddersfield
14 November 1949 – Palace, Halifax
21 November 1949 – Windsor,
Bearwood
28 November 1949 – Pavilion,
Newport
5 December 1949 – Kemble, Hereford

31 October 1949 – Empire, Swansea
Eve and Mary Harvey, Josef Locke,
The Martell Sisters, Leslie Sarony,
Arthur Dowler, Herschel Henlere,
M&W, The Four Kentons.

24 December 1949–4 March 1950 –
Opera House, Leicester
Little Red Riding Hood: Freddie
Frinton, Bill Burke, M&W, Doreen
Lavender, Greta Fayne, Bert Platt,
Martin Benson, Paula Marshall,
Carol Marr, Anna Marinova, Luke
Stan and Andy, J. W. Jackson Girls,
Mari Bici Juveniles.

13 March 1950 – Empire, Edinburgh
The Piddingtons, Jon Pertwee, the
Radio Revellers, Albert Whelan,
the Falcons, Semprini, M&W,
Macdonald and Graham.

20 March 1950 – Hippodrome,
Birmingham
Cilla's Dogs, Anne Shelton, Les
Ritchie and Wendy, Jimmy James
and Co, M&W, Dorothy Ward,
The Hurricanes, Eddie Gray, Leslie
Sarony.

27 March 1950 – Royal, Portsmouth
Peek-A-Boo: Phyllis Dixey, Howard
de Courcy, Jack and Stern, Irving
and Girdwood, Veronica Martell,
Jack Tracy, M&W.

3 April 1950 – Alhambra, Bradford
The Martell Sisters, Lee Lawrence,
Two Valettos, Georgie Wood and
Dolly Harmer, M&W, Manley and
Austin, Terry Hall, Dick Henderson,
Don Saunders.

10 April 1950 – Empire, Sheffield
Freda Wyn, Mack Triplets, Irene and
Stanley Davis, Georgie Wood and
Dolly Harmer, Jackie, Leslie Sarony,
M&W, Three Jokers, Mackenzie
Reid and Dorothy.

17 April 1950 – Empire, Liverpool
Peggy Ryan and Ray McDonald, Jon
Pertwee, Boris, Herschel Henlere,
Two Virginians, M&W, the Flying
Cromwells, the Skating Typhoons.

24 April 1950 – Metropolitan,
Edgware Road
Billy Reid and Dorothy Squires, Nino
Realtor, the Wonder Dogs, Ernest
Arnley and Gloria, Arthur English,
Milton Wood and Millicent Cooper,
Meg and Joan Mangean, M&W, the
D'Artagna.

1 May 1950 – Palace, Chelsea
Billy Reid and Dorothy Squires, Nino
Realtor, the Wonder Dogs, Four
Graham Brothers, M&W, Frank
and Lucille Preston, Max Seymour,
Three Spallas.

8 May 1950 – Palace, Grimsby
Ivy Benson and band, M&W, Betty
and partner, Ken Barnes and Jean,
Reid Twins, Five Adamarios, Jothia
and Joan.

19 June 1950 – Playhouse, Colchester
Morton Fraser and his Harmonica
Gang, Wilson Keppel and Betty,

Hilda Heath, Louise Loyal and
Mickey Mouse, Terry Hall and
Micky Flynn, M&W, Hill Billy
Polecats, Al Raie and Binnie.

26 June 1950 – Palace, Manchester
Reg Dixon, Joyce Golding, M&W,
Kay Cavendish, Two Kent Brothers,
Manley and Austin, Flying Comets,
Roger Carne, Two Valettos.

10 July 1950 – Hippodrome, Dudley
Ronnie Leslie, Medlock and
Marlowe, M&W, Swan and Leigh,
Hamilton Conrad and his Pigeons,
McKenzie Reid and Dorothy, Terry
O'Neill, Johnny Hutch and Stan,
Jack Ledair, Freda Wyn.

17 July 1950 – Palace, Ramsgate
The Radio Revellers, M&W, Felovis,
Hilda Heath, Kent Bros, Karlson
Three, Juliet.

24 July 1950 – Empire, Nottingham
Georges and Lennette, the Nicholas
Brothers, Kay Kortz and Eugene,
Freddie Forbes and Angela Barrie,
Keeffe Brothers and Annette, Saveen
with 'Daisy May', M&W, Willy
Woltard, the Wonder Wheelers.

31 July 1950 – Empire, Wood Green
Lee Lawrence, Alec Pleon, Billy
Thorburn, The Two Sophisticates,
Richman and Jackson, Two Valors,
M&W, Len Taylor, Chris Sands.

21 August 1950 – Regal, St Leonard's
Elsie and Doris Waters, Melody and
Joy, Freddie Stobbs, Louise Loyal
and Mickey Mouse, M&W, Irving
and Girdwood, Eric Williams, Two
Columbus.

28 August 1950 – Empire, Leeds
A. J. Powers, Nicholas Brothers, Allen and Lee, the Radio Revellers, M&W, Ivor E. Keys, Don Phillippe and Marta, Two Columbus, Madge Kent.

4 September 1950 – Empire, Dewsbury
Western Brothers, Freddie Mirfield and his Garbage Men, M&W, Craig and Voyle, Ed Royale, Freddie Stobbs.

25 September 1950 – Hippodrome, Manchester
Phyllis Dixey, Lester Ferguson, Bob Bromley, Howard de Courcy, Table Tennis, M&W, Ballet Parisienne.

2 October 1950 – Empire, Sunderland
Peek-A-Boo: Phyllis Dixey, Jack Tracy, Delbary and Partner, Howard de Courcy, M&W, The Kovacs.

23 October 1950 – Royal, Portsmouth
Alan Clive, George Mitchell Glee Club, Bernard Miles, Jane, M&W, Walthon and Dorraine, Del Monico Dancers.

30 October 1950 – Empire, Hackney
Peek-A-Boo: Phyllis Dixey, Jack Tracy, Howard de Courcy, Bob and Alf Pearson, Freddie Bamberger, Morecambe and Wise.

13 November 1950 – Empire, Swansea
Elwardos, Sam Costa, Georgie Wood and Dolly Harmer, M&W, Gloria and Splendid, the Skating Meteors, Walthon and Dorraine, Swan and Leigh, Andre Twins and Sandra.

20 November 1950 – New, Cardiff
Allan Jones, Ernest Arnley and Gloria, Tovarich Troupe, Tattersall with Jerry and Co, M&W, Cooke's Pony Revue, Eva and Lilian, Linda and Lana.

4 December 1950 – Empire, Finsbury Park
Billy Cotton and his Band, Alan Breeze, Doreen Stephens, Clem Bernard, Chris Sands, Johnny Lawson Trio, Donald B. Stuart, Joyce Golding, Ganjou Brothers and Juanita, Carsony Brothers, M&W.

23 December 1950–3 February 1951 – Hippodrome, Golders Green
Red Riding Hood: Rosalind Melville, Leo Franklin, Reg Varney, Doreen Lavender, M&W, Bert Platt, Bill Futter, Sylvia Lane, Luke Stan and Andy, Anna Marinova, the Jackson Girls, the Ada Foster Children.

12 February 1951 – Empire, Croydon
Elsie and Doris Waters, the Angelos, Annell and Brask, M&W, Four Aces, Two Ledas, Raydini, Hazel and Audrey Ross.

19 February 1951 – Hippodrome, Norwich
Wilson Keppel and Betty, Jane of the Daily Mirror, Delmonico Dancers, M&W, Verdini, Two Stankiews, Victor Seaforth, Two Burgos.

12 March 1951 – Empire, York
Jane of the Daily Mirror, Delmonico Dancers, M&W, Two Stankiews, Verdini, Two Burgos, Wilson Keppel and Betty, Victor Seaforth.

19 March 1951 – Hippodrome, Boscombe

Wilson Keppel and Betty, Jane of the *Daily Mirror*, Delmonico Dancers, M&W, Verdini, Two Stankiews, Victor Seaforth, Two Burgos.

26 March 1951 – Hippodrome, Hulme
Dorothy Squires, Gene Crowley, Carsony Brothers, Tattersall with Jerry, M&W, Frances Duncan, Lupi and Partner, Dancing Hollands.

2 April 1951 – Pavilion, Liverpool
Sheriff Johnny Denis and his singing ranchers, Ali Bey, Jane of the *Daily Mirror*, M&W, David Powell, Richman and Jackson, Delmonico Dancers.

9 April 1951 – Hippodrome, Birmingham
M&W, the Five Smith Brothers, Five Varias, G. H. Elliott, Tommy Jover and company, Michael Bentine, Joyce Golding, the Andre Twins and Sandra.

16 April 1951 – Hippodrome, Brighton
M&W, Sam Costa, Ruddy Bolly, the Nitwits, Alan Clive, the Beverley Sisters, the Five Varias, Floyd and B'Nay.

23 April 1951 – Empire, Glasgow
Red Ingle and Company – Frantic Four, Charles Ancaster, Shirley, Sharon and Wanda, Olga Varona, Jean Kennedy, M&W, the Falcons, Fred Lovelle, Linda and Lana.

30 April 1951 – Empire, New Cross
Sam Costa, the Nitwits, M&W, the Reco Sisters, Three Colorados, Lynn and Lee, Mereaux and Liliane.

7 May 1951 – Hippodrome, Chesterfield
Girls, Don't Blush: Bryan Michie, Dick Montague, Penny Lee, Freddie Brent, Juggling Junes, Lilian Brown, Wee Toddy, Eleanor Beams Television Girls, M&W.

14 May 1951 – Windsor, Bearwood
The Nitwits with Sid Millward, Jimmy Kidd and June, Peter Raynor, Frank Marx and Iris, Roy Walker, M&W, Cawalini's Dogs.

21 May 1951 – Empire, Kingston
Sam Costa, the Nitwits, M&W, Three Curzons, Lynn and Lee, Yvonnette Trio, Ruddy Bolly.

4 June 1951 – Grand, Southampton
Peter Cavanagh ('The voice of them all'), Jane of the *Daily Mirror*, Delmonico Dancers, Jimmy Gay, the Mongadors, Williams and Shand, Adrian and Spero, Dumarte and Denzar, M&W.

11 June 1951 – Savoy, Clacton
Webster Booth and Anne Ziegler, Hazel and Audrev Ross, Eddie Arnold, Walthon and Dorraine, M&W, Two Valors, Christine and Moll.

16 July 1951 – Empire, Finsbury Park
M&W, Anton Karas, Joan Turner, Teddy Johnson, Trio Daley, Bob and Alf Pearson, Leslie Welch, Joy Joy and Joy.

23 July 1951 – New, Cardiff
Lee Lawrence, Michael Bentine, Jane, Billy Thorburn, M&W, Two Condons, Delmonico Dancers.

6 August 1951 – Empire, Newcastle
Sugar Chile Robinson, Arthur
  Worsley, Two Arvings, Iris Sadler,
  M&W, Walthon and Dorraine, Olga
  Varona, Joy Joy and Joy.

1 October 1951 – Opera House,
  Belfast
Compagnons de la Chanson, Rob
  Murray, Two Arvings, M&W, Les
  Hellyos, Eddie Arnold, Richards
  Sisters.

8 October 1951 – Empire,
  Middlesbrough
Dorothy Squires, M&W, Les Hellyos,
  Paula Coutts, Michael Harvey, Rita
  and Jill Clyde, Joyce Golding, Paul
  and Pauline.

15 October 1951 – Empire, Leeds
M&W, Arthur Lucan and Kitty
  McShane, Rob Murray, Kitty Bluett,
  Williams and Shand, Hazel and
  Audrey Ross, Syd Seymour and his
  band with Constance Evans and Pat
  O'Brien.

23 October 1951 – Empire,
  Shepherd's Bush
Lee Lawrence, Peter Sellers, Billy
  Thorburn, Chuck Brown and Rita,
  Jose Moreno and assistant, M&W,
  Richard Sisters.

30 October 1951 – New,
  Northampton
Billy Cotton and his Band, Eddie
  Gordon and Nancy, M&W, Arthur
  Dowler, Walthon and Dorraine,
  Mills and Belita.

12 November 1951 – Empire,
  Sheffield

M&W, Dr Crock and his Crackpots,
  Flack and Lucas, Afrique, Billy
  Danvers, Suzette Tarri, Two Nadias.

19 November 1951 – Empire,
  Glasgow
Three Romanos Brothers, Bonar
  Colleano, M&W, Teddy Johnson,
  Wilson Keppel and Betty, Winifred
  Atwell, Noele Gordon, Mills and
  Belita.

26 November 1951 – Hippodrome,
  Manchester
Billy Cotton and his Band, M&W,
  Two Ledas, Elkins Sisters, Rob
  Murray, Arthur Dowler, Mills and
  Belita.

3 December 1951 – Royal,
  Portsmouth
Elsie and Doris Waters, Peter
  Cavanagh, Mister Sachs's Song
  Saloon with Geoffrey Hibbert,
  Lisa Lee, Bill Owen, Eleanor
  Summerfield, Leonard Sachs, Edric
  Connor, M&W, Williams and
  Shand, Richard Sisters, Syd Amoy.

22 December 1951–1 March 1952 –
  Empire, Dewsbury
Red Riding Hood: Harry Shiels,
  Sheila Bennett, Joe Black, Thelma
  Mace, M&W, Shirley Hills, the
  Melomaniacs, Manley and Austin,
  Mollie O'Connor, Evan Williams,
  Ravic and Rene, Florence Whiteley's
  Zio Angels, Peggy Glen's 12 Junior
  Misses.

10 March 1952 – Hippodrome,
  Norwich
Semprini, M&W, Four Siblons, Five
  Internationals, Eddie Arnold, Ford
  and Lenner, Ross Twins.

17 March 1952 – Empire, Sunderland
Hazel and Audrey Ross, Anton
  Karas, Dr Crock and his Crackpots,
  M&W, Manley and Austin, Joe
  King, Frances Duncan.

24 March 1952 – Empire, Croydon
Eddie Calvert, M&W, Malcolm
  Mitchell Trio.

31 March 1952 – Empire, Hackney
Phyllis Dixey, Billy West and his
  Harmony Group, Billy Danvers,
  M&W, George Martin, Jack Tracy,
  Ballet Parisienne.

7 April 1952 – Hippodrome,
  Birmingham
Phyllis Dixey, Walthon and Dorraine,
  Michael Bentine, Jack Tracy, Billy
  West and company, M&W, Varga
  Models, Eddie Gordon and Nancy.

14 April 1952 – Empire, Shepherd's
  Bush
Phyllis Dixey, Hall, Norman and
  Ladd, Billy Banks, George Martin,
  M&W, Terry Hall, Jack Tracy, Ballet
  Parisienne, Bernie Winters.

21 April 1952 – Hippodrome, Derby
Billy Cotton and his Band, M&W,
  Arthur Dowler, Frances Duncan,
  Mills and Belita, Nadias.

28 April 1952 – New, Cardiff
Phyllis Dixey, Billy Banks, Billy
  Thorburn, George Martin, M&W,
  Frances Duncan, Jack Tracy, Ballet
  Parisienne.

12 May 1952 – Empire, Chatham
Phyllis Dixey, Dandy Mery, M&W,
  George Martin, the Condons, Bobby
  Dennis.

19 May 1952 – Empire, Leeds
Phyllis Dixey, Gwen Liddle, Jack
  Tracy, Two Condons, M&W, Three
  Saytons, George Martin, Eddie
  Arnold.

26 May 1952 – Palace, Leicester
Dorothy Squires, Anton Karas,
  M&W, Les Marchisio, Claud
  Williams, Dandy Mery, Two
  Sterlings.

2 June 1952 – Hippodrome, Brighton
Billy Cotton and his Band, Mills and
  Belita, Three Saytons, the Angelos,
  M&W, Arthur Dowler, Will Carr
  and partner.

9 June 1952 – Embassy, Peterborough
Billy Cotton and his Band, M&W,
  Paula Coutts, Arthur Dowler,
  Original Peter, Angelos, Mills and
  Belita.

16 June 1952 – Derby Castle,
  Douglas
Dudley Dale, M&W, Two Cromwells,
  Charlie Clapham, Patricia
  Rossborough, Potter and Carole,
  Borstal Boys, Taro Naito, Stanley
  Watson.

23 June 1952 – Empire, Glasgow
Lena Horne, Clayton and Ward,
  Jack Parnell and his Music Makers,
  Paula Coutts, Song Pedlars, Evy and
  Everto, M&W.

30 June 1952 – Empire, Liverpool
Lena Horne, Two Sterlings, Jack
  Parnell and his Music Makers, the
  Angelos, Song Pedlars, the Condons,
  M&W.

7 July 1952 – Empire, Sheffield
Josef Locke, Trois Paulee, Nixon
  and Dixon, Les Marchisio, M&W,
  Krista and Kristel, Tattersall and
  Jerry, Paula Coutts.

14 July 1952 – Empire, Edinburgh
Gypsy Rose Lee, Clayton and Ward,
  Scott Sanders, Edna and Jimmy
  Webster, Three Saytons, Paula
  Coutts, M&W, Two Angelos.

21 July 1952 – Empire, Newcastle
Sugar Chile Robinson, Bea and Jill
  Clyde, M&W, the Angelos, Len
  Young, Three Saytons, AJ Powers,
  Paula Coutts, the Condons.

28 July 1952 – Empire, Finsbury Park
Gypsy Rose Lee, Adelaide Hall,
  George and Anne Doonan, the
  Shamvas, Les Trois Poupee, Two
  Alfreros, M&W, Francis Duncan.

4 August 1952 – Empire, Nottingham
Gypsy Rose Lee, M&W, Scott
  Sanders, Three Saytons, Paula
  Coutts, Two Angelos, Condons, Rex
  and Bessie.

11 August 1952 – Hippodrome,
  Manchester
Sugar Chile Robinson, Len Young,
  M&W, Three Franks, Beryl and
  Bobo, Joe King, Two Condons,
  Hamilton Twins.

18 August 1952 – Opera House,
  Belfast
Gypsy Rose Lee, Billy Banks, Claude
  Chandler, Les Marchisio, Ann and
  Bobby Black, Alan Kaye and Gloria,
  Two Condons, Hazel and Audrey
  Ross, M&W.

8 September 1952 – Regal, St
  Leonard's
Billy Cotton and his Band, Alan
  Breeze, Doreen Stephens, Clem
  Bernard, M&W, Nadias, Two
  Condons, Irene and Stanley Davis,
  Claud Williams.

22 September 1952 – Globe, Stockton
Josef Locke, Michael Bentine, Wilson
  Keppel and Betty, Vogelbein's Bears,
  Seven Volants, M&W, Jackie Allen
  and Barbara, Two Virginians.

29 September 1952 – Hippodrome,
  Birmingham
Harry Roy and his Band, Bebe and
  Belle, Vogelbein's Bears, Mereaux
  and Liliane, Fred Lovelle, Allen Bros
  and June, M&W.

6 October 1952 – Winter Gardens,
  Morecambe
Five Skyliners, Tom Katz Saxophone
  Six, Two Williams, Dolores and
  Leonardo Ferroni, Jimmie Elliott,
  Trio Eleanor, M&W.

13 October 1952 – Hippodrome,
  Boscombe
George Martin, Willy Paterson,
  Wilson Keppel and Betty, M&W,
  etc.

20 October 1952 – Empress, Brixton
Dr Crock and his Crackpots, the
  Beverley Sisters, M&W, George and
  Lydia, Jackie Ross, Los Marentos,
  the Two Sterlings.

27 October 1952 – Palace, Chelsea
Terry – Thomas, M&W, Two Pirates,
  Les Valettos, Claude Williams,
  Angelos, Beryl and Bobo, Nadias.

3 November 1952 – Palace, Plymouth
Hal Monty, Wilson Keppel and Betty,
M&W, Trio Elenor, Two Condons,
Nadias, Trio Bogino, etc.

17 November 1952 – Hippodrome,
Dudley
Charlie Chester, M&W, Alan Clive,
Trio Bogino, Beryl and Bobo, The
Condons, Roy Stevens, Eight Larry
Gordon Girls.

1 December 1952 – Palace, Halifax
Gladys Morgan and Co, Sisto and
Partner, Les Ricards, M&W, Joan
Laurie, Lester Sharpe and Iris, Les
and Len Rogers, Austin Sisters.

24 December 1952–28 March 1953 –
Lyceum, Sheffield
Dick Whittington and his Cat: Ken
Platt, Tom Heaton, Lynnette Rae,
M&W, Lorandos, Musical Elliotts.

30 March 1953 – Hippodrome,
Norwich
Eric Barker, M&W, Ron Parry,
Mundy and Earle, Jackie, David and
Jimmy Demon, Merle and Marie.

6 April 1953 (two weeks) –
Palladium, London
Tennessee Ernie Ford, Annell and
Brask, Florence Desmond, Madame
Louise with her Dogs and Pony,
Zero Mostel, M&W, Beverley
Sisters, Jack Durant, Palladium
Girls, Skyrockets Orchestra.

20 April 1953 – Royal, Portsmouth
Ken Platt, Doreen and Victor, Penny
Nichols and Billy Merrin, Harry
Worth, Flack and Lucas, M&W, Al
and Vic Farrell, Joan St Paul.

27 April 1953 – Empire, Leeds

Ken Platt, Cynthia and Gladys, Penny
Nichols and Billy Merrin, Flack and
Lucas, M&W, Laurie Watson, Four
Ds, Kerbsiders.

18 May 1953 – Empire, Newcastle
Ken Platt, Penny Nichols and Billy
Merrin, Flack and Lucas, M&W,
Laurie Watson, Four Ds, Kerbsiders,
Cassandras.

25 May 1953 – Alhambra, Bradford
Ken Platt, Penny Nichols and Billy
Merrin, Flack and Lucas, M&W,
Laurie Watson, Four Ds, Kerbsiders,
Cassandras.

8 June 1953 – Empire, Nottingham
Ken Platt, Dennis Brothers and June,
Penny Nicholls and Billy Merrin,
Four Ds, M&W, Harry Worth,
Kerbsiders, Cassandras.

25 June 1953–3 October 1953 –
Winter Gardens Pavilion, Blackpool
Something to Sing About: Allan Jones,
Ken Platt, M&W, Harry Worth,
Morlidor Trio, Rob Murray, Three
Coltas, Jean Baylesa, Malcolm
Goddard, Claudine Goodfellow,
Annette's Beau Belles.

2 November 1953 – Globe, Stockton

9 November 1953 – Palace,
Newcastle
M&W, Three Singing Scott Brothers,
Pop, White and Stagger, King
Brothers, Pauline and Eddie, Six
Starlets, Apex Four.

30 November 1953 – Theatre Royal,
Barnsley

24 December 1953–20 March 1954 –
Lyceum, Sheffield

Babes in the Wood: Freddie Sales, Stan Stennett, M&W, June Bishop, Mary Millar, Welcome Singers.

15 July 1954 – Hippodrome, Manchester
David Hughes, G. H. Elliott, M&W, Shipway Twins, Billy Danvers, Fayne and Evans, Manning and Joy Lea, Lorraine, Glamorous Roy Belles.

2 August 1954 – Grand Opera House, Belfast
Billy McCormack, M&W, Authors and Swinson, Cooper Twins, Walt Petz, Olga Varona, Billy Thorburn, Shirley Abicair.

9 August 1954 – Palace, Blackpool
M&W, Peter Cavanagh, Dick James, Max Geldray, Renee Strange, Jolly and Partner, Three Henrys, Dennis Bros and June.

16 August 1954 – Hippodrome, Birmingham
David Hughes, Jill, Jill and Jill, Yale and Diane, Des O'Connor, Avril Angers, Suzette Tarri, Tony Fayne and David Evans, Manning and Lee, Trio Tobas, M&W.

23 August 1954 – Empire, Sunderland
Frankie Vaughan, M&W, Radio Revellers, Trio Tobas, Shane and Lamar, Valento and Dorothy, Keefe Brothers and Annette, Manning and Lea.

30 August 1954 – Hippodrome, Wigan
M&W, Johnny Lockwood, Courtneys, Aerial Kenways, Gloria's Educated Dogs, Joe Crosbie, Rolg Hansen, Hal and Winnie Mack.

6 September 1954 – Empire, Middlesbrough
M&W, Garry Miller, Copa Cousins, Reg Russell with Susie, Tommy Lockley, Billy Bartholomew, Nicolettes, etc.

13 September 1954 – Royal, Hanley
Alma Cogan, M&W, etc.

20 September 1954 – Palace, Halifax
M&W, David Berglas, Stan White and Ann, Edmond Brothers, Paul Berrie, Six International Lovelies, Eve Boswell, Francois and Zandra, Gladys Morgan and Co, Keefe Bros and Annette, M&W, Randolph Sutton, Fayne and Evans, Ossie Morris, Bruce Forsyth.

27 September 1954 – Empire, Glasgow
Ray Ellington Quartet, Eve Boswell, M&W, Les Marthys, The Marvels, Norman Vaughan, Dot and Maureen, Tommy Lockey.

4 October 1954 – Empire, Edinburgh
Ray Ellington Quartet, Eve Boswell, M&W, Royale Trio, Tommy Lockey, Les Marthys, The Marvels, Norman Vaughan.

11 October 1954 – Empire, Newcastle
Ray Ellington Quartet, Eve Boswell, M&W, Royale Trio, Tommy Lockey, Manning and Lee, Les Marthys.

18 October 1954 – Empire, Sheffield
Ray Ellington Quartet, M&W, Gary Miller, Mayfairs, Norman Vaughan, Marvels, Manning and Lee, Les Marthys.

25 October 1954 – Empire,
Nottingham
Ray Ellington Quartet, Eve Boswell,
M&W, Conway and Day, Norman
Vaughan, Marvels, Manning and
Lee, Les Marthys.

1 November 1954 – Empire, Leeds
Ray Ellington Quartet, Eve Boswell,
M&W, Marvels, Norman Vaughan,
Manning and Lee, Les Marthys,
Jackson Bow and Darnell.

8 November 1954 – Empire,
Liverpool
Ray Ellington Quartet, Eve Boswell,
Les Marthys, Kay and Katrina,
M&W, Marvels, Norman Vaughan,
Manning and Lea.

15 November 1954 – Queen's,
Blackpool
Piccadilly to Paris: Jimmy Bryant,
M&W.

29 November 1954 – Empire,
Finsbury Park
Ray Ellington Quartet, Rex and
Bessie, Marvels, Eve Boswell, Les
Marthys, M&W, Norman Vaughan,
Tommy Lockey.

6 December 1954 – Hippodrome,
Hulme
M&W, Paul and Peta Page,
Johnny and Suma Lamonte, Billy
O'Sullivan, Two Yolandas, Lou
Campara, Keefe Bros and Annette,
Two Sterlings, etc.

24 December 1954–12 February
1955 – Hippodrome, Derby
Babes in the Wood: Stan Stennett,
M&W, Rex Holdsworth, the
Welcome Singers, Gladys Joyce,
Mary Miller, Shirley Cook, Sandra

and Mary, the Westway Corps de
Ballet, Alan Curtis.

7 March 1955 – New Royal,
Bournemouth
M&W, Four Jones Boys, Tex James
and his Ponies, Sandow Sisters,
Wyn Calvin, Yolanda, Jimmy Scott,
Lorraine and Gaye.

14 March 1955 – Empire, Glasgow
Frankie Vaughan, Two Sterlings,
Albert and Les Ward, Des
O'Connor, Jerry Allen Trio, Skylons,
M&W, Jat Herod.

21 March 1955 – Hippodrome,
Bristol
Ruby Murray, M&W, Jimmy Wheeler,
David Berglas, Harry Worth,
Skylons, Vera Cody and her Wonder
Horse, Norman Vaughan, Jackson
Bow and Darnell.

28 March 1955 – Empire, Chiswick
Joan Regan, M&W, Jimmy Wheeler,
Ted and George Durante, Jat Herod,
Harry Worth, Des O'Connor, Shane
and Lamar.

4 April 1955 – Empire, Sunderland
Ronnie Harris, Yale and Diane,
Bobbysoxers, M&W, Hollywood
Marionettes, Jimmy Edmundson,
Treble Tones, Jerry Harris, Gold and
Cordell.

13 April 1955 (one night) – New
Opera House, Blackpool
Reginald Dixon, Lupino Lane,
George Truzzi, Peter Glaze, Kenneth
Sandford, Pamela Bromley, Vera
Day, The John Tiller Girls, The
Victoria Palace Girls and Boys,
Kathryn Moore, The Flying De
Pauls, The Barbour Brothers and

Jean, The Amandis, The Crazy Gang, M&W, Bill Waddington, Josephine Anne, The Showgirls, Arthur Askey, Geraldo and his Orchestra, Jewel and Warriss, Littlewood's Girls' Choir, Joan Regan, Alma Cogan, Five Smith Brothers, George Formby, 1st Battalion The Liverpool Scottish (T. A.) (Queen's Own Cameron Highlanders), Beryl Grey with John Field, Jack Tripp with the John Tiller Girls, children from the Blackpool Tower Ballet, Charlie Cairoli with Paul, Wilfred and Mabel (Pickles), Albert Modley, Flanagan and Allen, Eddie Fisher with the BBC Northern Orchestra, Al Read.

18 April 1955 – Hippodrome, Manchester
Ruby Murray, M&W, Freddie Sales, Jat Herod, Ted and George Durante, Harry Worth, Des O'Connor, Aerial Kenways, Shane and Lamar.

25 April 1955 – Alhambra, Bradford
Beverley Sisters, Morgan and Manning, M&W, Skylons, Harry Worth, Freddie Harrison, Keefe Bros and Annette, Victor Seaforth.

9 May 1955 – Hippodrome, Birmingham
Ruby Murray, Shane and Lamar, Jimmy Wheeler, Flying De Pauls, M&W, Skylons, Ted and George Durante, Audrey Jeans, Harry Worth, Tommy Locky.

16 May 1955 – Empire, Nottingham
Ruby Murray, Kenways, M&W, Francois and Zandra, Audrey Jeans, Ted and George Durante, Jack Watson, Bruce Forsyth.

21 May–21 October 1955 – Central Pier, Blackpool
Let's Have Fun: M&W, Ken Dodd, Kenny Baker, Jimmy Clitheroe, The Kordites, Joy Harris.

23 October 1955 – Opera House, Belfast
M&W, Howard Jones and Reg Arnold, Jill Day, Jean and Joy Bernley, Austral, Les Ricards.

30 October 1955 – Empire, Sunderland
David Hughes, Francois and Zandra, M&W, Peggy Cavell, Chic Murray and Maidie, Audrey Jeans, Keefe Brothers and Annette.

6 November 1955 – Empire, Chiswick
Joan Regan, M&W, Audrey Jeans, Ted and George Durante, Harry Worth, Keefe Brothers and Annette, Tommy Locky, Francois and Zandra.

13 November 1955 – Gaumont, Southampton
Alma Cogan, M&W, Tommy Fields, Musical Elliotts, Ken Morris and Joan Savage, Rih-Aruso, Trio Rayros, Flack and Lucas.

20 November 1955 – Empire, Liverpool
David Whitfield, Horler Twins, M&W, Trio Ravros, Janet Brown, Wilson Keppel and Betty, Billy Maxam.

27 November 1955 – Hippodrome, Bristol
Eve Boswell, Francois and Zandra, Gladys Morgan and Co, Keefe Brois and Annette, M&W, Randolph

Sutton, Fayne and Evans, Ossie
Morris, Bruce Forsyth.

5 December 1955 – Hippodrome,
Derby
Issy Bonn, M&W, Harry Worth,
Mundy and Earle, Billy Guest and
Caroline, Hollywood Marionettes,
Scott's Sea lions, Gale and Clarke.

24 December 1955–25 February
1956 – Empire, Swansea
Babes in the Wood: Stan Stennett,
M&W, Leslie Hatton, Gladys Joyce,
Mary Millar, etc.

19 March 1956 – Empire, Edinburgh
Chic Murray and Maidie, Granger
Brothers, Four Jones Boys, Bill
Wareham and Barbara, M&W,
Harry Worth, Billie Wyner, Bruce
Forsyth.

26 March 1956 – Hippodrome,
Birmingham
Joan Regan, McAndrews and Mills,
M&W, Nenette Mongadors and
Anne, Tony Fayne and David Evans,
Wilson Keppel and Betty, Richards
and Yolands, Bobby Limb.

2 April 1956 – Empire, Finsbury Park
Three Monarchs, Anton and Janetta,
M&W, Walthon and Dorraine, Tony
Fayne and David Evans, Bobbie
Kimber, Kazan and Katz.

9 April 1956 – New, Cardiff
Four Jones Boys, M&W, Johnny
Stewart, Billie Wyner, Jack Francois,
Keefe Brothers and Annette,
Delicados, Cynthia and Gladys,

2 July 1956 – Regal, Great Yarmouth
Teddy Johnson and Pearl Carr,
M&W, Sally Barnes, Billy Maxam,

Frances Duncan, Winston Foxwell,
Lane Twins.

9 July 1956 – Empire, Liverpool
Yana, Mayfairs, M&W, Lester Sharpe
and Iris, Cherry Wainer, Frank
Cook, Marion and Eddie Rose,
Tattersall and Jerry.

16 July 1956 – Winter Gardens,
Morecambe
Yana, M&W, El Granadas, Eleanor
Gunter and partner, Tony and
Pauline Derrick, Freddie Harrison,
Granger Brothers.

23 July 1956 – Empire, Glasgow
Issy Bonn, Gold and Cordell, M&W,
Romaine and Claire, Billie Anthony,
Freddie Bamberger and Pam, Phil
Darban and Wendy.

30 July 1956 – Hippodrome,
Birmingham
Yana, Granger Brothers, M&W,
Freddie Harrison, Cherry Wainer,
Eleanor Gunter and Partner, Eddie
Gordon and Nancy.

6 August 1956 – Palace, Manchester
Yana, Granger Brothers, M&W,
Romaine and Claire, Walthon and
Dorraine, Max Geldray, George
Melton.

13 August 1956 – Coventry Theatre,
Coventry
Yana, M&W, Cherry Wainer, Allen
Brothers and June, Walthon and
Dorraine, Jackie Ross, Helen.

20 August 1956 – Ritz, Cleethorpes
Dickie Valentine, M&W, Eddie Rone
and Marion, Eleanor Gunter, Lane
Twins, Tony and Pauline Derrick,
Richman and Jackson.

10 September 1956 – Empire, Newcastle
David Whitfield, Kay and Valerie Glynn, M&W, Kelroys, Janet Brown, Archie Glen, Joan and Ernest.

17 September 1956 – Savoy, Lincoln
Joan Regan, M&W, Sally Barnes, Walthon and Dorraine, George Melton, Lane Twins, Tattersall and Jerry.

24 September 1956 – Rialto, York
Dickie Valentine, M&W, Musical Elliotts, Les Mallini, Freddie Harrison, Rita Martell, Ballet Montparnasse.

8 October 1956 – Pavilion, Liverpool
M&W, Penny Nicholls, Billy McCormack, Dandy Brothers, Two Pirates, Skylons, Peter Raynor, Bill Wareham and Barbara, etc.

15 October 1956 – Alhambra, Bradford
Dickie Valentine, M&W, Evy and Everto, Martin Granger, Freddie Harrison, Nadias, Ann and Val Shelley.

29 October 1956 – Empire, Glasgow
Anne Shelton, Floyd and B'Nay, M&W, Cooper Twins, Dickie Henderson, King Brothers, Skylons, Ann and Bobbie Black.

5 November 1956 (two weeks) – Prince of Wales, London
Hylda Baker, Peggy Ryan and Ray McDonald, Derek Roy, Charlie Cairoli and Paul, M&W, Four Jones Boys, Billie Anthony, Joe Church, Jo Jac and Joni, Marcellis.

24 December 1956–2 March 1957 – Hippodrome, Dudley
Dick Whittington: Stan Stennett, Mrs Shufflewick, M&W, Doreen Croft, Janet Wall, Alan Curtis, Peter Young, Nicholas Rogers, Ken Swales, Prudence Rodney, Lehmiski Ladies, Latour Babes, 7 Volants, Maple Leaf Four, Jimmy Currie's Rocking Cabin.

1 April 1957 – Metropolitan, Edgware Road
April Fools: Jon Pertwee, M&W, Glen Mason, Fe Jover, Henri Vadden and Partner, Les and Len Rogers, Fred Atkins, Tony Gilbert and Sylvia.

8 April 1957 – Empire, Chiswick
David Whitfield, M&W, Vera Cody and Company, Frank Cook, Elites, Three Paulos, Ron and Rita.

15 April 1957 – New Royal, Bournemouth
M&W, Gary Miller, Brazilianos, Shipway Twins, Lloyd and Vi Day, Georgette, Two Vinces, Harry Arnold, Ray and Ronjay.

29 April 1957 – Empire, Nottingham
Yana, Renee Dymott, M&W, the Weldens, Hollander and Hart, The Raymils, Pharos and Marina.

3 June–12 October 1957 – Central Pier, Blackpool
Let's Have Fun: M&W, Kenny Baker, Dennis Spicer, Joan Turner.

21 December 1957–29 March 1958 – Coventry Theatre, Coventry
Puss in Boots: Harry Secombe, M&W, Janie Marden, Terry Kendall, Gillian Lynne, Tony Sympson, Three Tarragonas,

George Mitchell Choir, Julia Sutton, Herbert Hare, John Wright, Charles Rowley, Betty Fox Babs, Corps de Ballet.

31 March 1958 – Hippodrome, Birmingham
Johnny Duncan, Ann and Val Shelley, M&W, Carlo Sisters, Southlanders, Manetti Twins, Freddie Earle.

7 April 1958 – Empire, Chiswick
Alma Cogan, M&W, the Hedley Ward Trio, Three Paulos, Ray Alan with Steve and Skippy, Ron and Rita, Norman and Nikki Grant.

12 May 1958 – Empire, Newcastle
Marvin Rainwater, Candy Sisters, M&W, Carlo Sisters, Phil Fernando, Freddie Earle, Falcons.

19 May 1958 – Hippodrome, Hulme
M&W, Dennis Spicer, Nordics, Marcia Owen, Steve Martin, Carter and Doray, Kemp Sisters.

16 June 1958 – Royalty, Chester
Rush Hamilton, M&W, Barbara Law, Verdini, Gillian and June, Christine Martell, Leslie Bryant.

23 June 1958 – Granada, Shrewsbury
Eddie Calvert, Rosemary Squires, Rush Hamilton, M&W, Londonaires, Margo and John, Pinky and Perky, Mandy and Sandy.

7 July–23 August 1958 – Winter Gardens, Morecambe
Resident summer revue
Alma Cogan, Ken Platt, M&W, Semprini, Albert Sturm, Audrey Mann, Kendor Bros, Munks Twins.

7 October–6 December 1958 – Tivoli, Melbourne
Rocking the Town: Winifred Atwell, M&W, Gaston Palmer, Two Earls, Ross and Howitt, Jack and Doreen Rees Puppets, Trio Sylverkings, Vic Sabrino, Lorraine Bransgrove, Beverly Urquhart.

15 December 1958–21 February 1959 – Tivoli Sydney
Rocking the Town: Winifred Atwell, M&W, Gaston Palmer, Two Earls, Ross and Howitt, Jack and Doreen Rees Puppets, Trio Sylverkings, Vic Sabrino, Lorraine Bransgrove, Beverly Urquhart.

16 March 1959 – Empire, Glasgow
Alma Cogan, Edorics, M&W, Maurice French and Joy, Alan Clive, Marcellis, Frank Cook.

13 April 1959 – Hippodrome, Birmingham
Joan Regan, Ballet Montmartre, M&W, Stan Stennett, Ronnie Collis, Tommy Wallis and Beryl, Richards and Volanda, Nico Ferry and Co.

20 April 1959 – Empire, Finsbury Park
Joan Regan, M&W.

16 May–26 September 1959 – Central Pier, Blackpool
Let's Have Fun: Jimmy James, M&W, Trio Vedette.

9 November 1959 (two weeks) – Empire, Finsbury Park
Diamond Jubilee Show: Michael Holliday, De Vere Girls, Joan Regan, Dennis Spicer, Mistin Juniors, M&W, Gilbert, Billy Dainty.

23 December 1959–20 February 1960 – Empire, Liverpool
Jack and the Beanstalk: Hylda Baker, Jimmy Clitheroe, Lorrae Desmond, Jill Westlake, M&W, Tony Melody, Arnaut Joan and Arnaut, Arthur Clarke, Yuiles.

2 June 1960 – North Pier, Blackpool
Show Time: Standing in for Bruce Forsyth.

10 June–17 September 1960 – Alexandra Gardens, Weymouth
Show Time: Anne Shelton, M&W, Gladys Morgan and Co, Daisy May and Saveen, The Kingpins, Kendor Brothers, Show Time Lovelies, Louis Mordish Trio.

17 October 1960 (six weeks) – Coventry Theatre, Coventry
The Birthday Show: Arthur Askey, M&W, Yana, Roy Castle, Ken Morris and Joan Savage, the Dallas Boys, Kazbek and Zari, the Amin Brothers, the Debutantes, the Debonnaires.

24 December 1960–4 March 1961 – Alexandra, Birmingham
Sinbad the Sailor: George Lacy, M&W, Lynnette Rae, Johnny Stewart, the Four Playboys, the Three Ghezzis, Hans Bela and Mary, Anton and Janetta, Linda Lee, Sylvia Briar, Derek Royle, William Avenell, Arthur Tolcher, the Lehmiski Ladies, the Roselli Singers.

18 April 1961 (six weeks) – Palace, Manchester
The Spring Show: Alma Cogan, the Charlivels, M&W, the Dallas Boys, Rosemary Squires, Billy Dainty,

Freddie Frinton, Three Ghezzis, Kazbek and Zari, the Debutantes, the Debonaires.

7 June–30 September 1961 – Princess, Torquay
Show Time: Joan Regan, Tommy Cooper, M&W, Edmund Hockridge, Ugo Garrido, Munk Twins, Patricia Stark, George Mitchell Four, The Lovelies.
Producer: Ernest Maxin.

6 November 1961 – Prince of Wales, London
Royal Variety Performance

26 December 1961–10 March 1962 – Grand, Leeds
Sleeping Beauty: David Whitfield, M&W, Tony Heaton, Patricia Lambert.

1 June–8 December 1962 – Palladium, London
Every Night at the Palladium: Bruce Forsyth, M&W, Teddy Johnson and Pearl Carr.

21 December 1962–23 February 1963 – Empire, Liverpool
Sleeping Beauty: David Whitfield, M&W, Eddie Molloy, Carol Layton, Dorothy Dampier, Charles Harris, Eric Greenall, Winstanley Babes, Kirby's Flying Ballet, Bill Shepherd Singers, the Empire Boys and Girls.

31 May–5 October 1963 – North Pier, Blackpool
Bernard Delfont presents *Show Time*: M&W, Matt Monro, Lena Martell, Saveen, Strong Bros, San Remo Trio, Paul Burnett and Orchestra, Show Time Lovelies.

24 December 1963–7 March 1964 –
Hippodrome, Bristol
Sleeping Beauty: M&W, Edmund
Hockridge, Eddie Molloy, Erica
Yorke, Elizabeth Alys, Betty Emery,
Nicholas Smith, James Hinson,
Bristol Babes, Hippodrome Dancers,
Derek Taverner Singers.

5 June–26 September 1964 –
Wellington Pier, Great Yarmouth
Bernard Delfont presents *Show Time*:
M&W, Bert Weedon, Barbara Law,
Daniel Remy, Paul and Peta Page,
the San Remo Trio, Herbert Hare,
Pavilion Lovelies, Des O'Connor at
the Britannia.

12 July 1964 (one night) – Floral
Hall, Scarborough
M&W, Stanley Watson, Julius
Nehring, Sylvia Eaves, Michael
Collins, Roy Douglas, Stanley
Ashforth and his Orchestra.

26 December 1964–3 April 1965 –
Palace, Manchester
Sleeping Beauty: M&W, Edmund
Hockridge, Eddie Molloy, Dorothy
Dampier, Denny Dayviss, Herbert
Hare, Betty Emery, Leon Bartell
Dancers, Winstanley Babes.

5 June–25 September 1965 – ABC,
Blackpool
The Morecambe and Wise Show:
M&W, Mark Wynter, Anna
Dawson, The Three Hermanis, The
Alfrero, Marvo and Delores, Pamela
Devis Dancers.

30 May 1966 – Coventry Theatre,
Coventry
Two of a Kind: M&W, Teddy
Johnson and Pearl Carr, Eddie
Calvert and Arthur Worsley.

16 July–2 September 1966 – Winter
Gardens, Bournemouth
The Morecambe and Wise Show:
M&W, Susan Maughan, Arthur
Worsley, Eric Delaney and his Band,
Ivor Emmanuel, the Aristons, Jimmy
Lee, Valerie Shelton, 10 Dancing
Lovelies.

26 December 1966–11 March 1967 –
Hippodrome, Birmingham
Sleeping Beauty: M&W, Eddie
Molloy, Patricia Bredin, Kevin Scott,
Jimmy Lee, Dororthy Dampier,
Betty Emery, Betty Fox Babes.

24 June–23 September 1967 – ABC,
Great Yarmouth
The Morecambe and Wise Show:
M&W, Ivor Emmanuel, David and
Marianne Dalmour, Eric Delaney
and his band, Saveen and Daisy
May, Pamela Devis Dancers, Jimmy
Lee.
The Morecambe and Wise Show –
tour sponsored by Ovaltine: M&W,
Eric Delaney and his Band, Pearl
Carr and Teddy Johnson, Anna Lou
and Maria, Saveen and Daisy May,
Ballet Montparnasse.
1 April 1968 – New, Cardiff
8 April 1968 – Palace, Manchester
15 April 1968 – Hippodrome, Bristol
22 April 1968 – Empire, Liverpool.

13 May 1968 (two weeks) – O'Keefe
Centre, Toronto
The London Palladium Show: M&W,
Pearl Carr and Teddy Johnson.

10 November 1968 – Variety Club,
Batley
Week cut short by Eric's heart attack.

Endnotes

Chapter 1

1 *Eric and Ernie: The autobiography of Morecambe and Wise* by Eric Morecambe and Ernie Wise, with Dennis Holman (WH Allen, London, 1973), p17.

2 Ibid, p22.

3 'The Nig Nog Club – Uncle Mac Talks', *Morecambe Guardian*, 7 December 1929, p11.

4 'Nignog Revue Wins Again – Best Ever Show – Old Favourites and New – Happiness the Keynote', *Bradford Observer*, 31 March 1936, p5.

5 Ibid.

6 *Eric and Ernie: The autobiography of Morecambe and Wise*, p28.

7 'Young Stage "Hopefuls" – Few Bradford "Discoveries"', *Bradford Observer*, 20 May 1938, p3.

8 *The Best of Jazz 2* by Humphrey Lyttelton (Robson Books, London, 1981).

9 Author's conversation with Hugh Mendl, 1 May 2002.

10 *40 Minutes: The Importance of Being Ernie* (BBC1, tx: 27 April 1993).

11 Ibid.

12 *Eric and Ernie: The autobiography of Morecambe and Wise*, p6.

13 Ibid.

14 Ibid, p12.

15 Ibid, p6.

16 Ibid, p10.

17 Ibid, p7.

18 Ibid, p5.

19 'Meeting People: Why Eric would not like to read a lesson in church...' by Scarth Flett, *Sunday Express*, 1 February 1981, p3.

20 *Liverpool Echo*, 17 June 1940, p1.

21 *Eric and Ernie: The autobiography of Morecambe and Wise*, pp4 and 14.

22 *Melody Maker*, 2 March 1940.

23 Author's conversation with Gary Morecambe, 6 November 2013.

24 Ibid.

25 *Eric and Ernie: The autobiography of Morecambe and Wise*, p33.

26 Author's conversation with Ernest Maxin, 9 November 2005.

27 *Eric and Ernie: The autobiography of Morecambe and Wise*, pp34–5.

28 Ibid, p35.

29 *The Best of British Laughs* (R4, tx: 5 December 1971).

30 *Eric and Ernie: The autobiography of Morecambe and Wise*, p38.

31 Ibid, p49.
32 'Prince of Wales Theatre: Strike a New Note', *The Stage*, 25 March 1943, p1.
33 *Eric and Ernie: The autobiography of Morecambe and Wise*, pp49–50.
34 Included in *The Morecambe and Wise Special* (Weidenfeld and Nicolson, London, 1977).
35 *Eric and Ernie: The autobiography of Morecambe and Wise*, p51.
36 Ibid, p50.
37 Ibid, p49.
38 *London Town* (1946).
39 *Hudson and Halls*, BBC1, 1 September 1989.
40 Author's conversation with Stanley Baxter, 31 May 2006.
41 Author's conversation with John Ammonds, 14 April 2005.

Chapter 2

1 *Eric and Ernie: The autobiography of Morecambe and Wise* by Eric Morecambe and Ernie Wise, with Dennis Holman (W. H. Allen, London, 1973), p62.
2 Ibid, p66.
3 *Wells Journal*, 16 May 1947, p2.
4 *Wiltshire Times and Trowbridge Advertiser*, 10 May 1947, p4.
5 *Eric and Ernie: The autobiography of Morecambe and Wise*, p57.
6 *Still On My Way to Hollywood*, by Ernie Wise and Trevor Barnes (Duckworth, London, 1990), p69.
7 *Eric and Ernie: The autobiography of Morecambe and Wise*, p63.
8 Author's conversation with John Bouchier, 25 September 2020.
9 'Round the Halls', *The Stage*, 27 April 1950, p5.
10 *Eric and Ernie: The autobiography of Morecambe and Wise*, p106.
11 Ibid, p108.
12 Ibid, p106.
13 Author's conversation with Alan Grahame, 24 February 2020.
14 *Yorkshire Evening Post*, 18 October 1949, p5.
15 'Round the Halls', *The Stage*, 9 June 1949, p5.
16 Author's conversation with Barry Cryer, 22 March 2020.
17 *Over the Limit* by Bob Monkhouse (Century, London, 1998), pp34–5.
18 Author's conversation with John Ammonds, 14 April 2005.
19 Author's conversation with Peter Pilbeam, 26 June 2020.
20 *Eric and Ernie: The autobiography of Morecambe and Wise* by Eric Morecambe and Ernie Wise, with Dennis Holman (WH Allen, London, 1973), p129.
21 Memo from Ronnie Taylor to Patrick Newman, BBC Written Archives file RCONT1, Morecambe and Wise Artists 1947–1954.
22 Memo from Patrick Newman to Ronnie Taylor, 25 November 1953, BBC Written Archives file RCONT1, Morecambe and Wise Artists 1947–1954.
23 Letter from Ernie Wise to Miss Boxall, variety department bookings assistant, 20 September 1955, BBC Written Archives file RCONT2, Morecambe and Wise Artists 1955–1962.
24 Letter from Patrick Newman to Morecambe and Wise, BBC Written Archives file RCONT2, Morecambe and Wise Artists 1955–62.
25 Letter from Morecambe and Wise to Patrick Newman, BBC Written Archives file RCONT2,

Morecambe and Wise Artists
1955–62.

26 Author's conversation with Alan
Grahame, 24 February 2020.

27 *One Pair of Eyes: No, But
Seriously* (BBC2, tx: 7 June 1969).

28 Author's conversation with James
Casey, 17 June 2009.

29 Author's conversation with Gary
Morecambe, 6 November 2013.

Chapter 3

1 'Would you laugh at these? I SAY
YES!' George Campey, *London
Evening Standard*, 9 November
1953.

2 Letter from Frank Pope to Ronnie
Waldman, 9 November 1953, BBC
Written Archives file TVART1 –
Morecambe and Wise 1948–61.

3 'Who will be foremost in drama
and television?', *Picture Post*, 2
January 1954, pp10–11.

4 Letter from Frank Pope to Ronnie
Waldman, 8 January 1954, BBC
Written Archives file TVART1 –
Morecambe and Wise 1948–61.

5 Letter from Ronnie Waldman to
Frank Pope, BBC Written Archives
file TVART1 – Morecambe and
Wise 1948–61.

6 'Running Wild is about right',
Daily Mirror, 22 April 1954, p4.

7 'TV News' by Kenneth Baily, The
People, 25 April 1954, p8.

8 'Three Nation Show a courageous
effort', *Sunderland Daily Echo*, 23
April 1954, p8.

9 *Daily Herald*, 22 April 1954, p3.

10 Gilbert Harding's Notebook,
Picture Post, 22 May 1954.

11 Letter from Frank Pope to Ronnie
Waldman, 17 June 1954, BBC
Written Archives file TVART1 –
Morecambe and Wise 1948–61.

12 Letter from Ronnie Waldman to
Frank Pope, 17 June 1954, BBC
Written Archives file TVART1 –
Morecambe and Wise 1948–61.

13 Author's conversation with John
Ammonds, 14 April 2005.

14 *The Show Goes On* (BBC Light
Programme, tx: 24 May 1955).

15 *The Goon Show: The Greenslade
Story*, script by Spike Milligan,
(BBC Light Programme, tx: 20
December 1955).

16 Johnny Speight interview with Ian
Potter, 9 June 1995.

17 *Eric and Ernie: The autobiography
of Morecambe and Wise* by Eric
Morecambe and Ernie Wise, with
Dennis Holman (W. H. Allen,
London, 1973), p136.

18 'Why Bother?' *The Stage*, 5 July
1956, p12.

19 'Keynote Speed', *Radio Times*,
11–17 August 1957, p5.

20 Gladys Morgan from Edward
Taylor to John Ammonds, 5 May
1959, BBC Written Archives file
N18/3414/1 North Region – Artist
– Morecambe and Wise 1949–65.

21 Memo from Eric Miller to B.
W. Cave-Browne-Cave, Head
of North Region Programmes,
3 February 1959, BBC Written
Archives file N18/3414/1 North
Region – Artist – Morecambe and
Wise 1949–65.

22 Memo from B. W. Cave-Browne-
Cave, Head of North Region
Programmes, 18 February
1959, BBC Written Archives file
N18/3414/1 North Region – Artist
– Morecambe and Wise 1949–65.

23 Author's conversation with Gary
Morecambe, 6 November 2013.

24 Letter from John Ammonds to
Edward Taylor, 5 June 1959, BBC
Written Archives file N18/3414/1

North Region – Artist –
Morecambe and Wise 1949–65.

25 *This Particular Show* (ATV, tx:
26 December 1959).

Chapter 4

1 Memo from Frank Muir and
Denis Norden to Eric Maschwitz,
head of light entertainment, 6
October 1960 – BBC Written
Archives – TVART1 – Morecambe
and Wise – file 1 – 1948–1961.

2 Letter from Billy Marsh to Tom
Sloan, assistant head of light
entertainment, 8 February 1961 –
BBC Written Archives – TVART1
– Morecambe and Wise – file 1 –
1948–1961.

3 Author's conversation with Jack
Parnell, 24 January 2004.

4 *Bruce: the Autobiography* by
Bruce Forsyth (Sidgwick and
Jackson, London), pp84–5.

5 'Equity shows its teeth', *The Stage*,
27 April 1961, p1.

6 *Eric and Ernie: The autobiography
of Morecambe and Wise* by Eric
Morecambe and Ernie Wise, with
Dennis Holman (W. H. Allen,
London, 1973), p157.

7 'Hughie Green', Aberdeen *Evening
Express*, 10 November 1961, p2.

8 *Late Night Line-Up*, BBC2, 20
November 1966.

9 *Eric and Ernie: the autobiography
of Morecambe and Wise*, p156.

10 'He makes it sound so easy!', by
Marjorie Bilbow, *The Stage*, 12
March 1964, p10.

11 'Colour and gaiety', *The Stage*, 9
November 1961, p9.

12 *Best of British Laughs* (BBC R4,
tx: 5 December 1971).

13 Ibid.

14 *Best of British Laughs* (BBC R4,
tx: 5 December 1971).

Chapter 5

1 'Now Morecambe and Wise want
to buy British Lion' by Ned Grant,
Daily Mirror, 19 February 1964,
p3.

2 *Points West*, BBC Bristol, 1964,
exact date uncertain.

3 'Morecambe and Wise reach for
world stardom with screen debut',
Coventry Evening Telegraph, 28
November 1964, p7.

4 'The Joyful Spell of Julie: New
Films' by Dick Richards, *Daily
Mirror*, 26 March 1965, p24.

5 'The New Films: If you're young
in heart – then this is for YOU'
by Ernest Betts, The *People*, 28
March 1965, p15.

6 Reviews, *Sunday Mirror*, 28
March 1965, p29.

7 Author's conversation with
William G. Stewart, 22 March
2006.

8 'Whatever happened to the vital
touch?' by Dick Richards, *Daily
Mirror*, 25 March 1966, p21.

9 'An Alfie Elkins worth a better
film', *The Times*, 24 March 1966,
p16.

10 *Late Night Line-Up* (BBC2, tx: 20
November 1966).

11 'Demy's Hollywood-style musical'
by John Russell Taylor, *The Times*,
6 July 1967, p8.

12 'Why must they break up Eric and
Ernie?' by Dick Richards, *Daily
Mirror*, 7 July 1967, p19.

13 *One Pair of Eyes: No, But
Seriously* (BBC2, tx: 7 June 1969).

14 *Desert Island Discs* (BBC R4, tx:
21 October 1990).

Chapter 6

1 'What the stars foretell' by Alasdair Buchan, *Daily Mirror*, 21 April 1979, p9.
2 Author's conversation with John Bouchier, 25 September 2020.
3 Author's correspondence with Roger Ordish, 11 November 2020.
4 *Parkinson* (BBC1, tx: 11 November 1972).
5 Author's conversation with Gary Morecambe, 6 November 2013.

Chapter 7

1 Author's conversation with Sir Bill Cotton, 29 September 2004.
2 *Desert Island Discs* (BBC R4, tx: 21 October 1990).
3 Author's conversation with John Fisher, 11 May 2006.
4 Author's conversation with Stuart Lindley, 29 January 2021.
5 Author's conversation with Gary Morecambe, 6 November 2013.
6 Eric Morecambe's diary entry, 30 August 1967, quoted in *Eric Morecambe Unseen*, edited by William Cook (HarperCollins, London, 2005).
7 Author's conversation with John Ammonds, 14 April 2005.
8 Author's conversation with Terry Henebery, 6 November 2004.
9 Author's conversation with Con Cluskey, 20 June 2009.
10 *Look Back with Laughter, Volume Two* by Mike Craig, pp192–3.
11 Ibid, p194.
12 *Eric and Ernie: The autobiography of Morecambe and Wise* by Eric Morecambe and Ernie Wise, with Dennis Holman (W. H. Allen, London, 1973), p202.

13 Author's conversation with Ernest Maxin, 9 November 2005.
14 *Does the Team Drink* (BBC R4, tx: 6 August 2019).
15 'Is it funny or isn't it?' by Marjorie Bilbow, *The Stage*, 4 February 1965, p12.
16 'Laughter makers switch to ITV' by Martin Jackson, *Daily Express*, 21 March 1969, p11.
17 *Eric and Ernie: The autobiography of Morecambe and Wise*, p205.

Chapter 8

1 *The Book What I Wrote* by Eddie Braben (Hodder and Stoughton, London, 2004), p40.
2 *A Royal Gala* (ITV, tx: 4 December 1966).
3 'Eric's back' by Kenneth Eastaugh, *Daily Mirror*, 21 May 1969, p9.
4 *The Morecambe and Wise Show* (BBC2, tx: 27 July 1969).
5 *Parkinson* (BBC1, tx: 11 November 1972).
6 *The Book What I Wrote*, p4.
7 *The Morecambe and Wise Christmas Show* (BBC1, tx: 25 December 1973).
8 Author's conversation with Barry Cryer, 15 September 2010.
9 *Omnibus: Fools Rush In* (BBC1, tx: 18 February 1973).
10 'Back – and better than ever' by James Thomas, *Daily Express*, 28 July 1969, p8.
11 *The Morecambe and Wise Show* (BBC1, tx: 8 April 1971).
12 *The Morecambe and Wise Show* (ATV, tx: 25 April 1964).
13 'I Love You All: the biggest star of TV tells the lot', *Sunday Mirror*, 8 July 1973, pp10–12.

14 'Now fashion thinks big' by Moya Jones, *Liverpool Echo*, 10 November 1970, p6.

15 'Not now Arthur' by Val Marriott, *Leicester Chronicle*, 18 October 1974, p2.

16 Author's conversation with Eddie Stuart, 16 October 2020.

17 Author's conversation with Alan Plater, 25 February 2009.

18 Audience Research Report, Morecambe and Wise Christmas Show 1970, 2 February 1971 – BBC Written Archives file T12/1392/1 – Morecambe and Wise Christmas Special 1970.

19 *The Morecambe and Wise Christmas Show* (BBC1, tx: 25 December 1971).

20 Ibid.

21 Author's conversation with Eddie Stuart, 16 October 2020.

22 Author's conversation with Ernest Maxin, 9 November 2005.

23 *Morecambe and Wise Christmas Show* (BBC1, tx: 25 December 1971).

24 Author's conversation with John Ammonds, 14 April 2005.

25 Author's conversation with Barry Cryer, 23 March 2020.

26 *The Book What I Wrote*, p37.

27 *The Morecambe and Wise Show*, series 9, show 6 (BBC1, tx: 19 April 1976).

28 Ibid.

29 *Morecambe and Wise Christmas Show* (BBC1, tx: 25 December 1972).

30 '"Let's stop the knock", says Des' by Ken Irwin, *Daily Mirror*, 8 March 1975, p15.

31 *Christmas with Eric and Ernie* (Thames, tx: 25 December 1979).

32 'Des at 79: "I used to send Eric and Ernie jokes"' by Jane Clinton, *Sunday Express*, 2 October 2011, p52.

33 Author's correspondence with Susan Belbin, 25 February 2021.

34 Author's conversation with John Ammonds, 14 April 2005.

35 *Ask Aspel* (BBC1, tx: 17 August 1977).

36 *There's No Answer to That!* by Eric Morecambe and Ernie Wise with Michael Freedland (Coronet, London, 1981), p19.

37 Ibid, p44.

38 Ibid, p18.

39 Author's conversation with John Bouchier, 25 September 2020.

40 *There's No Answer to That!*, p155.

41 Ibid, p154.

42 *The Morecambe and Wise Show*, series 3, show 3 (ATV, tx: 29 June 1963).

43 *Morecambe and Wise: Live 1973* (Polygram Video).

44 *The Morecambe and Wise Show* (BBC1, tx: 27 July 1974).

45 Author's conversation with John Ammonds, 14 April 2005.

46 Author's conversation with Ernest Maxin, 9 November 2005.

47 Visual Effects Requirements form, sent by Susan Belbin, 11 February 1976, BBC Written Archives file T12/1401/1, Morecambe and Wise Show 1976 shows 3 and 4.

48 Author's conversation with Eddie Stuart, 16 October 2020.

49 *There's No Answer To That!*, p18.

50 Author's conversation with Paul Maxin, 17 March 2020.

51 Author's conversation with Ernest Maxin, 9 November 2005.

52 Ibid.

53 Ibid.
54 Author's conversation with Paul Maxin, 17 March 2020.
55 *The Crystal Bucket* by Clive James (Picador, London, 1981), p91.
56 Author's conversation with John Ammonds, 14 April 2005.
57 *Double Bill* by Bill Cotton (Fourth Estate, London, 2000).

Chapter 9

1 *There's No Answer to That!* by Eric Morceambe and Ernie Wise with Michael Freedland, (Coronet, London, 1981), p110.
2 *The Morecambe and Wise Show* (Thames, tx: 18 October 1978).
3 Author's conversation with Chris Dean, 8 November 2020.
4 Author's correspondence with David Hamilton, 20 April 2020.
5 *There's No Answer To That!*, pp148–9.
6 *Parkinson* (BBC1, tx: 11 November 1972).
7 Author's conversation with Barry Cryer, 22 March 2020.
8 'Eric goes to hospital, but has a laugh', *Daily Mirror*, 21 January 1979, p3.
9 *There's No Answer to That!*, p118.
10 '"I'll have to go it alone", says Ern' by Steve Bailey, *Sunday Mirror*, 22 April 1979, p24.
11 Author's conversation with Bill Cotton, 29 September 2004.

12 'Meeting People: Why Eric would not like to read a lesson in church...' by Scarth Flett, *Sunday Express*, 1 February 1981, p3.
13 *Mr Lonely* by Eric Morecambe (Methuen, London, 1981), p10.
14 Ibid, p87.
15 Ibid, p59.
16 Author's conversation with John Ammonds, 14 April 2005.
17 *Morecambe and Wise* by Graham McCann (Fourth Estate, London, 1998), p283.
18 *There's No Answer to That!*, p128.

Chapter 10

1 'Sir John – Poet of the People', *Sunday Mirror*, 20 May 1984, p15.
2 *Desert Island Discs* (BBC R4, tx: 21 October 1990).
3 Ibid.
4 *The Book What I Wrote* by Eddie Braben (Hodder and Stoughton, London, 2004), p256.
5 *Desert Island Discs* (BBC R4, tx: 21 October 1990).
6 Ibid.
7 Ibid.

Chapter 11

1 Author's conversation with Gary Morecambe, 6 November 2013.
2 Ibid.

Acknowledgements

When Richard Milbank and Anthony Cheetham at Head of Zeus suggested that this book should exist, I very briefly had reservations. So many words have been written about Morecambe and Wise over the years, was there anything more to say?

An answer in the affirmative came when I revisited the transcripts of the interviews I had undertaken with Johnny Ammonds and Ernest Maxin for my book *Turned Out Nice Again*. Although these had been general overviews of these two distinguished producers' careers, Eric and Ernie, naturally, figured heavily, and there was far more there than I had been able to use. In addition, the Magnificent Two had cropped up in numerous other interviews I had conducted over the years.

Then there was the BBC Written Archives Centre at Caversham, where Louise North was once again able to open up the files for me. My two-day raid there was facilitated by my dear friend Charlotte Ross, who put me up overnight and gave me curry.

I am indebted to John Adams, Susan Belbin, John Bouchier, Barry Cryer, Chris Dean, Alan Grahame, David Hamilton, Stuart Lindley, Roger Ordish, Peter Pilbeam and Eddie Stuart for the insights they gave me on knowing and working with

Eric and Ernie, and to Gail Renard for her theory about the all-too-frequent inclination towards ill health of British comedians, which came up in my Radio 4 documentary *Does the Team Drink?*

Thanks also to friends like Steve Arnold, David Brunt, Pete Cater, Simon Coward, Adam Cumiskey, Martin Fenton, Ian Greaves, George Grimwood, Simon Harries, Jason Hazeley, Andy Hollingworth, Patrick Humphries, Georgy Jamieson, Adam McLean, Matt Owen, Ian Potter, Gareth Randall, Hamstall Ridware, Gary Rodger, Simon Scott, Jonathan Sloman, Ed Stradling, Gavin Sutherland, Vicky Thomas, John Williams and Rob Williams, all of whom provided archive material or informed thoughts on the matter in hand. In addition, I must express profound gratitude to the faintly mysterious @eric_ernie_col on Twitter, a one-person Morecambe and Wise Archive. I can vouch for his existence, as we sat together at Ernest Maxin's funeral, and sang 'Bring Me Sunshine' with the rest of the congregation.

Then there are those who were closest to me during the strange, fractured stretch of history in which this book came to be: Sali Earls, Alanna Lauder, Susannah Godman, my daughter Primrose and my mum. My conversation with John Bouchier happened purely because of a chance conversation between Sali and a woman who turned out to be his daughter in a swimming pool in West Wales.

At Head of Zeus, it was a delight to work once again with the aforementioned Richard Milbank, as well as encountering Matilda Singer, Anna Nightingale and Kate Appleton, all of whom have been clever, kind and patient. Meanwhile I send fifteen per cent of my thanks to my agents David Smith and Annette Green.

Finally, some sad news. Midway through the writing of

this book, my long-serving research assistant Lyttelton died. She was seventeen, which isn't a bad age for a Jack Russell/ Cavalier cross, but she was my constant companion, and I miss her terribly. Thankfully, her apprentice Jessamy Beagle learned well and has been invaluable throughout. Any errors are hers, obviously.

Aberdare
May 2021

Index

Names of television, radio and theatre shows and record albums are in *italics*. Titles of books are in *italics* followed by the author's name in parentheses. Titles of songs and comedy sketches are in single quote marks. Topical subentries, in alphabetical order, are found under 'Morecambe, Eric,' 'Morecambe and Wise', *'Morecambe and Wise Show* (BBC)' and 'Wise, Ernie'.